EDITOR TO AUTHOR

THE LETTERS OF
MAXWELL E. PERKINS

EDITOR TO AUTHOR

The Letters of

MAXWELL E. PERKINS

Edited by John Hall Wheelock
Preface by Marcia Davenport

CHARLES SCRIBNER'S SONS / NEW YORK

1987

EDITOR'S NOTE

Grateful acknowledgment is here made to Mr. Edward C. Aswell, Administrator, C.T.A., of the Estate of Thomas Wolfe, for permission to include in this collection a letter from Thomas Wolfe to Maxwell E. Perkins dated August 12, 1938; to Mr. Van Wyck Brooks, for his kindness in placing at my disposal a copy of the letter addressed to him with which this collection opens; to Irma Wyckoff (Mrs. Osmer Muench), secretary to Maxwell E. Perkins for twenty-seven years until the time of his death, for unfailing help in the selection of material and in supplying factual data and background; to Louise Saunders Perkins (Mrs. Maxwell E. Perkins), for her encouragement and for invaluable suggestions.

Library of Congress Cataloging-in-Publication Data

Perkins, Maxwell E. (Maxwell Evarts), 1884-1947.
    Editor to author.

    Reprint. Originally published: New York: Scribner,
1979, c1950.
    1. Perkins, Maxwell E. (Maxwell Evarts), 1884-1947—
Correspondence. 2. Editors—Correspondence.
I. Wheelock, John Hall, 1886-   . II. Title.
[PN149.9.P4A34 1987]   070.5'2'0924 [B]   86-22040
ISBN 0-684-18840-6 (pbk.)

Manufactured by Haddon Craftsmen, Scranton, Pennsylvania
Jacket art and design by Stacey Farley

First Paperback Edition 1987

CONTENTS

(The name of the person written to
has, in some cases, not been included)

PREFACE BY	*Marcia Davenport*	xiii
INTRODUCTION BY	*John Hall Wheelock*	1
MAY 20, 1914	*Van Wyck Brooks*	10
MARCH 27, 1916	*E. H. Sothern*	14
MARCH 5, 1917	*Arthur Train*	16
APRIL 30, 1919	*James Huneker*	18
SEPTEMBER 16, 1919	*F. Scott Fitzgerald*	20
SEPTEMBER 23, 1919	*F. Scott Fitzgerald*	21
OCTOBER 22, 1919	*Arthur Train*	23
NOVEMBER 18, 1919	*James Huneker*	25
NOVEMBER 1, 1920	*James Huneker*	25
NOVEMBER 5, 1920	*James Huneker*	26
FEBRUARY 11, 1921	*John Galsworthy*	27
AUGUST 2, 1921	*John Galsworthy*	29
DECEMBER 12, 1921	*F. Scott Fitzgerald*	30
DECEMBER 31, 1921	*F. Scott Fitzgerald*	31
JULY 2, 1923	*Ring W. Lardner*	32
MARCH 31, 1924	*Edward Bok*	33
JUNE 5, 1924	*F. Scott Fitzgerald*	36
JUNE 11, 1924	*Ring W. Lardner*	37
NOVEMBER 20, 1924	*F. Scott Fitzgerald*	38
DECEMBER 1, 1924	*James Boyd*	41
DECEMBER 5, 1924	*Will James*	42
MAY 26, 1925	*Struthers Burt*	44

v

JANUARY 29, 1926	*Stark Young*	45
APRIL 27, 1926	*F. Scott Fitzgerald*	46
JANUARY 6, 1927	*James Boyd*	49
MARCH 14, 1927	*James Boyd*	50
OCTOBER 11, 1927	*John W. Thomason, Jr.*	52
JANUARY 3, 1928	*Willard Huntington Wright*	53
MARCH 30, 1928	*Without name*	54
MAY 9, 1928	*John W. Thomason, Jr.*	55
JUNE 20, 1928	*Roger Burlingame*	56
AUGUST 28, 1928	*Without name*	58
OCTOBER 22, 1928	*Thomas Wolfe*	61
MARCH 15, 1929	*Stark Young*	61
NOVEMBER 27, 1929	*Without name*	62
DFCEMBER 13, 1929	*John Galsworthy*	63
DECEMBER 30, 1929	*James Boyd*	65
FEBRUARY 26, 1930	*Erskine Caldwell*	66
MAY 22, 1930	*Leon Trotsky*	67
JUNE 3, 1930	*Thomas Wolfe*	68
AUGUST 28, 1930	*Thomas Wolfe*	69
SEPTEMBER 10, 1930	*Thomas Wolfe*	70
NOVEMBER 12, 1930	*Thomas Wolfe*	72
JUNE 27, 1931	*Allen Tate*	73
NOVEMBER 16, 1931	*Morley Callaghan*	74
JANUARY 14, 1932	*Ernest Hemingway*	77
JULY 22, 1932	*Ernest Hemingway*	78
NOVEMBER 23, 1932	*Chard Powers Smith*	80
JANUARY 17, 1933	*Without name*	80
JANUARY 31, 1933	*Without name*	82
OCTOBER 27, 1933	*Marjorie Kinnan Rawlings*	83

CONTENTS

NOVEMBER 15, 1933	*Marjorie Kinnan Rawlings*	85
JANUARY 16, 1934	*Caroline Gordon*	86
FEBRUARY 1, 1934	*Marjorie Kinnan Rawlings*	87
JUNE 25, 1934	*James Boyd*	89
JUNE 28, 1934	*Ernest Hemingway*	90
AUGUST 10, 1934	*Marjorie Kinnan Rawlings*	92
OCTOBER 1, 1934	*Ernest Hemingway*	94
NOVEMBER 28, 1934	*Ernest Hemingway*	95
JANUARY 21, 1935	*Thomas Wolfe*	99
FEBRUARY 8, 1935	*Thomas Wolfe*	100
MARCH 14, 1935	*Thomas Wolfe*	101
APRIL 15, 1935	*Caroline Gordon*	103
AUGUST 30, 1935	*Thomas Wolfe*	104
SEPTEMBER 10, 1935	*Hamilton Basso*	105
SEPTEMBER 16, 1935	*A. S. Frere-Reeves*	106
JANUARY 10, 1936	*Without name*	107
MARCH 6, 1936	*Without name*	109
APRIL 3, 1936	*Without name*	109
APRIL 22, 1936	*Thomas Wolfe*	110
AUGUST 5, 1936	*Marjorie Kinnan Rawlings*	113
OCTOBER 7, 1936	*John W. Thomason, Jr.*	114
NOVEMBER 17, 1936	*Thomas Wolfe*	115
NOVEMBER 18, 1936	*Thomas Wolfe*	116
NOVEMBER 18, 1936	*Thomas Wolfe*	116
DECEMBER 9, 1936	*Ernest Hemingway*	117
JANUARY 13, 1937	*Thomas Wolfe*	119
JANUARY 14, 1937	*Thomas Wolfe*	121
JANUARY 16, 1937	*Thomas Wolfe*	121
JUNE 18, 1937	*Nancy Hale*	126

CONTENTS

JULY 22, 1937	*Arthur Train*	127
AUGUST 23, 1937	*Hamilton Basso*	130
SEPTEMBER 7, 1937	*Caroline Gordon*	130
SEPTEMBER 17, 1937	*Will James*	131
NOVEMBER 20, 1937	*Thomas Wolfe*	133
DECEMBER 7, 1937	*Hamilton Basso*	134
DECEMBER 13, 1937	*Marjorie Kinnan Rawlings*	135
MAY 4, 1938	*Robert Briffault*	136
JUNE 21, 1938	*Arthur Train*	138
JULY 25, 1938	*Fred Wolfe*	140
AUGUST 12, 1938	*Maxwell E. Perkins*	141
AUGUST 19, 1938	*Thomas Wolfe*	142
NOVEMBER 23, 1938	*Taylor Caldwell*	142
DECEMBER 13, 1938	*Nicholas Murray Butler*	145
JULY 17, 1939	*Charles Townsend Copeland*	145
JULY 26, 1939	*Waldo Peirce*	146
AUGUST 15, 1939	*Allen Tate*	147
AUGUST 28, 1939	*Ward Dorrance*	148
JANUARY 3, 1940	*Charles Townsend Copeland*	149
JANUARY 5, 1940	*Marjorie Kinnan Rawlings*	150
JANUARY 19, 1940	*Ernest Hemingway*	152
FEBRUARY 14, 1940	*Ernest Hemingway*	153
APRIL 24, 1940	*Ernest Hemingway*	156
MAY 22, 1940	*F. Scott Fitzgerald*	158
JULY 18, 1940	*Hamilton Basso*	159
JULY 18, 1940	*Charles Townsend Copeland*	160
JULY 26, 1940	*Marjorie Kinnan Rawlings*	163
AUGUST 7, 1940	*Dawn Powell*	164
AUGUST 12, 1940	*Sherwood Anderson*	165

AUGUST 21, 1940 · *Sherwood Anderson* 167
AUGUST 23, 1940 *Dixon Wecter* 168
AUGUST 30, 1940 *Ray Stannard Baker* 169
SEPTEMBER 9, 1940 *Ray Stannard Baker* 171
SEPTEMBER 20, 1940 *Ernest Hemingway* 174
SEPTEMBER 20, 1940 *Marjorie Kinnan Rawlings* 175
OCTOBER 14, 1940 *John W. Thomason, Jr.* 180
DECEMBER 4, 1940 *Dixon Wecter* 182
DECEMBER 16, 1940 *William B. Wisdom* 183
MARCH 11, 1941 *Without name* 184
AUGUST 8, 1941 *James Truslow Adams* 185
AUGUST 19, 1941 *William B. Wisdom* 187
SEPTEMBER 3, 1941 *Charles Townsend Copeland* 189
SEPTEMBER 26, 1941 *James Truslow Adams* 190
NOVEMBER 19, 1941 *Nancy Hale* 191
DECEMBER 12, 1941 *Annie Laurie Etchison* 192
JANUARY 29, 1942 *Chard Powers Smith* 194
FEBRUARY 17, 1942 *Without name* 195
MARCH 30, 1942 *Marcia Davenport* 196
MAY 26, 1942 *Ann Chidester* 199
JUNE 8, 1942 *Ernest Hemingway* 200
AUGUST 13, 1942 *Ernest Hemingway* 203
SEPTEMBER 4, 1942 *Ernest Hemingway* 204
SEPTEMBER 21, 1942 *William Lyon Phelps* 207
OCTOBER 13, 1942 *Without name* 208
OCTOBER 21, 1942 *Nancy Hale* 209
NOVEMBER 2, 1942 *Without name* 210
DECEMBER 2, 1942 *Alden Brooks* 214
FEBRUARY 18, 1943 *Raymond Thompson* 215

MARCH 10, 1943	*Betty Grace Boyd*	216
APRIL 1, 1943	*William Lyon Phelps*	218
APRIL 8, 1943	*William Lyon Phelps*	220
APRIL 12, 1943	*Maxwell Geismar*	222
JUNE 14, 1943	*William B. Wisdom*	223
JUNE 17, 1943	*Without name*	226
JUNE 28, 1943	*Edith Pope*	230
JULY 15, 1943	*Ann Chidester*	232
AUGUST 30, 1943	*Without name*	233
SEPTEMBER 2, 1943	*Ernest Hemingway*	234
APRIL 19, 1944	*Marjorie Kinnan Rawlings*	236
MAY 19, 1944	*Without name*	238
MAY 23, 1944	*Without name*	241
MAY 25, 1944	*Without name*	242
MAY 31, 1944	*Without name*	245
JULY 17, 1944	*Alice D. Bond*	246
JULY 26, 1944	*Joseph Stanley Pennell*	248
SEPTEMBER 19, 1944	*Without name*	249
SEPTEMBER 22, 1944	*William B. Wisdom*	250
OCTOBER 3, 1944	*Without name*	251
NOVEMBER 3, 1944	*Without name*	253
NOVEMBER 13, 1944	*Without name*	255
DECEMBER 4, 1944	*Geoffrey Parsons*	257
DECEMBER 13, 1944	*Christine Weston*	259
DECEMBER 26, 1944	*Without name*	262
JANUARY 24, 1945	*Without name*	263
FEBRUARY 9, 1945	*R. W. Cowden*	264
APRIL 19, 1945	*Ernest Hemingway*	264
MAY 17, 1945	*John H. Mulliken, Jr.*	266

JUNE 22, 1945	*James Boyd, Jr.*	268
DECEMBER 19, 1945	*Nancy Hale*	269
JANUARY 4, 1946	*James Boyd, Jr.*	270
JANUARY 31, 1946	*Ann Chidester*	271
MARCH 27, 1946	*James Jones*	273
MAY 31, 1946	*Without name*	274
JUNE 10, 1946	*Marjorie Kinnan Rawlings*	275
JUNE 26, 1946	*Nicholas Murray Butler*	277
AUGUST 16, 1946	*Without name*	279
SEPTEMBER 27, 1946	*G. P. Brett, Jr.*	280
NOVEMBER 18, 1946	*Taylor Caldwell*	281
DECEMBER 31, 1946	*Taylor Caldwell*	282
JANUARY 6, 1947	*Ann Chidester*	283
FEBRUARY 17, 1947	*Without name*	284
APRIL 28, 1947	*Marcia Davenport*	286
MAY 6, 1947	*Alan Paton*	294
MAY 9, 1947	*James Jones*	295
MAY 28, 1947	*James Jones*	297
MAY 29, 1947	*Without name*	300
JUNE 4, 1947	*Katharine Newlin Burt*	302
JUNE 4, 1947	*Without name*	303
INDEX		305

PREFACE

By Marcia Davenport

It would be impossible for a writer whose editor was Maxwell Evarts Perkins to write impersonally of Max. And since I am about the last of those who were so fortunate as to have Max Perkins for our editor from our beginnings until his death, I cannot take an editorial colleague's or a biographer's view of Max. Both of those have been ably presented, the first in the introduction to the original edition of this book of Max's letters, the second in a recent widely commended biography. I see Max Perkins as I feel for him, with devotion that has outlasted more than thirty years of his absence; with a sense of necessity to refer to him that keeps on my desk the famous photograph of him in his office, cigarette in hand, surrounded by piles of books, telephone and Rough-Rider-hat ashtray beside him, Teddy Roosevelt's picture on the wall behind him; in my own words, the reserved, laconic man with the sensitive face and the extraordinary eyes. I met him in this unforgettable setting just less than fifty years ago. I was timid but not shy; Max was shy but not timid.

I came to see him because I wanted to write a biography of Mozart, and I was afraid to begin the project, quitting my job as a reporter on *The New Yorker*, without some assurance that somebody would be interested in publishing such a book. Of course I had no right to seek that assurance, but I was too ingenuous, perhaps too lucky, to have shared the fate of most beginning writers — the inchoate short story or first novel and the inevitable sequence of rejections. I had written only journalism. I had nothing to show Mr. Perkins (the first and the last time that I so referred to him) to validate my desire to write that book. I had no idea that I would ever write a novel — Max, of course, had — but I did not know that then. My native milieu was music, and Max had no interest whatever in music or its personalities present or past. He cared primarily about fiction and those who had talent for it. He was dedicated to finding that talent. His essential quality (I am paraphrasing myself) was always to say little, but by powerful instinct for writers and books to draw out of them what they had it in them to say and to write. He drew from me my reasons for wanting to write my book. Then he said, "Go ahead and write it. We will publish it."

From my very long view, that was the most extraordinary experience I have ever had. Writers are egocentric. What happens to a writer happens to him and to nobody else. It might be that others have known moments like that thunderclap for me, but nothing can diminish the intensity with which a writer experiences such a supreme emotion, and later lives by its recollection. It is the fact that I have never heard of another unknown young aspirant who was assured of publication by a great editor and publishing house before a word was written. But Max's promise to me bore out what he said at different times to different people: "You can tell more about a writer by listening to him than by reading something he wrote." He did suggest that I write a few pages of the proposed book and let him see them, but I never knew what clinched his decision about me until three years after his death, when this collection of his letters was first published.

One hundred and eighty-eight letters were selected for this book from the thousands that Max wrote in some thirty years, dictating to his amanuensis, Irma Wyckoff, herself inseparable from memories of Max. The letters reveal very much the man;

they reflect the problems, choices, convictions, decisions, and, above all, the relations of a great editor to the writers who relied on him. Speech must have come readily to Max only in dictating, for his fluency and incisiveness in letters were a surprising contrast to his reticence in face-to-face talk. So at this time, when the 'legend' of Max Perkins has been expanded by a long book about him, it is important that his letters should be currently accessible to contemporary readers and writers to whom his name and achievements are in truth legendary.

There is always fascination in pursuing the mystery of genius. In my lifetime, circumstance has given me the privilege of knowing intimately and living under the influence of two men who were defined in their totally different arts as 'genius', and who remain so defined twenty and thirty years after their deaths. One was Arturo Toscanini and the other was Maxwell Perkins. How can I possibly relate the two? At first glance the idea is preposterous. There could be no more extreme contrast between two individuals. It is almost absurd to see any resemblance between the world's most eminent musician, the scintillant, hyper-articulate, plebeian-born Italian, and the most renowned of literary editors, the diffident, silent, New England patrician. Nor would either in the least have understood the other. Then what did the two men share; what emboldens me to make this curious statement? Simply that both possessed the ability to evoke from people of talent the best that they had in them; the ability to get out of them better work than they ever otherwise did; the mysterious spell of personality which gave performers (writers too, in this sense) confidence, and encouraged them to do what, they often said, they did not know they had it in them to do. The analogy is necessarily inexact. Its premise is the question of talent, its distortion that professional musicians must have a consistently high degree of execution while writers, especially novelists, must slough around in the rough, their successive productions uneven and their problems perpetually renewed. In a word there is little similarity between interpretive and creative talent, except that both can be inspired by presiding genius to rise above their own limitations.

People have asked us who knew Max just what it was that he did as our editor; how he differed from any other editor. The difference was Max himself, of course. What he did was *be with us*, in mind, in mood, in the commonplaces of existence as much as in the notable experiences. He was with us in retrospection when we dealt with remembered experience, and in anticipation when we were grappling with the still unformed mass of what we aimed at. He gave us infinite, tolerant understanding which built a floor under the isolation and solitude that are the writer's life. Writers elect that life and thereafter suffer with it, often in terrible discouragement and despair, sometimes in elation that is only momentary. Max said and, more typically, wrote to all of us, in one phrase or another, "It is the good book that gives a writer trouble." "All you lack in regard to this book is confidence." "Writing a novel is a very hard thing to do." "I know it is a terrible task." "Don't lose courage." His patience was prodigious. The idea of a deadline or of hurrying a writer was unthinkable to him. Also he stayed with you, with me in this instance, in the long dead intervals between books, reassuringly the friend before the editor. Then when you were once again in the agonies of writing, he knew by a magical instinct exactly when to call you on the telephone and ask you to meet him next day for lunch or for 'tea'. He might say, "How are you getting on?" That was always the moment when your answer was, and would have been for perhaps six weeks past, "I'm stuck. The whole thing is a horrible mess."

So I would meet him and sit with him in the small bar at the old Ritz. We sat, I have written elsewhere, and drank our drinks and talked not very much. If I mentioned the problem I had been wrestling with, Max somehow changed the subject and the change often ended up on the head of Franklin Roosevelt. Max did not admire him, nor did he like the New Deal. Or he talked about Louise, his wife, or his five daughters, or about one of his other authors. Often he did not talk at all. We just sat there and thought. Suddenly he would say, "Time for my train," pick up from under the table his briefcase full of manuscripts, and bid me a hasty good-bye as he started down Madison Avenue to Grand Central Station. In my memory those afternoons were usually rainy. I would go home, feeling both calm and exhilarated, and next morning my problem would have disappeared. Others have agreed that they had the same experience.

It seems quixotic, if not frivolous, to say of a man whose life was communication that he was somewhat inarticulate in speech. But this appeared to be the case if you expected Max to talk about your work in progress or about a problem in the book that you were writing. The genius part was his waiving of these specifics, and his spanning the problems with his phrase, "Just get it all down on paper and then we'll see what to do with it." "We" of course was Max himself, but Max's avoidance of "I" was as much part of his personality as the famous ever-present hat, the thick, loosely-knotted necktie, the lisp in his muffled enunciation, the slight deafness, the advice to every one of us (each, I think, believed it was special in his case) to read *War and Peace* constantly. He advised me to read it every other year, alternately with *Anna Karenina*, and I have done so ever since.

But the tangible art of Max as editor came after a writer had got it all down on paper. The letter on page 286 of this book

was selected as the perfect example of Max in action after he
had read a completed but not yet a finished manuscript. It is
only coincidental that the letter was written to me; it might
have been to another novelist, to various others. It throws a
penetrating beam of comprehension and perspective through
the two banks of fog that confuse and obstruct a novelist: the
central theme of the whole book, and the details of characterization, action, dialogue (dialogue *is* action, said Max many
times); the interworkings of memory, imagination, suscepti-
bility to place and to physical impressions: Max saw more
clearly what a writer meant to do than the writer could see
himself. That letter was the last such work that Max did, only
six weeks before he died. Everyone who knew him well had
been increasingly concerned about his visible exhaustion, the
pallor and the trembling hands that showed his failing health;
but his death after only two days' acute illness was a shattering
shock. Marjorie Kinnan Rawlings had become a dear friend of
mine — Max had brought us together years before — and in
our letters we agreed that our first reaction of grief and panic
was that we would never write another book. But that would
be a denial of all that Max had done for us. So we knew that
we would indeed write more books and that they would never
be the books they could have been.

The original edition of this collection of Maxwell Perkins's
letters was prepared by the late John Hall Wheelock, the poet,
who was also an editor at Scribners and a long-time colleague
of Max's. Nearly thirty years ago, reasons of taste and conven-
tion — perhaps of potential trouble, too — led Mr. Wheelock
to omit the names of certain recipients of the letters. These
excisions today seem quaint, anachronistic, even pedantic. It
is no longer the fashion to consider people's privacy as John
Wheelock did. So reference has been made to the original

letters in the Scribner archives, with the possible intention of restoring the omitted names as contemporary usage might expect. But it has been decided that the excisions remain, because the anonymities concerned would have little or no meaning in the present day. They would probably no longer be alive. Their usefulness is that their letters to Max Perkins elicited from him replies which enshrine his magnificent defences of freedom of speech and writing, his statements of conscience and dedication to the responsibilities of publishing, his opposition to censorship in any form. One whose name was omitted was Everett Perry, to whom two letters on pages 80–83 sum up the heart and soul of Max's beliefs. Some letters, like the masterpiece on page 238, are replies to the cranks who plague all writers and publishers; the founts of intolerance and prejudice; the ones who read social, racial, or religious slurs into every realistic approach to the human amalgam and angrily demand retraction or, much worse in Max's view, censorship. Max's repudiation of censorship in any form was perhaps the most passionate of his convictions and Max, despite his Yankee reserve, his diffidence and modesty, his desire for self-effacement, was a passionate man. He had passion for talent. Passion for truth. Passion for tolerance. Passion for the good writer's necessity to write what he must.

Max became and remains renowned through the fame of his most conspicuous writers, Fitzgerald, Hemingway, and Wolfe. Up to a point that is interesting, but beyond that point overemphasis on three writers, however important, rather than on Max himself, deprives literary posterity of the opportunity to know Maxwell Perkins and his views in the entirety of his letters. Since the letters fortunately took the place of much that he left unsaid in person, the interested reader and, more importantly, the writer, published or still unpublished, who seeks for the magic in Max which drew their best work out of so many authors, will come closest to that discovery in reading the letters of Maxwell Perkins without the intervention of any expositor.

And finally, as though in answer to the questions of would-be writers who grope and hope and seek the key to the dream of "I want to write," there is the letter on page 266 of this book. It was written to a young man who wanted to write fiction. This letter should be a rubric to any young person who wants to be a writer. The more carefully and often these words of Max's are studied, the more they reveal. They dismiss procedures and practices which obstruct, rather than clear, the way to writing fiction. They tell what the aspirant ought to know and do, and too often does not. They tell it all. So does the concluding paragraph of the next letter, on page 269, to another young man: "What really makes writing is done in the head, where impressions are stored up, and it is done with the eye and the ear. The agony comes later, when it has to be done with the hand, and that part of it can gain greatly from seeing how others do it, by reading."

This is Maxwell Perkins, the great editor, enduring in American writing not in the reflection of celebrated novelists, but in his own words.

January 1979

INTRODUCTION

By John Hall Wheelock

For thirty-seven years Maxwell Evarts Perkins was associated with the House of Scribner, during the last twenty as its head editor, a title, however, which he, in his modest and unassuming way, never acknowledged. When he died, in 1947, he was generally regarded as the most far-sighted and creative editor of his time. The letters brought together in this book have been taken from the Scribner files from the large number written by him throughout the years of his editorship, selected with a view to showing a great editor at work. Few letters have been included that do not, directly or indirectly, serve this purpose. The letters are arranged chronologically. The man who wrote these letters was a man with a passion for good writing, a passion for the true, for the intensely felt, the completely realized — in other words, for talent. Nothing, throughout a working lifetime, swerved him from that allegiance. For him, reading with those watchful, those ever hopeful eyes, no honest writing was without interest. How many a bulky manuscript, unpublishable for one reason or another, was laid on his desk, with a report noting perhaps certain passages that showed promise! For Max, that was enough. The work might not be publishable, but there were glimmerings of talent. Into his already swollen briefcase it would go; a weekend was devoted to it, in the hope, not always unrewarded, that something could be salvaged.

With this deep care for talent, there went, in Max's case, an intuitive perceptivity that was uncanny. On manuscripts involving scholarship, abstract thinking or ideas, his judgment might go astray. Where writing was concerned, the kind of observation, thinking and feeling that go into an imaginative creation, little that was meretricious, however plausible, or second-rate, however deft, got past that eagle guard. By the same token, he seldom failed in recognition of work of a high order: he knew it instantly when he came across it in the manuscripts of writers now famous, but at the time unknown or little known, who had through him their first publication.

Another attribute which went into the making of a great editor was Max's selfless devotion. The recognizing, the encouraging, the guiding of talent — this, in his view, was a sacred task worth any amount of effort, of risk, of time expended. I recall the visit of a certain eminent critic and a dispute over the merits of Thomas Wolfe as a writer. His faults, thought the eminent critic, were so many and so serious as to render his work unworthy of the amount of labor and attention Max was giving it. And I remember Max's answer, flaring into rage: "Well, then you just don't care about talent!" Max did. And he had the courage of his convictions, then and always. That, perhaps, must come first among the qualifications necessary to a great editor, one who would foster that fragile film of articulate spirit which overlies our mortality, and survives it.

Max's ambition at one period was to be a writer. While a reporter on the New York *Times,* he made his mark not only by his enterprise and devotion to his work but by the quality of the writing he turned in. As an undergraduate at Harvard he had read widely. Defoe and Swift made a lasting impression; Tolstoi's "War and Peace" became a book that he re-read regularly every few years. Napoleon had, early, been one of his heroes; later, General Grant, and it was at this time that he developed his lifelong interest in military strategy, in the campaigns of the American Civil War, and in American history and politics, in general. He did a good deal of writing, too. He had, as the letters in this collection will show, a natural gift of expression, and though he soon abandoned the idea of writing as a career, the fact that he was, at heart, himself a writer, gave him sympathy and insight, put him as it were on the writer's side. This turned out to be a valuable asset when he entered the publishing field. From the moment he took up his work as editor he knew he had struck his vocation. Thereafter he never faltered. His gifts of temperament and equipment made him the ideal father-confessor, the listener, wise and sympathetic, whose understanding, often conveyed without words, acted as a catalyst, precipitating in many a writer the definite self-discovery which till then had been vast but formless aspiration.

The job of editor in a publishing house is the dullest, hardest, most exciting, exasperating and rewarding of perhaps any job in the world. Most writers are in a state of gloom a good deal of the time; they need perpetual reassurance. When a writer has written his masterpiece he will often be certain that the whole thing is worthless. The perpetrator of the dimmest literary effort, on the other hand, is apt to be invincibly cocksure and combative about it. No book gets enough advertising (the old superstition regarding its magic power still persists), or it is the wrong kind. And, obviously, almost every writer needs money and needs it before, not after, delivery of the goods. There is the writer whose manuscript proves that Shakespeare's plays are merely an elaborate system of political code; another has written a book to demonstrate that the earth is round, but that we are living on the inside of it; still another has completed a novel in five volumes, entitled "God." Through it all Max kept his countenance. To the many aspects of an editor's work he brought a tremendous seriousness, masculine drive and energy, daring coupled with shrewd judgment, quiet strength, and a self-effacement and delicacy of feeling almost feminine in character. But he brought a sense of humor too. After the departure of some particularly excited visitor he could burst out in laughing desperation: "What sort of a madhouse is this, anyway! What are we supposed to be — ghost-writers, bankers, psychiatrists, income-tax experts, magicians?" And in the letters that follow, there are some amusing anecdotes: of the author with whom he dined, from time to time, in her so-called "studio" (a magnificent and richly appointed apartment), in order to work with her later on the manuscript of her book, and who mingled violent enthusiasm for communism and a "classless society" with shouts over her shoulder at the maid in the pantry, "God-damn it, Kate, stop rattling those dishes"; of the writer who called up in tears to say, "My cat, John Keats, is dying — you must send a veterinary," and, when advised to get one in the neighborhood, inquired: "But will you pay for it?" And he did.

Among an editor's various rôles, one of the most important is that of the listener. Much of what he hears is interesting and some of it is important. But there are talkers the weight of whose message seems to be in inverse proportion to the length of time it takes to convey it. Amid elaborate explanations as to how a book came to be written, and just what the author has tried to do, the mind tends to wander and the interest to confine itself to the one essential question: "Did you put your name and address on the manuscript?" Max, as has already been pointed out, had talent as a listener. A New Englander, and reserved, he was naturally inclined to silence. But his silence was attentive, perceptive, helpful to the talker, a positive kind of silence, charged with the awareness and judgments of a superior intelligence. When he did speak, it was briefly — and not always in agreement. Coming after so much silence, what he had to say gained weight and force. When he felt that the talker made sense, Max would give him free rein. There were days when his entire time in the office was given over to this silent listening. That silence could, on occasion, be terrifying and, when driven to desperation by some long-winded speaker, Max would sometimes puncture it with an irritable, "Well, what about it?" which usually served to bring things to a head. He was not by any means always amiable.

The letters in the collection that follows give us the clue to Max's creed as an editor. The function of an editor, he feels, is to serve as a skilled objective outsider, a critical touchstone by recourse to which a writer is enabled to sense flaws in surface or structure, to grasp and solve the artistic or technical problems involved, and thus to realize completely his own work in his own way. The ideas or theories of an editor should not be obtruded, a writer must not substitute them for his own solution. Over and over, in these pages, that warning is implied or stated, as in an early letter to Scott Fitzgerald, with its striking first sentence, "Do not ever defer to my judgment" (a thing Fitzgerald had threatened to do). Further, an editor is important as a means only and he should remain in the background. Max carried this idea a bit far perhaps, in his refusal to speak in public or on the air, to write for publication, or to be interviewed if he could possibly help it. In one of the letters he remarks that if it be true, as the old adage has it, that children should be seen and not heard, an editor should not even be seen.

Other passages in the letters have bearing on Max's conception of the function of a publisher. He frequently stresses the fact that fiction is not mere entertainment but, at its best, a serious interpretation of reality, comprehending within its scope the evil and the ugly side of things, as well as the good and the beautiful, and subject to such limitations only as are imposed by the conscience of art. Where ideas are concerned, a publisher as such must not be partisan, but should offer to any honest and fresh viewpoint, worthily presented, a chance to take its place in the free commonwealth of thought. Is it of interest to the public? If so, the public is entitled to know about it and to pass upon it. The public, not the publisher, is to be the judge.

There will also be found among these letters a few making comment upon specific elements or episodes in a manuscript or outlining detailed plans for its reorganization. They reveal an extraordinary insight, a wealth of creative criticism far beyond the range of the usual editorial routine. It is not surprising that many well-known authors welcomed suggestions so perceptive and, later, came to feel that these had played an important part in the final achievement. There were some who even went so far as to claim that whatever they knew about writing they had learned from Max — a statement which always upset and irritated him. His irritability was part of his charm.

What comes through these letters, in the end, is a personality. One feels it on every page. This personality was a curious blend of diverse, and sometimes conflicting, qualities. In Max, the Puritan and the Cavalier, the shrewd Yankee and the generous and disarming artist, were subtly and perpetually at war. Gentleness, consideration for others to the point of self-abnegation, was combined with a stubbornness of conviction, a crag-like obstinacy, that at times was maddening. He was shy but very daring, would lie awake with excitement over the discovery of a new writer, but had a Vermonter's distaste for the display of emotion in music or poetry. Male dancers embarrassed him. A conservative in politics, he was suspicious of hotheads and zealots, who, he felt, did nothing but harm. His mistrust of human nature at its present level and of all callow idealism was perhaps another Yankee trait. Then, there was his New England conscience. When Max was on the Mexican border, with his squadron, at the time of the trouble there, he wrote Mr.

Scribner asking him to dock his pay by twenty dollars a month, the amount he was getting in the army, as he did not wish to profit financially by absence from his work. His was a lonely pride. His, also, and all too often, were lonely enthusiasms.

Headlong admiration for work well done, unflinching courage in backing it, quite a few crotchety prejudices and quirks of unreason, a will "immutable and still as stone" — that was Max. To many writers, some famous, some as yet unknown, he had become, in a sense, a spiritual father. Many depended on him; many would give a great deal to be able to do so again. One can go back to familiar places. Not always to one's friends. Not now to him. Time has a valve.

It is too soon to measure the achievement of an editor like Maxwell Perkins. That achievement is a part of the literary history of our day here in America. Throughout a third of a century he gave proof of his remarkable gift. The development of American talent and literature, that was where his main interest lay. To the oncoming talents in countries other than his own, he was less alert. Fiction was his principal concern and, within that classification, his temperament inclined him toward the inventive and experimental, occasionally at the expense of work in the great tradition equally distinguished. Science and abstract thinking interested him less than did books on controversial subjects or those based upon the application of a theory or idea. His passion was for the rare real thing, the flash of poetic insight that lights up a character or a situation and reveals talent at work. And his judgment, as attested by many a name now famous or book on its way to becoming a classic, was almost unerring in its clairvoyance. He loved the best but was no literary snob. His appreciation found room for the story well told, the narrative with a primarily popular appeal, the novel that gave pleasure to the less critical taste. The great books, he used to say, stand somewhere between the precious and the trashy, between what speaks to the literati only and what appeals to the masses. The great books reach both.

Max knew what he was about. In a period divided between imitative admiration for English and European models on the one hand and cynical disparagement of American materialism and ineptitude on the other, he had a large part in arousing the growing consciousness of the value and importance of our native note and in introducing to the world a group of American writers of sound worth. In this movement he was a pioneer, a discoverer whose forward-looking vision did not lead him to mistake the merely new for the authentic or blind him to the validity of the great traditions and standards of the past. To the publishing house which he served so ably and so long he has left the priceless legacy of his example and of his influence. He took on heavy burdens, exhausting labors, spending himself gallantly to the end. Was it worth it? His selfless consecration to the cause of contemporary letters resulted in bringing together, to their mutual advantage, the reading public and writers of whom our time has reason to be proud. Taine says somewhere that the great editor is an artist whose medium is the work of other men. Max's spirit lives on in the work of the writers he helped to full self-realization; his influence will be implicit in the work of writers still to come.

This collection opens with a letter from Maxwell Perkins to Van Wyck Brooks. The friendship between the two men had begun while they were schoolboys, at Plainfield, New Jersey, and was continued during their undergraduate days at Harvard University. The letter was handwritten by Perkins from a hospital bed, where he was convalescing after an appendectomy. It is dated May 20, and the year is not given, but was probably 1914. Brooks, who had already published four books and was well on the way to his place among the chief writers and critics of our time, was then living in England. Through Perkins, he had submitted to Scribners for publication the manuscript of his "America's Coming-of-Age." On the advice of William Crary Brownell, eminent critic, then senior editor at Scribners, the book was declined. It was issued in 1915 by B. W. Huebsch.

This opening letter is of particular interest in the glimpse it gives us into the mind of the youthful Perkins. He was not yet actually an editor. After several years with the Advertising Department of Scribners, he was about to begin, with that House, his long and brilliant career in the field so suited to his talents. The letter is, obviously, that of a young man but it reveals the combination of thoughtfulness, wary common-sense and a natural gift of expression, that was later to be put to such good use in the service of writers and of writing.

TO VAN WYCK BROOKS

MUHLENBURG HOSPITAL, MAY 20th

DEAR VAN WYCK:

Thanks for your letter, which came the night before my operation, a matter so simple and comfortable as to call for no comment here and now. I had already — after reading but a few pages of it — given your manuscript[1] to the Editorial Department;[2] and they had decided against it, although strongly impressed by the cleverness and mental independence of the writer; and therefore put by it into an attitude of welcome toward any other thing you may send in. I gathered that the chief objection was that "you swept these fellows into the dustbin of the past with a contemptuousness of gesture which was at least pre-mature" — Mr. Brownell's[3] words, spoken with an appreciative smile and the assertion that you were certainly a "live wire." I think this will enable you to understand their position.

I hope to be in the office for one day on June first and will then pass the manuscript on, personally, to some other publisher, Henry Holt or Stokes, I should think, and will keep in touch with them. When I go back to work, a week later, it will be in the Editorial Department, not the Advertising. Hoppin[4] is leaving to become a partner of Duffield,[5] and I shall fill his place, more or less.

Why don't you write something in "lighter vein" about the sort of life you are seeing in England, from an American point

[1] *America's Coming-of-Age*, B. W. Huebsch, 1915.   [2] Of Charles Scribner's Sons. [3] William Crary Brownell, the critic (1851–1928), senior editor at Scribners at that time.   [4] Frederic T. Hoppin (1875–1946), formerly an editor at Scribners, president of Duffield & Co. from 1918 to 1925.   [5] Pitts Duffield (1869–1936), president of Duffield & Co. from 1905 to 1918.

of view; for you are seeing an aspect of English life not often commented upon, if ever, at first hand, for Americans. And send it to *Scribner's Magazine* via me.

I started once to write you at length about an idea which has bothered me for months — but bothered less and less, in one way, as it became gradually more and more convincing to me and acted to give life, in general, a purpose, and the world a meaning. It ought to be set forth by one standing or sitting, not by one lying on a bed. But I will state it roughly.

Resolved: — that should man stand entirely free of the regime of competition in the widest sense, the motive forces acting upon him would be so utterly different from those that now compel him as to mould him into an entirely different creature from that which he now is. Indeed, that this change may be that new environment which evolution requires (always) to produce a higher type of being, a real superman; and so to advance life a step nearer perfection.

Now if this is true, then the terribly depressing historical theory — so hard to resist — that man is now intrinsically no better than he was four thousand years ago, may imply nothing for the future. . . .

This idea depends upon one we discussed last Spring—that of an era in which the production of necessities would be so apportioned among men that an almost negligible part of a man's time would be given to this purely material work — a conception principally supported by the fact that the power of machinery is now so great as to make possible such a reduction of actual man-work. In that case, a leisure class could be based not, as in the past, on slavery only, but on machinery; and this class could include everybody.

Now all men agree that, in theory at least, the material things in life are only valuable as means, and that the true ends are the immaterial, i.e., the intellectual and spiritual things. And if such an era of leisure from material pursuits would turn man to these unmaterial pursuits we can at last read a satisfactory answer to that puzzling question which, as Rousseau showed, could be answered before at least as well by a "no" as by a "yes" — the question, "Has the progress of science done man any real good?" If it has merely made him physically more comfortable, luxurious, even more healthy, it has not improved him intrinsically. If it has made possible his emancipation from the animal demands of existence to such an extent that his powers are therefore turned into spiritual channels, it will be the cause of the most extraordinary improvement in man's estate. And, in that case, the purpose of all this otherwise futile inventing of engines, etc., is clear as daylight.

But most men will contend that this now possible emancipation from material toil would simply reduce man to sloth or libertinism, according as he was individually made. And I answer, that appears to be so because you can only regard man through a competitive atmosphere! How can you even guess how radically he would change in the utterly different noncompetitive atmosphere? You can only be sure of the tendency, not the extent of the change. You can be sure that those qualities demanded for success in a competitive regime would weaken and tend to die; and that those qualities that weaken and die now would tend to grow vigorous and to gain control. The qualities of competition are selfish, brutal, beast-like qualities as compared with the softer, generous qualities whose presence in a man handicaps him under the competitive regime; and therefore the change that would take place in him would be from selfishness toward generosity, and from material aims to spiritual aims — from the endeavour to become eminent through the power of wealth and the display of possessions, to the endeavour to perfect one's self in whatever art one was by nature driven towards, were it only that of sympathizing with all sorts of people, were it even that of writing epic poems.

But, you object, do you observe any such change in those few men who inherit wealth and, so, have leisure? No. Because they are virtually as much the creatures of competition as anyone. They have no other air to breathe but that of competition; and even the very great are circumscribed by the prevailing order. Consider the enormous power of merely local and temporary regimes over men, how the aristocracy was always, for ever so long, accepted as a permanent fact — a superior race to be obeyed and reverenced, so that its destruction was unthinkable. And the terror of the French on being at first without a king! Men had adjusted their whole existence to the regime of royalty, and those qualities in them that would have rebelled had lain dormant or died.

But how far greater and more all-pervasive is this regime of competition, which has always, everywhere, existed; has ever been the one great principle on which life operated among men. Can anyone doubt but that it has bred up a certain set of qualities and worked to suppress and repress any other qualities incompatible with it and disadvantageous to have under it; that it has held up for honor and respect those qualities whose presence in a man made him pre-eminent in it, and held up for contempt those characteristics — even though Christ put some of them first of all — which held man down in it, just as in periods of war certain characteristics, now distasteful, become the great and all-admirable ones.

And just as in those war eras men were from very babyhood taught to develop those war-qualities and to choke such as conflicted with them, so now it is in competition: from the moment of birth, consciously or otherwise, by parents, teachers and society, the qualities that further a man in the competitive way of life are nurtured and the others held down, rooted out, or allowed to remain rudimentary. Now what would happen if this great influence that pulls up one set of qualities and pulls down the other were removed: all the rudimentary ones — (who can say how many are not even recognized at all now) — would come to natural growth and the others would *not* come, as now, to *un*natural growth. Then men would not run to sloth and dissipation, for the growth of these other tastes and interests — spiritual and intellectual — would make those things repulsive, or at least would furnish infinitely more enjoyable substitutes. It would be found that all men had in them — though now so often totally repressed — a love for some pursuit now often held contemptible. (Do we not largely here, now, hold contemptible all the arts — at least we did yesterday — and is it not because the love of them curbs a man in competition, partly?)

Now there is no positive evidence of what I hold. There could not be, since competition has always been the great prevailing influence. But there is the case of Athens, when the influence of competition was partially excluded. And did not the very things happen, to some extent, that I have named — did they not hate vice and love virtue and beauty? But how much more would this be so if competition were banished from the whole world and there was no slavery. What might not man then become?

If you understand this, it will be chiefly by imagination. I have not been able to say it fully or well, and now my pencil is used up entirely.

Yours as ever,

TO E. H. SOTHERN

DEAR MR. SOTHERN: MARCH 27, 1916

In the idea of publishing your reminiscences[1] early in the fall

[1] *The Melancholy Tale of "Me,"* Scribners, 1916.

we are engaged in the preliminaries to putting the manuscript in the printer's hands, such as determining the most suitable format, etc. And we are therefore writing you, in view of the possibility that you may have some suggestions to make of changes or omissions or the ordering of the chapters; and also, with the question of the length of the book in mind, upon the wisdom of including certain of the chapters. Our interest and pleasure in the material, as you know, are such that we need hardly assure you that it is not due to a failure to appreciate the intrinsic qualities of the chapters, "Came We to Camelot," "Let Us Be Unreasonable," "Why," and "Begot of Nothing but Vain Phantasy," that we suggest their omission, but mainly to the impression that their retention would tend to detract from the harmony of the narrative, and that they are not so thoroughly successful as to be on quite the same level with the rest of the book: they would prevent it from being as well proportioned, harmonious, and unified as it would otherwise be. The informality and discursive manner of the narrative are qualities that contribute largely to its charm; and we recognize that they are partly derived from the presentation of matters not apparently related according to the logical methods of formal memoirs but actually contributory to the main theme; but we think these particular chapters could be omitted with advantage when viewed extrinsically, in relation to the whole, with the mechanical question of the length of the manuscript in mind. Their omission would shorten it by about 15,000 words and would leave it about 115,000 words in length.

In recommending the omission of "Let Us Be Unreasonable" — the chapter on critics — we have also this other motive: it is so open to misinterpretation, at least by *reviewers and critics,* as to be exposed to unjustifiable overemphasis and unintentional misrepresentation.

These matters are presented purely as suggestion: and we

would only wish you to consider our view and to let us know how you regard it as soon as may be convenient; and also, of course, to make any suggestions that occur to you.

Very sincerely yours,

TO ARTHUR TRAIN

MARCH 5, 1917

DEAR MR. TRAIN:

I am returning herewith the first part of your novel.[1] May we retain the second for a day or two, so that Mr. Scribner[2] may finish it? I have read the entire manuscript with very great interest and certain parts of it with a special delight. You suggested that I speak about two points — the length of the first part to the beginning of Tom's undergraduate life, and the title.

The quotation about the wisdom of Egypt, and that of a mother, I cannot find. In fact, they don't seem to have attached so much importance to mothers, in the Bible. Nor is there the one I had in mind about gold refined by the furnace, although I am sure that that does exist somewhere. As for "Spindrift," if that has been used on a volume of poetry, I think there would be no impropriety or disadvantage on that account, because the volume was not copyrighted in this country but only imported, evidently, in a small edition from England where it was published. It certainly could not be injured by the use of the title on your book and the title would not have been injured by its use on that book, which has had a very small, insignificant circulation, as near as I can judge. "Spindrift," however, is not an ideal title for this book, because the significance of the book is Tom's denunciation of the vain and frivolous. But, simply as a title, "Spindrift" is excellent.

[1] *The World and Thomas Kelly*, Scribners, 1917. [2] Charles Scribner, Senior (1854–1930), president of Charles Scribner's Sons.

As for shortening the first part, I think the novel would be much strengthened if this were done, even to the extent of more than one-third. One reason for this is that the characterization of the Bostonian environment, and that of the summer resorts, is so effectively done that many passages could be dispensed with as simply renewing the impression already or thereafter given by others. Another is that a good deal of what is expressed in the early pages might well be left to the Harvard part, where the social creed of Boston is revealed in and by the narrative — is woven into the very fabric of the story. Still another is that, it seems to me, the characters, Tom and his mother, are injured by the great weight of the emphasis that in the early pages falls upon the environment rather than upon them as individuals. I think that both of them would become more clearly individualized to a reader if there were not so much to divert his attention from them in these early pages.

In fact, I thought that all of the characters in the book were pictured with great success except Tom's mother and Tom, the child. She was, I understand, a negative kind of person in the design of the story: but, even as such, could she not by an occasional touch, by emphasis upon her characteristics, her peculiarities perhaps, be made more realizable — this because the reader does not sufficiently comprehend the significance of her death. She is not enough of a reality to him.

I think this may be because in the first part of the book, after which she little appears and in which she is especially portrayed, the emphasis is so heavy upon the Bostonian environment, etc.; she hardly gets her share; and Tom, I think, would largely profit throughout, if he were then individualized in boyhood as he later is — just by an incident or two, I mean; because when the reader encounters him as a freshman he is a little surprised to find him the kind of person he is: he has not become individualized before.

Some minor points in the book, I think, are exceedingly effective. For instance, Parradyn's views on "sex" were excellent and required expression; and though he is an admirable character — I mean in a literary sense — and everything he says has point, this passage particularly will be noted by readers and quoted by reviewers. I thought the Harvard part was bully. The "egg" was an inspiration — so telling an example of the tremendous effect upon a person's life of a chance trifle would be hard to find. In fact, these things are hard to find in literature anyway, though common enough in life. It is one of those things that make you laugh with pleasure because so true. I think the way you handled Leslies, and his band in the office, was a rare piece of skill: he started off quietly and calmly, and I suppose meant to continue so but gradually was mastered by the review of the situation, which so involved his emotions and ended in rage. That's the way it *happens*.

But I've very much exceeded your suggestion of comment. I only thought that, as this novel is to be read, it might interest you to know how certain points of it strike a fairly typical reader.

Very sincerely yours,

TO JAMES HUNEKER

APRIL 30, 1919
DEAR MR. HUNEKER:

We are sorry that we put you to the trouble of writing a letter while you were ill and we shall, of course, let the matter rest until we hear from you, which we hope will be soon, both because of the great interest which we feel in "Steeplejack"[1] and because it will show that you are well again. We shall then

[1] Huneker's autobiography, 2 volumes, Scribners, 1920.

hope, too, to make apparent to you the appreciation we have always had for your books — indeed, we think that on account of the thought and care we have put into their publication we may claim some share in the responsibility for these offers which you speak of. We do not know offhand exactly how the matter stands with libraries but we do know that your books have had interested attention, in every instance, by our Library Department,[1] and that there is no library in the country but is completely informed about every one of them. We shall be glad to discuss this whole question with you whenever you wish.

As for "Steeplejack." We know we can satisfy you, both in the matter of terms and in the matter of exploitation, and shall look forward to being able to do so. "Steeplejack" is a fetching name for a book of this kind; and we are glad to know that the volume headed by Mary Garden[2] is also concerned in the question. The publication of a big work like "Steeplejack" — if everything comes out all right and we are its publishers — will give us an opportunity for bringing forward all of your books in a more effective way than would simply the publication of another uniform volume.

Very sincerely yours,

When the manuscript of "This Side of Paradise" first reached Scribners, Perkins, who was greatly impressed by it, felt that it needed revision and reorganization. It was, in its original version, declined by Scribners, and Perkins, who had been asked to do so by Fitzgerald, submitted a slightly revised version of the manuscript to various publishers, hoping that it would not be accepted, because he was aware of its extraordinary quality

---

[1] A department that sells the books of all publishers to university, college and public libraries. [2] A volume of mixed essays, to be entitled *Mary Garden*, was scheduled for publication by Scribners on February 1, 1920, but was never completed.

and felt that with further, more complete, rewriting it could be made a work of real importance and distinction. The publishers to whom the slightly revised version was sent returned it without comment, and Fitzgerald eventually rewrote the whole thing. This final version when submitted to Scribners was accepted, in the letter which follows, and shortly thereafter the book, now so well known, was published.

TO F. SCOTT FITZGERALD

SEPT. 16, 1919

DEAR MR. FITZGERALD:

I am very glad, personally, to be able to write to you that we are all for publishing your book, "This Side of Paradise."[1] Viewing it as the same book that was here before, which in a sense it is, though translated into somewhat different terms and extended further, I think that you have improved it enormously. As the first manuscript did, it abounds in energy and life and it seems to me to be in much better proportion. I was afraid that when we declined the first manuscript, you might be done with us conservatives. I am glad you are not. The book is so different that it is hard to prophesy how it will sell, but we are all for taking a chance and supporting it with vigor.

Hoping to hear from you, we are,

Sincerely yours,

P.S. Our expectation would be to publish your book in the early Spring. Now, if you are ready to have us do this, and have the time, we should be glad to have you get together any publicity matter you could for us, including a photograph. You have been in the advertising game long enough to know the sort of thing.

[1] Scribners, 1920.

In his letter of September 18 to Perkins, Fitzgerald had writ-ten: "Would it be utterly impossible for you to publish the book ["This Side of Paradise"] before Xmas or, say, by February?"

TO F. SCOTT FITZGERALD

DEAR MR. FITZGERALD:

SEPT. 23, 1919

I was very glad to get your letter of the 18th and to know that everything was ready with regard to "This Side of Para-dise";[1] and we are now making an estimate upon the book preliminary to putting it in hand, which we shall do within a short time if the printers' strike does not make it impossible to put anything in hand.

It is this way about publishing before Christmas: there are two book seasons in the year and the preparations for each one are begun long before the season opens. The publishers' travel-ers go out in July and August over the country with trunks filled with dummies and samples of the Fall books, which are to have their greatest sale in the Christmas season. The Adver-tising Department and the Circularizing Department get up their material in August and early September to make these books known considerably before publication and at the very time of publication. The advertising that is done from the first of September on is supposed to have its great effect in De-cember, although the book may have appeared in August or September or October and may have sold considerably then. Now, if a book is accepted after all this preliminary work is done and comes out in November, as yours would have to do at the earliest, it must make its own way altogether: it will get no preliminary advertising; it will not be presented to the trade by salesmen on the basis of a dummy; and it will come

[1] Scribners, 1920.

to the bookseller, who is already nearly mad with the number of new books and has already invested all the money he can in them, as a most unwelcome and troublesome thing and will suffer accordingly. Even if it is a book by an author who has been selling well for years, it will be very considerably injured by this.

The next book publishing season is the Spring season. The moment the Christmas rush is ended, the travelers go out once more and see all the booksellers, equipped with samples, etc. The bookseller has made his money out of the previous season and is ready to begin afresh and to stock up on new books. The Advertising and Circularizing departments have prepared their work on it, and their accounts of the author, etc., and have advertised it in the trade magazines to reinforce the salesmen's selling argument. Then, when the book does appear in February, March or April, the trade is ready for it and knows about it and it can be competently advertised because the publicity force of the house has become familiar with it.

These are the reasons why there is no question but it would damage your book exceedingly to try to rush it out before Christmas. Whether or not it can be printed in February we cannot yet say, but it certainly can be published in that month or March and we shall remember that you want it to be as early as possible.

About the story,[1] I know that Mr. Bridges[2] would want to read it. He has been much interested in you and what you have done already and I hope he may have a chance at this.

"The Demon Lover"[3] sounds good. Everybody ought to read Samuel Butler's "Note Books."   Sincerely yours,

---

[1] Fitzgerald had written Perkins that he was writing "quite a marvellous after-the-war story" and inquired whether Bridges would care to see it. [2] Robert Bridges (1858–1941), poet and essayist, then editor of *Scribner's Magazine*. [3] Tentative title of a novel Fitzgerald was at work on. It was published by Scribners in 1922 as *The Beautiful and Damned*.

OCT. 22, 1919

DEAR MR. TRAIN:

I have read the last four of the Tutt stories[1] which you had
sent to me — and with great enjoyment and considerable
laughter. Certainly there were never any stories nor any other
kind of writing, so far as I know, that gave such a picture of
the legal life in and about the criminal courts and the district
attorney's office, and that of the lawyers connected with them.
And certainly Mr. Tutt is a very real and sympathetic character. I now think you were probably right in letting his character develop incidentally, and in not subordinating the stories
to it, because in the aggregate they give you the character in
a truer way than would be the case had *that* been made in
every sense the main thing.

I do think that it would be well, though, to have some stories
that would be chiefly concerned in exhibiting his character;
but when it comes to suggesting them, I am afraid I cannot
help much. I have two very general ideas that might result in
something: the kind of a case Tutt would not handle might
furnish a story — a case for which rich clients wanted to retain
him and in which, because of the great fee, he became involved
up to a certain point, and then stuck upon the question of right
and wrong and dropped it. Would this be plausible? The other,
which would bring out the sympathy and sentiment of Mr.
Tutt, might be based on one of those not uncommon incidents
where a young man, or girl, comes to the city from the country
and gets into ways of crime, or semi-crime, mainly through
ignorance and greenness. I do not think you have referred to
Tutt's origin, and it might be that the element of reminiscence
— which has been rather overworked, it is true — by which a

---

[1] Included in a collection entitled *Tutt and Mr. Tutt*, Scribners, 1920.

man's sympathy is engaged because he recalls his own first contact with the city, could be effectively evoked. In such a story, might not Mr. Tutt ethically free the victim from the technicalities of law because of his conviction that his fault was due not to his nature but to his ignorance?

If we should select the stories, for a volume,[1] from those we now have, I think a good list would be these:

"The People Against Angelo Seraphino"
"Case No. 2"
"Case No. 5"
"People vs. Appleboy"
"Contempt of Court"
"Hocus-pocus"

These alone would amount to almost 68,000 words, which would be enough for a book, although a story or two more could be added. In making this selection I have left out some of the best stories, such as "Ways That Are Dark," "In Re Misella," "Sweet Land of Liberty." I have also omitted the sequel to the Barrows story, that is, "Barrows vs. Horses' Neck Extension Co." You also thought of doing a sequel story to "Case No. 5" about McFee. I was going on the theory of a second volume,[2] which should be as good as the first, but I thought it a good move to have that slight direct connection between the two volumes which there would be if certain stories in the second volume reached back to the first.

As to the advisability of publishing this Spring, it seems to me we should strike while the iron is hot. Serialization in big papers is a disadvantage generally, but we should make it an advantage for the moment by publishing in book form while serialization is still going on.

Sincerely yours,

---

[1] *Tutt and Mr. Tutt*, Scribners, 1920. [2] Eight or more collections of Tutt stories were subsequently published by Scribners.

Nov. 18, 1919

DEAR MR. HUNEKER:

We have been hoping to the end that the strike would be concluded in time to publish the books which were caught in an unfinished condition, in time for the Christmas season. But we now must acknowledge to ourselves that there is no longer any chance of this, and one of those, therefore, that we were most anxious to get out, your "Steeplejack,"[1] must go over. This is a great disappointment to you, but there is no help for it. It is a very large book, and one that would have to be made carefully, and we could not possibly have finished it in time to escape the strike even if we had known that it was coming. In the face of this situation, we should like to be able to discuss with you the best time for publication. We have thought, you know, to publish "Mary Garden"[2] early in the year — and, by the way, we should take up the question of illustrations for that — and so must consider carefully how we had better manage.

We have been in daily hope that you would bring in the manuscript of your novel.[3] What has happened to it?

Sincerely yours,

Nov. 1, 1920

DEAR MR. HUNEKER:

I'll bet you suspected the reason I did not return the Mencken article, which I read with great delight, was because I lost it.

---

[1] Huneker's autobiography, 2 volumes, Scribners, 1920. [2] A volume of mixed essays under this title, scheduled for publication by Scribners on Feb. 1, 1920, but never completed. [3] *Painted Veils*. This was eventually published by Liveright, in 1928.

At least, Mr. Brownell[1] thinks I lost it and *I* think *he* did. I gave it to him after reading it and he read it himself and gave it back, and then asked for it again and did not give it back. Anyhow, I return a copy of it herewith which I dug up from a pile of our own old papers in the magazine.[2] I hope you will forgive my delay.

Have you any comment on our advertising of "Steeplejack"?[3] I do not want you to feel dissatisfied and not say so. We certainly intend to keep this book in the front rack right along, and if we do not seem to you to be doing so, we want to know it.

Sincerely yours,

TO JAMES HUNEKER

DEAR MR. HUNEKER: Nov. 5, 1920

We have been asked to bring two authors to the Authors' Night at the National Arts Club in connection with the annual book exhibition there on November 17. I know you generally avoid such affairs but you will only have to autograph some copies of your books and perhaps — though probably not — make a very little speech. Your "Steeplejack"[4] is very well represented there and it is regarded as one of the very finest books of the year, on all accounts. I hope we may count on you. I hope to get Scott Fitzgerald to go and one reason is that I want him to meet you; and I think you will find him an interesting personality. You know he is the author of "This Side of Paradise,"[5] and he is a very attractive fellow.

If you will only say that you will go, we can arrange the details later.   Sincerely yours,

---

[1] William Crary Brownell (1851–1928), writer and critic, then senior editor at Scribners.   [2] *Scribner's Magazine.*   [3] By James Huneker, Scribners, 1920, 2 volumes.   [4] Scribners, 1920, 2 volumes.   [5] Scribners, 1920.

TO JOHN GALSWORTHY

Dear Mr. Galsworthy: February 11, 1921

Your views of "Awakening"[1] are exactly ours. We know the book is not for children at all, but for grown-up people, and unquestionably for mothers in particular. Our difficulty has not been a failure to understand this so much as it has been that of making the trade understand it; and even more than that, perhaps, the difficulty that comes from the superficial, the physical, character of the book. The truth is that it falls superficially into a class of books that almost does not exist here — that of gift books. There was a time when books of very much this form were published around Christmas in this country simply as gift books. They found a ready market then, but such books have almost entirely gone out now. People buy a great many books at Christmas but they are simply the outstanding books of the year, as a rule, or the standard books. The only class of books that sell at that time, rather than at any other, are what we call holiday books, which are generally standard works beautifully illustrated and designed for children primarily. The trouble is that "Awakening" seems to the bookseller to be one of these — a holiday book for young people; and, at first sight, the nature of the illustrations, seen without reading the text, as they are by a customer in a bookstore, rather tends to give the idea of a juvenile. We have tried to counteract this tendency but it is true that, in spite of the fact that it was extremely well distributed, it has not been handled in the way that its real character demanded. It sometimes seems almost impossible to prevent the trade from thinking altogether according to precedent and, with a book like this, which sells so much in the bookstores rather than by advertis-

[1] By John Galsworthy, Scribners, 1920.

ing, this consideration is important.

I think that our best plan for "Awakening" now is to emphasize its relation to "In Chancery"[1] and "To Let";[2] and we have sent out to the reviews a note explaining this, and are also putting an advertisement in *Scribner's*[3] to the same effect; — in *Scribner's* it is particularly suitable because all the readers of *Scribner's* are reading "To Let."

The sale of "In Chancery" is 20,800. It did not do as well as "Saint's Progress"[4] did in the same period, four months — probably because "In Chancery" is a sequel, which works against a book at first. But we shall be disappointed and surprised if in the end the sale of "In Chancery" is not altogether satisfactory. It is noteworthy that the sale of "A Man of Property,"[5] always one of the best of the older books, has very considerably improved since "In Chancery" appeared; and when "To Let" appears, so that we may present the whole design of the "Forsyte Saga,"[6] its sale should be still further advanced, and that of "In Chancery" should be markedly larger than would otherwise be the case. This will also act upon "Awakening" and we ought, eventually, to find some way of bringing "The Indian Summer of a Forsyte"[7] into its place in connection with the three novels.

We are having here a long rainy, misty period. Arizona must be a most pleasant contrast. I have very pleasant memories of Arizona, the only flaw I found in it was that any given point in the landscape always looked so much better than it was when you got to it.

Sincerely yours,

[1] By John Galsworthy, Scribners, 1920.   [2] By John Galsworthy, Scribners, 1921. [3] *Scribner's Magazine.*   [4] By John Galsworthy, Scribners, 1919.   [5] By John Galsworthy, Scribners, 1921.   [6] By John Galsworthy, Scribners, 1922.   [7] By John Galsworthy, included in *Five Tales*, Scribners, 1918.

TO JOHN GALSWORTHY

AUGUST 2, 1921

DEAR MR. GALSWORTHY:

Your letter and the proof of the short plays[1] arrived yesterday and we are today estimating upon it in the idea of putting it immediately in hand. It arrived just in time to let us make an announcement of the volume in our Fall list. I think we should do well with it.

We already have completed copies of "To Let,"[2] which we publish September 2, at the same time that it appears in England. I enclose herewith a number of our advertisements.

Scott Fitzgerald, returning to this country much sooner than he had expected, turned up the other day and spoke with the very greatest enthusiasm and interest of dining at your house and of the kindness of Mrs. Galsworthy and you. He told me of what you talked. He has the not very usual faculty of remembering things and turning them over in his mind, so that he gets much good out of anything that suggests an idea to him. I am delighted that he saw you and am very grateful to you for having allowed me to introduce him. I think it may turn out to have done him a great deal of good, for he needs steering.

I heard on all sides that the summer has been very uncomfortable and trying in England but I hope it may have been comfortable for you and Mrs. Galsworthy.

Very sincerely yours,

---

[1] *Six Short Plays*, Scribners, 1921.   [2] By John Galsworthy, Scribners, 1921.

TO F. SCOTT FITZGERALD

DEC. 12, 1921

DEAR FITZGERALD:

Don't ever *defer* to my judgment. You won't on any vital point, I know, and I should be ashamed, if it were possible to have made you; for a writer of any account must speak solely for himself. I should hate to play (assuming V. W. B.'s[1] position to be sound) the W. D. Howells to your Mark Twain.

It is not to the *substance* of this passage[2] that I object. Everyone of any account, anyone who could conceivably read this book, under forty, agrees with the substance of it. If they did not, there would be less objection to it in one way — it would then startle them as a revelation of a new point of view which, by giving a more solid kind of value, would lessen the objection on account of flippancy. (I hate the word. I hate to be put in the position of using such words as "respect" and "flippancy," which have so often enraged me, but there is some meaning in them.) The Old Testament ought not to be treated in a way which suggests a failure to realize its tremendous significance in the recent history of man, as if it could simply be puffed away with a breath of contempt, it is so trivial. That is the effect of the passage at present. It is partly so because Maury is talking and is talking in character; and that is the way men do talk too, so far as ability enables them, even when they fully appreciate every side of the matter. It is here that the question of the public comes in. They will not make allowance for the fact that a character is talking extemporaneously. They will think F. S. F. is writing deliberately. Tolstoi did that even, and to Shakespeare.

---

[1] Van Wyck Brooks, American critic, author of *The Ordeal of Mark Twain*, Dutton, 1920. In this book, the influence of Howells on Mark Twain is revealed as, on the whole, a restrictive and injurious one.   [2] In *The Beautiful and Damned* (Scribners, 1922), in which Maury makes light of the Old Testament.

Now, you are, through Maury, expressing your views, of course; but you would do so differently if you were deliberately stating them as your views. You speak of Galileo: he and Bruno showed themselves to have a genuine sense of the religious significance of the theories they broke down. They were not in a state of mind to treat the erroneous beliefs of men with a light contempt. France[1] does not so treat Christ in that story of Pilate in his old age. And "Whited Sepulchre" is an expression of a high contempt, although applied to an object which had no such quality of significance as the Bible.

My point is that you impair the effectiveness of the passage — of the very purpose you use it for — by giving it that quality of contempt, and I wish you would try so to revise it as not to antagonize even the very people who agree with the substance of it. You would go a long way toward this if you cut out "God Almighty" and put "Deity." In fact, if you will change it on the line indicated, by that change you will have excised the element to which I object.

I do agree that it belongs in Maury's speech; that it does bring it to a focus. But you could so revise it that it would do this without at the same time doing the thing to which we object.

I hope this gets over to you. If I saw you for ten minutes I know you would understand and would agree with me.

As ever,

TO F. SCOTT FITZGERALD

DEC. 31, 1921

DEAR FITZGERALD:

The letter from Reynolds[2] which you sent and which I return is rather pathetic, but so far as it concerns your writing, I think

[1] Anatole France. [2] Paul Reynolds, literary agent.

it represents a temporary condition. The time ought to come when whatever you write will go through and where its irony and satire will be understood. They will know what you stand for in writing, and they do not really know yet. It is in recognition of this that I want very much to have this book[1] so announced in our lists, and so on, that it will be regarded as "important" as well as the other things.

There is, especially in this country, a rootless class of society into which Gloria and Anthony drifted, a large class and one which has an important effect on society in general. It is certainly worth presenting in a novel. I know that you did not deliberately undertake to do this but I think "The Beautiful and Damned" has, in effect, done this; and that this makes it a valuable as well as brilliant commentary upon American society. Perhaps you have never even formulated the idea that it does do this thing, but don't you think it is true? The book is not written according to the usual conventions of the novel, and its greatest interest is not that of the usual novel. Its satire will not of itself be understood by the great, simple-minded public without a little help. For instance, in talking to one man about the book, I received the comment that Anthony was unscathed; that he came through with his millions, and thinking well of himself. This man completely missed the extraordinarily effective irony of the last few paragraphs.

As ever,

TO RING W. LARDNER

JULY 2, 1923

DEAR MR. LARDNER:

I read your story, "The Golden Wedding,"[2] with huge en-

---

[1] *The Beautiful and Damned*, Scribners, 1922.   [2] Published by Scribners, with other stories by Ring Lardner, under the title *How to Write Short Stories*, 1924.

joyment. Scott Fitzgerald recommended it to me and he also suggested that you might have other material of the same sort which, with this, could form a volume. I am therefore writing to tell you how very much interested we should be to consider this possibility, if you could put the material before us. I would hardly have ventured to do this if Scott had not spoken of the possibility, because your position in the literary world is such that you must be besieged by publishers, and to people in that situation their letters of interest are rather a nuisance. I am certainly mighty glad to have the chance of expressing our interest though, if, as Scott thought, you would not feel that we were merely bothering you. Would you be willing to send on any material that might go with "The Golden Wedding" to form a volume, or to tell me where I might come at it in periodicals?

Very truly yours,

TO EDWARD BOK

MARCH 31, 1924

DEAR MR. BOK:

I have read the [Woodrow] Wilson chapter and I think it an important and highly interesting addition to the book.[1] There are one or two points in it which I feel, for my part, doubtful about. But I would rather consider them again, on a second reading, before discussing them. I am delighted you did the chapter and I think it will be read with great eagerness. It will make many people think. It will be a revelation.

I have been looking over the manuscript and thinking about it. It seems to me that the great element of distinction in this book — and this was your intention — is the spiritual and philo-

[1] *Twice Thirty*, Scribners, 1924.

sophical element. You are trying to bring out the significant and valuable in life as it appears to a man of great experience at the age of sixty. But chapters dealing with abstractions are necessarily less interesting than those dealing with actualities, and we already have a sufficient number of chapters of that sort. And yet it seemed to me that there were certain topics that might well be discussed and would tend to increase the distinctive element in the book.

In the first place, I think your books as a whole run the danger of giving the impression that you overvalue *material* success. This book does not, perhaps, as it stands; but, at the same time, it does not emphatically present the other point of view. To present it in a disquisition would be preachy. It occurred to me, though, that you might present it, if your views and experience warrant it, by such a topic as "successful men who were poor." It is true men of character and talent are not likely to be poor, and yet there are many who are. For instance, Carlyle regarded his father, a peasant, as equal to any great man. He said he had known Burns, but that he would not put Burns above his father. His father, he thought, had as strong an intellect and noble a character as any hero, and Carlyle was not a sentimentalist. His father was a builder in a rough part of Scotland and he built honest buildings. Do you not remember men who in this same sense could be called great men, and successful men? There was old Evarts Greene of the Worcester *Spy*, who always looked threadbare, but he was a man of great influence for right in his community. I think that a chapter on this aspect of things, with some of those excellent portraits and character sketches that you give, would be a splendid addition to the book, and would enhance its spiritual quality. On the same line, could you not write a chapter on "The finest man I ever knew" — that is, the man who simply in himself, and apart from whatever he might be or might have done, gave the impression of moral force, of goodness? If there were any such single man, I think that a presentation of him would be of advantage. Of course, in these suggestions I have been working around to the expression of ideas through characters, in concrete terms, which is the way you do them best.

It also occurred to me that it might be possible for you to write in this book something further about "The Sanctuary"[1] and to what degree it was fulfilling its purpose — the purpose of the "Two Persons."[2] This you will be able to judge of in an instant. It depends simply upon whether there is yet anything to say, or anything further to say.

You have practically confessed, I think in "The Americanization,"[3] or in one way or another, to a rather low opinion of woman (an opinion to which I have no objection, since I share it) but this would make still more interesting a chapter by you upon "Women who have impressed me." Of course, you have talked about various distinguished women whom you have met, but mostly you have associated with men and have written about them. Could you not make a fine chapter on remarkable women you have known? I have known some extraordinary ones in vitality and will power and intellect too. I think this would have a tendency to round out this book, and to once more bring out your views in these concrete terms.

I did debate with myself the possibility of a chapter on rich young men. What ought they to do? But I could not decide, myself, exactly what they ought to do, and, upon the whole, I rather abandoned the idea. Possibly it will interest you. But we do not want to make the book *too* long.

So much for the present. It is very interesting to be able to act in this way in connection with the book, and it would have been impossible if you had not had it ready so far in advance.

Sincerely yours,

---

[1] A sanctuary for birds, established in Florida by Edward Bok.   [2] A book by Edward Bok, about his Dutch grandparents, Scribners, 1922.   [3] *The Americanization of Edward Bok*, Scribners, 1920.

TO F. SCOTT FITZGERALD

JUNE 5, 1924

DEAR SCOTT:

I was mighty glad to hear from you to say you had arrived, and I did whatever you asked me to do in the store — I have forgotten what it was — and then to get Zelda's[1] very spirited and amusing letter.

I am glad you are deep in Shelley and Byron. Trelawny wrote an exceedingly interesting book about both of them — perhaps you have read it. I came across it in college. He told about how Shelley not only had that physical peculiarity which prevented his heart from burning, but that other one of sinking to the very bottom of a pool when Trelawny told him that all a man needed to swim was self-confidence. No ordinary human being would, of course, sink to a depth of more than three feet or so. There was also a most interesting book by James Hogg about Shelley. Oh, I was a great Shelley fan, and I never fully got over it, though people think badly of him now.

I read your story[2] in the *Mercury* and it seemed to me very good indeed, and also different from what you had done before — it showed a more steady and complete mastery, it seemed to me. Greater maturity might be the word. At any rate, it gave me a more distinct sense of what you could do, possibly because I have not read any of your other stories in the magazines except, "How to Live on Thirty-six Thousand," which of course was a trifle. This seemed to show a remarkable strength and resource. I was greatly impressed by it.

Did you get the "War and Peace"? Don't feel any obligation to read it, because it is better that you should follow your inclination, and time is valuable. The reason I mention it is that

[1] Mrs. F. Scott Fitzgerald. [2] "Absolution" in *American Mercury*, June, 1924.

it did not get on the steamer, in spite of the assurances of office boys, etc., that it would, and so I had to send it by mail.

The reason I went down to Ring Lardner's — but I am ashamed to tell you about it. I meant to have a serious talk with him, but we arrived late and the drinks were already prepared. We did no business that night. He was very amusing. The book is out[1] — you will have had your copy of it. The reviews have been excellent and, so far as the reviewers are concerned, the title got across perfectly. I will pick out a bunch of clippings and send them, after certain others like H. L. M.[2] have been heard from. So far there has not been much of a sale, but all the publicity we have got ought to accomplish something for us.

Yours,

TO RING W. LARDNER

JUNE 11, 1924

DEAR RING:

I am enclosing some ads which perhaps you have seen, one from the *Post,* one from the *Times,* and one from *Scribner's.*[3] But chiefly I am writing to warn you to avoid 42nd Street opposite 4th Avenue for the next several days (though I imagine you are safely in Chicago, anyway), because you are likely to be recognized there on account of the fact that Liggetts have a large window display of "How to Write Short Stories," an enormous enlargement of your picture, and some pages of the preface. *Printer's Ink* had an article which was highly complimentary to the device of the title and preface, and comments on the stories as being a new way of putting out a product so as to distinguish it.

I wish you could manage to stop in here some time because

---

[1] *How to Write Short Stories* by Ring Lardner, Scribners, 1924. [2] H. L. Mencken. [3] *Scribner's Magazine.*

I want to have Mr. Scribner[1] meet you. He is very keen about the stories. He sent a copy to Barrie and I have sent one to Galsworthy.

Yours,

TO F. SCOTT FITZGERALD

NOVEMBER 20, 1924

DEAR SCOTT:

I think you have every kind of right to be proud of this book.[2] It is an extraordinary book, suggestive of all sorts of thoughts and moods. You adopted exactly the right method of telling it, that of employing a narrator who is more of a spectator than an actor: this puts the reader upon a point of observation on a higher level than that on which the characters stand and at a distance that gives perspective. In no other way could your irony have been so immensely effective, nor the reader have been enabled so strongly to feel at times the strangeness of human circumstance in a vast heedless universe. In the eyes of Dr. Eckleberg various readers will see different significances; but their presence gives a superb touch to the whole thing: great unblinking eyes, expressionless, looking down upon the human scene. It's magnificent!

I could go on praising the book and speculating on its various elements, and means, but points of criticism are more important now. I think you are right in feeling a certain slight sagging in chapters six and seven, and I don't know how to suggest a remedy. I hardly doubt that you will find one and I am only writing to say that I think it does need something to hold up here to the pace set, and ensuing. I have only two actual criticisms:

One is that among a set of characters marvelously palpable

---

[1] Charles Scribner, Senior (1854–1930), president of Charles Scribner's Sons.
[2] *The Great Gatsby*, Scribners, 1925.

and vital — I would know Tom Buchanan if I met him on the street and would avoid him — Gatsby is somewhat vague. The reader's eyes can never quite focus upon him, his outlines are dim. Now everything about Gatsby is more or less a mystery, i.e. more or less vague, and this may be somewhat of an artistic intention, but I think it is mistaken. Couldn't *he* be physically described as distinctly as the others, and couldn't you add one or two characteristics like the use of that phrase "old sport" — not verbal, but physical ones, perhaps. I think that for some reason or other a reader — this was true of Mr. Scribner[1] and of Louise[2] — gets an idea that Gatsby is a much older man than he is, although you have the writer say that he is little older than himself. But this would be avoided if on his first appearance he was seen as vividly as Daisy and Tom are, for instance — and I do not think your scheme would be impaired if you made him so.

The other point is also about Gatsby: his career must remain mysterious, of course. But in the end you make it pretty clear that his wealth came through his connection with Wolfsheim. You also suggest this much earlier. Now almost all readers numerically are going to be puzzled by his having all this wealth and are going to feel entitled to an explanation. To give a distinct and definite one would be, of course, utterly absurd. It did occur to me, though, that you might here and there interpolate some phrases, and possibly incidents, little touches of various kinds, that would suggest that he was in some active way mysteriously engaged. You do have him called on the telephone, but couldn't he be seen once or twice consulting at his parties with people of some sort of mysterious significance, from the political, the gambling, the sporting world, or whatever it may be. I know I am floundering, but that fact may help you to see

---

[1] Charles Scribner, Senior (1854–1930), president of Charles Scribner's Sons.
[2] Mrs. Maxwell E. Perkins.

what I mean. The *total* lack of an explanation through so large a part of the story does seem to me a defect — or not of an explanation, but of the suggestion of an explanation. I wish you were here so I could talk about it to you, for then I know I could at least make you understand what I mean. What Gatsby did ought never to be definitely imparted, even if it could be. Whether he was an innocent tool in the hands of somebody else, or to what degree he was this, ought not to be explained. But if some sort of business activity of his were simply adumbrated, it would lend further probability to that part of the story.

There is one other point: in giving deliberately Gatsby's biography, when he gives it to the narrator, you do depart from the method of the narrative in some degree, for otherwise almost everything is told, and beautifully told, in the regular flow of it, in the succession of events or in accompaniment with them. But you can't avoid the biography altogether. I thought you might find ways to let the truth of some of his claims like "Oxford" and his army career come out, bit by bit, in the course of actual narrative. I mention the point anyway, for consideration in this interval before I send the proofs.

The general brilliant quality of the book makes me ashamed to make even these criticisms. The amount of meaning you get into a sentence, the dimensions and intensity of the impression you make a paragraph carry, are most extraordinary. The manuscript is full of phrases which make a scene blaze with life. If one enjoyed a rapid railroad journey I would compare the number and vividness of pictures your living words suggest, to the living scenes disclosed in that way. It seems, in reading, a much shorter book than it is, but it carries the mind through a series of experiences that one would think would require a book of three times its length.

The presentation of Tom, his place, Daisy and Jordan, and

the unfolding of their characters is unequaled so far as I know. The description of the valley of ashes adjacent to the lovely country, the conversation and the action in Myrtle's apartment, the marvelous catalogue of those who came to Gatsby's house — these are such things as make a man famous. And all these things, the whole pathetic episode, you have given a place in time and space, for with the help of T. J. Eckleberg and by an occasional glance at the sky, or the sea, or the city, you have imparted a sort of sense of eternity. You once told me you were not a *natural* writer — my God! You have plainly mastered the craft, of course; but you needed far more than craftsmanship for this.

As ever,

TO JAMES BOYD

DEC. 1, 1924

DEAR MR. BOYD:

I have just received your letter of the 28th. I had been waiting to write you until the question of the wrap[1] was wholly settled. We thought that Mrs. Boyd's suggestion of using the pines was an excellent one and we therefore began the whole wrap over again and have made it somewhat different. We abandoned the colonial troops and have put in, among the pine tree trunks, an irregular line of mounted men which might be military and might be merely a pack train such as that described early in the book. We have in this way worked in the coonskin caps as well. We thought that this was wise because the title "Drums" is so distinctly military that the effect with the use of the marching troops would be too wholly military. The general effect still is military, but not to so emphatic a degree.

[1] For his book *Drums*, published by Scribners in 1925.

I have sent you now sixty-nine galleys, which is a very large part of the book, and as the others will follow very rapidly, I should think you would be justified in beginning your reading. By the time you finish what is now in your hands, you will have a great deal more and will therefore be able to read the whole book without interruption.

As for Mr. Brownell,[1] he has been laid up lately, but he will soon be in and I shall try to get from him some general comments — although he had less to say critically upon this book than upon almost any that I can remember his reading.

About young authors I do not feel in the least as you suggest. Far from it. It is with them that our great hopes lie. We know what the old authors can do and, although some of them do admirably, they seldom surprise us. But the young writers may do anything — at least several of them may, and you are certainly one of those several.

If Mrs. Boyd was "scared" it must have been of ——,[2] of whom I also am scared. But of me not even my own children are scared — while I am still always scared when confronted by a charming young woman. But don't tell anybody this, because it is not a suitable characteristic for an editor.

Sincerely yours,

TO WILL JAMES

DEAR MR. JAMES: DEC. 5, 1924

I suppose you have seen enough reviews of "Cowboys North and South"[3] to know with what enthusiasm the critics and literary observers have received it, and as much on account of the text as the pictures. I enclose a review that has just come from

---

[1] William Crary Brownell, at that time senior editor of Charles Scribner's Sons.
[2] A member of the Scribner organization, nameless here.   [3] Scribner's, 1924.

Struthers Burt; but the comments of the ordinary unliterary citizen, who is the really important critic in the end, would probably interest you more, and, if so, those I have heard would please you much. As for the sale, it goes well and promises to go better.

Anyway, the outcome of the publication has already been such, it seems to us, as to give you any assurance you may have wanted of marked success in book writing; I hardly think you could have had any doubts at all upon the matter of illustrating. I am therefore writing to suggest that you consider following this book with another, written in the same manner but different in design, a continuous narrative with as much or as little plot as you thought best, which would bring into the compass of a single story the adventures and incidents characteristic of a young cowboy's career, related in his own words. Really the book I have in mind — for unsatisfactory as comparisons are, one can never altogether avoid them — is "Huckleberry Finn." There was very little plot to it, you probably remember. Its great interest was simply in the incidents and scenes of the trip on a raft down the Mississippi, told in the language of a boy. Of course, "Huckleberry Finn" is primarily a boy's book and it would be better if what you would do were not altogether that, but the great thing is that any such consecutive narrative would give your unquestionable talent for graphic human writing a chance beyond that which this book gave. And we suspect that it would show an equal skill in making types and characters realizable as individuals. Won't you consider this? We should then have a book the novel size, to sell as a novel, and would be quite justified in having great expectations for it. We, of course, see it also as illustrated with your own pictures. I have talked to Mr. Chapin[1] about this and he is in hearty accord with the plan. Sincerely yours,

[1] Joseph Hawley Chapin, at that time head of Scribner's Art Department.

TO STRUTHERS BURT

MAY 26, 1925

DEAR STRUTHERS:

I swear I do not know anybody writing poetry who gives the purely lyrical thrill you give in these poems[1] of yours many times; and certainly there is nobody who has ever combined that quality with the homely sense of common humanity. I think you have done something very unusual indeed in this collection — and, what is more, the value of the individual poem gains by its place in the volume as a whole. The poems all work together to express a point of view that is genuinely human as well as aware of unexpected beauty in all sorts of things. And, added to all this, there is frequent originality of form. There is, however, one poem that I think is not up to the others and that the collection would be better without. That is number XV — "Renewal." I hope you won't want me to explain, but somehow this poem does seem to me to fail — not to "get across." I do distinctly urge its omission. But, of course, it is up to you altogether. Other than that, I have only made a few suggestions where I did not understand the irregularity in meter. I marked others, here and there, and then rubbed out the marks because, after reading them over carefully, I thought the irregularity was part of the quality of the poem and should therefore not be changed.

Now I have read over all of these poems several times and the older ones, the ones which you had in the magazine,[2] half a dozen times at least. This is a great test for poetry, and these poems stand it. They give me the ecstasy of the first reading, if anything intensified. On the whole it is a wonderfully even collection. I got Dunn[3] to read them, and Jack Wheelock,[4] and

---

[1] *When I Grew Up to Middle Age*, Scribners, 1925.   [2] *Scribner's Magazine.*
[3] Charles F. Dunn, an editor at Scribners.   [4] John Hall Wheelock, an editor at Scribners.

each of them picked different favorites, but everyone agrees on "When I Grew Up to Middle Age," "The Lovely Lady" and "The River." The one that I remember Jack spoke of particularly was the little poem "Beauty Persists," and those that Dunn was most taken with were "Dust" and "Pursuit." It is easy to agree with them, but among those that I did not know so well and liked especially — although "Mountain Prayer" I read a long time ago — were *that,* which is one I care for most, "The Countryside," and "Pack Trip."

Certainly the book should make an impression.

Tell Walter Gilkyson[1] I had a note from him and was delighted to get it, and I will answer it soon. Just to put his brand upon the title we got out a note saying that he was again in Europe in connection with the preparation of a novel to be called, "The Lost Adventurer."[2]

Yours as ever,

TO STARK YOUNG

JAN. 29, 1926

DEAR STARK:

Of course "Heaven Trees"[3] is lovely, and it has the note of authenticity. It has the charm and the pathos of that which was, long ago, and will never again be. The chapters are curiously and, I judge, artfully, cumulative in their effect, and, as suggestions I thought to make at first came later to be superfluous, so a couple of points of question I still have may vanish with the later chapters. May these come soon. I waited to write on account of the Magazine,[4] to whom I showed some manuscript; but they have not read it. I shall write more later.

As ever,

---

[1] Author of *Toward What Bright Land, Oil, The Lost Adventurer*, published by Scribners. [2] *The Lost Adventurer*, Scribners, 1927. [3] By Stark Young, Scribners, 1926. [4] *Scribner's Magazine.*

TO F. SCOTT FITZGERALD

APRIL 27, 1926

DEAR SCOTT:

The picture is bad and caused us to hesitate. But that it was so widely printed showed the chance there was for a picture, and we could not forego that chance. The truth is we have no picture of you but those old ones, which ought not any longer to be used even if they could be — they are too widely known. Anyway, the chief value of pictures is simply that of catching the eye. People hardly expect likenesses in a newspaper, but they do look at a picture and read the caption, and, in this instance, are reminded that they have not yet met All the Sad Young Men. That bit of obvious psychology accounts for our use of pictures in the enclosed "ads"; they serve solely to draw attention, are only thereby justified.

As for sales, they are something over 10,000 to date. We have printed 15,000. The prospects are good. I don't enclose reviews — your clipping agency will furnish them.

The Galsworthys[1] passed through New York on the way to England. I gave them your book, and *she* was much pleased. So was he, but he talked of it (between ourselves) with less judgment. He did speak of "Gatsby" as "a great advance"; but he's not really in sympathy with things today. The books he most admires — I won't mention the one I'm thinking of because it's ours — are laid out on the old lines and are not expressive of present thought and feeling. This is much less true of Mrs. Galsworthy, it seemed to me; it may be that women, living much more in the present, from day to day, don't get rooted in a period as men almost inevitably do.

The other day I assigned to you "all right, title and interest in and to the motion picture rights" of "The Great Gatsby,"

---

[1] Mr. and Mrs. John Galsworthy.

that Reynolds[1] might sell them. So that will bring you something, and not a little.

The O'Brien[2] book did not contain any of your stories, but some of them were listed as follows:

> ***Absolution
> **Adjuster
> *Baby Party
> Love in the Night
> *One of My Oldest Friends
> **Our Own Movie Queen
> **Pusher-in-the-Face
> Sensible Thing

Molly Colum's article[3] drew considerable written comment and was vocally much discussed — which in itself proves nothing except that it was good for *Scribner's,* as having been, in what criticism it has printed, too classical and academic. I detest argument and, though I cannot restrain myself often from a verbal one, I can from a written, and so do now.

I'm almost afraid to tell you about a book that I think incredibly interesting — Spengler's "Decline of the West" — for you'll tell me it's "old stuff" and that you read it two years ago — for it was published eight years ago in Germany, and probably six, in France, and has been a long time translating into English. I'm trying for time to read that and Clarendon's "History of the Rebellion," which long ago attracted me through quotations from it I was always encountering in other books.

Our really great success this spring promises to be Thomason's "Fix Bayonets!"; for, although its price is $3.50, it's already well on toward a sale of ten thousand copies, and we're

---

[1] Paul Reynolds, literary agent. [2] *The Best Short Stories of 1925,* edited by Edward O'Brien. [3] Mary M. Colum, "A Critical Credo," in *Scribner's Magazine,* April 1926.

printing five thousand more. Sullivan[1] is also going strong. I think Hemingway's[2] book will look well when done: we've made several good cuts to stand on the half-title pages; but it's the novel that I'm most eager to see, "The Sun Also Rises"![3] They say Dreiser is anxious to leave Liveright, who has certainly done well by him. In fact, there's a story about that he threw a cup of coffee into Liveright's face, but if it had been true it would have been confirmed, for the ―― was the alleged scene of the encounter ― a broadcasting station if ever there was one.

Van Wyck Brooks has been in New Canaan for several months; but, although I've seen much of him, there was little fun in it because he is so depressed ― and the chief cause is (in confidence) that he's stuck in his book on Emerson.[4] He can't finish it and declares it's a failure. I read it and suggested a scheme to apply to it which would give the structure it totally lacks. But Van Wyck won't adopt it ― at least not as yet. Perhaps he will in the end. So he says he must get a *job;* and I say, "What a shame at your age, with a foundation of reputation well laid. Set down the names of ten lesser American writers as titles for articles and I'll sell them at five hundred a piece, and the result will be a book that will outsell any you've done." But he says he cannot write that way, and so we get no further. What he wants, of course, is a "part time" job, but such a one, if it continues, will suck a man under. Van Wyck could also, and profitably, lecture; for he has a body of ideas all related to U. S. "civilization" and letters, and he could get up a series which would be altogether in line with his literary motives. But I ought not to bother you with his problem.

We had a grand winter at New Canaan. Skating on most of the week-ends and hockey, and over New Year's, for three

---

[1] *Our Times: The United States, 1900–1925*, Vol. I, by Mark Sullivan, Scribners, 1926. [2] *The Torrents of Spring*, Scribners, 1926. [3] By Ernest Hemingway, Scribners, 1926. [4] *The Life of Emerson*, Dutton, 1932.

windless days, the whole three-mile lake, a sheet of flexible black ice.

As ever your friend,

JAN. 6, 1927

DEAR JIM:

I sent you yesterday the first fourteen galleys.[1] I am reading the duplicate, and I shall certainly have nothing of importance to say up to this point, excepting that I think they are beautifully done in every respect. My inclination to write to you sometimes about larger matters in respect to the novel is thwarted by the fear that I may only confuse you and trouble you. I speak, for instance, of not having got the impression of the great length and long-drawn grinding hardship of the Civil War, but that I thought I might have got this if I had read it all at one time, or at several times close together. You certainly give, in the prison chapter, an idea of great length of time, and it may be that this is the case with all the War. When I spoke of portraits of the privates, I did not mean that you had not enough actual soldier *characters* in the story, like those members of the company whom one even sees when the company is first formed, and then throughout. I only meant that the great skill in portraiture which you showed in Stonewall Jackson might be given more play by introducing glimpses of individuals of a characteristic sort — little incidents, just like that of Jackson, but not of the leaders. If you put in the leaders, it would become like the old-time historical novel, where the hero encountered everybody of importance in an altogether impossible way. In all my comments, my idea is not so much that there are deficiencies, but that you have abilities that might get

---

[1] Of his *Marching On*, published by Scribners in 1927.

fuller play. That is what prompted me mainly in commenting on the war chapters.

There is one other idea I thought you might think over. I do not know whether James, who immediately wins the affection of the reader, and his respect too, is not made too simple throughout; whether he ought not to develop a more positive character than he does. He is a little perplexed and bewildered when he first comes into the world from his little farm, and this is altogether right and admirable, but I question whether he ought not to develop more than he does under experience. His captain saw that he had the stuff in him for an officer, but he did not himself particularly exhibit the qualities perceived. I liked your note making him an officer, because to do that would have been to follow the old historical romance. I merely want to suggest the idea now that the growth of his character might be, in some way, emphasized in the latter part of the book.

The rest of the galleys will follow rapidly.

As ever yours,

TO JAMES BOYD

MARCH 14, 1927

DEAR JIM:

Sorry to have troubled you with the telegram. I supposed you had followed the letter with the pages,[1] because you have always acted promptly about proof.

Now I have a strong demand from our advertising department to urge you to give them some material for use at the time the book appears. They hope that they might even get a

---

[1] Page-proof of his *Marching On*, published by Scribners in 1927.

story in the daily press, some new views about the war that
your research for "Marching On" turned up.

I remember your saying two things that struck me as extremely interesting: one, that the class freed by the war was
not so much the slaves, as the non-slaveholding whites; and the
other, that the South might yet have won the war had not the
people lost their will to win.

The first idea seemed to me very interesting indeed, and even
though, of course in a way, it has been discussed by historians
— at least I suppose it must have been — it would strike most
people as quite a new idea, I believe. And, as for the second,
it might provoke indignation in the South, but I remember your
saying there were great supplies of material and of food in the
northern part of the South, which could have been used to keep
the army going through the summer. I thought that you might
take one of these points, and that from there you might go into
some of the interesting little sidelights that you had unearthed
in diaries, etc. At any rate, I put the question up to you for
some consideration. You are to be here on the 25th and, if you
had thought there was a possibility, you could have turned it
over mentally, and would then be able to put it in shape.

I always feel unfair in asking an author to do anything more
than to write such a book as this one. It seems as though the
publisher should feel himself compelled to do all the rest, to say
the least, but we cannot do what I am now asking you to do.

We were to go to Struthers'[1] today, but he said you were to
be away, and we would much rather wait until you were back
again. But the news that you were to be away made me hope
that perhaps you were coming up here. If so, do please let me
know, because nowadays I am compelled to make various little
trips to Boston and Philadelphia, and I would want to arrange

---

[1] Struthers Burt, poet, essayist and novelist. He and his wife, the novelist Katharine Newlin Burt, lived not far from the Boyds, in Southern Pines, North Carolina.

them so as not to conflict with any chance of seeing you and your wife.

As ever yours,

TO JOHN W. THOMASON, JR.

OCT. 11, 1927

DEAR THOMASON:

I just bought the *Cosmopolitan* with your story "The Killer." I suppose you will soon have written enough stories for another book, but what would you think of this idea? — To take some fine Southern figure of the Civil War who is not too well known in general, and yet played a significant part, and one of strong military interest, and simply write the story of his career, with plentiful illustrations. Even so well known a figure as Stuart,[1] if he appealed to you, would do very well, and I suppose you would have to take someone notable in order to have one who cut sufficient figure as a soldier. This would give you a chance, I should think, to write highly interesting military history, and yet to give scope for presenting the quality of the time, and for character drawing, and for showing the old South — all things that you can do so well. It would also result in a book of a kind of writing that is particularly popular at present — a free sort of biography in which all that is historically true is so presented, but in which there is also scope for the imagination working on the basis of the known facts.

Anyhow, I thought I would put this idea before you in order that you might think it over. When the vacation epidemic is ended, we can talk it over, among other things. I believe that the *Cosmopolitan,* if you thought you ought to consider them, would be sympathetic to this idea, because I know Ray Long[2]

---

[1] Captain Thomason's book, *Jeb Stuart,* was published by Scribners in 1930.
[2] Editor of *The Cosmopolitan.*

believes in biography. Anyhow, I am sure that *Scribner's* would be more than sympathetic.

Ever yours,

TO WILLARD HUNTINGTON WRIGHT

JAN. 3, 1928

DEAR WRIGHT:[1]

I think "The Greene Murder Case" magnificent. I did not suppose that any story could keep me reading until 3:30 A.M., but this one did.

There are two possible points that might be considered. More reasons could be easily given, I suppose, for Ada's adoption, about which the reader is left with a little curiosity. And I think it highly doubtful that one could count upon killing another instantly with a 32 caliber. You often read of a suicide shooting himself in the head or heart with even a larger caliber, and not dying for hours or even days.

But neither of these points is important. Consider in the proof whether Philo Vance's memorandum of the known facts ought not to be in larger type. And do the facts, when re-arranged as Vance did, and as you show in a footnote, really indicate the guilty party pretty well? If statements of fact are open to such manipulation, I can tell you how you might make another fortune with a better than the cross-word puzzle book and such. Simply invent some twenty-five crimes. In each case, state that so and so was found murdered under such and such circumstances, in a couple of paragraphs. Then, that after an investigation the following facts were revealed. Set down these twenty or thirty facts as they were discovered and suggest that, when put in the right order, the criminal would be indi-

---

[1] Willard Huntington Wright, author, under the pen-name S. S. Van Dine, of the Philo Vance mysteries.

cated. Think of the happy competitions around the family hearths all over the country, and of the busy ladies and gents on the commuting trains.

Hoping soon to see you, I am,

Ever yours,

MARCH 30, 1928

DEAR ——:

We received yours of the 24th informing us that you intend to destroy a copy of "——." We very much regret that it should have displeased you, and we value your opinion and thank you for expressing it.

A publisher is not, as such, a partisan and we shall not argue the merits of the book. We feel, however, that we may rightly point to the extraordinarily enthusiastic reception which this book has had from practically every one of the great papers of the country, and from practically all of the leading critics. In order to show this, we enclose herewith a number of quotations. It seems to us, as publishers, that this also represents a body of opinion which we should not ignore.

Literary and artistic considerations aside, there are two positions commonly taken with regard to books of this kind: one is, that vice ought never to be presented in literature as it actually is, because it is unpleasant, and the other is that the presentation of it as it is, actually, is valuable because it is, actually, repulsive and terrible, and if known to be so will be hated. But if ignored and concealed, it takes on a false glamour which is seductive.

It has not yet been decided which of these positions is the right one. A great deal can be said for each of them, and we respect the one to which you adhere, and value the expression of it.   Very truly yours,

MAY 9, 1928

DEAR THOMASON:

It was mighty pleasant to hear that you are getting on so well. I should think you would take your full leave though. You do not get many chances for rest in this world. Whether or not you do a novel, I hope we can work out a plan for something in a large unit, some continuous narrative, whether history, biography, or fiction. It would give you a larger scope for expression and for the development of character, and things of that sort, that you have shown ability in, and have not had room to develop.

I was in Southern Pines for a week last year, staying with the Burts,[1] and I saw Jim Boyd's[2] house, which is charming. My only objection to Southern Pines was that the warmth, and the perfumed air and all, put me into a kind of somnolent condition, where I could not even converse. It seemed to me inconceivable that anybody could do any work at all in that climate, but that if one had none to do, there was no climate so pleasant to be in. The atmosphere even suppressed a New England conscience which makes it always seem incumbent on one to be busy.

I am glad you and Jim took so well to each other. I felt sure you would. Struthers always is in a state of excitement, and climate has no effect upon him. I will send you a book of his indignant essays when it comes out, "The Other Side" it is called.

[1] Mr. and Mrs. Struthers Burt (Struthers & Katharine Newlin Burt). [2] James Boyd.

I do not think that Tom Boyd[1] really had such a bad experience with officers in the war. I know he almost worshipped one called Johnny the Hard, a major you must know of named Hughes. He was in his battalion. Tom is an individualist. Any discipline would be irksome. He has a natural hate for all restraints. I think he really admires the Marine Corps highly, and that he really liked the war in many ways. I know he told me that although he did not believe in war at all, he would certainly go to the next one if he were young enough.

With remembrance to your wife, I am,

Ever yours,

TO ROGER BURLINGAME

JUNE 20, 1928

DEAR ROGER:

Last week was a hard week. D—— had an idea that he ought to meet all the literary people and I told him recklessly, a month ago, that if he would spend a week in New York, I would see that he did. When the time drew near I asked Chapin,[2] whom I knew to be the gayest dog in this outfit, if he could devote an evening to him. He went far beyond my proposal: he devoted a night to him, and to me as well. I merely wanted D—— to see the crowd at the Players, at dinner time. Chapin wanted him and me first to see the Book Club, where they have one large bookcase containing twenty books, or maybe twenty-one, and a complete assortment of drinks. The head of this Book Club is an Irishman with profound views on the Roman Catholic Church, and we did not leave there until 8:30. Chapin

---

[1] Thomas Boyd, author of *Mad Anthony Wayne, Through the Wheat,* and other books published by Scribners.   [2] Joseph Hawley Chapin, at that time head of Scribner's Art Department.

then wanted us to stop, on the way to the Players, at the Murray Hill Merchants and Manufacturers Club, which was formerly known as the Bengal Bicycle Club. There they have a bar with a foot rail and a red-headed bar tender, who really was very amusing, though not nearly as much so as Chapin and D—— thought. He tried to turn on the radio without effect, and then swore at it and said, "You can't even get static on it," which D—— thought excessively funny, but which I firmly believed to be an old one. But the bartender was an eloquent Irish boy, who spoke well for Al Smith.

It was nearly ten when we got to the Players and found, among others, more or less reclining on the bar, Mr. Reginald Birch,[1] who immediately launched into one of those stories that he gradually develops after the manner of the eighties. This delighted D——, who had not before encountered him, so we gathered him up and proceeded to the dining-room, where we found Clive Weed, the cartoonist, and several others. Weed I always did like much, so that saved the dinner for me. D—— had the time of his life. We started for home at about 11:30, when Chapin proposed that we visit a certain night club where he said he knew the girls. I felt I must go along in line of duty, but I never would have if I had supposed we would stay in an underground, airless place until four in the morning . . . Chapin did know the girls, but there was not much to boast of in that: they were very easy to know.

The next day, Charlie[2] and I gave D—— a luncheon in the board room at the Harvard Club. Canby[3] sat on his right and Hansen[4] at his left. We had a dozen people there, practically all the literary editors. The thing went off very well, and D—— was very much pleased. On the two succeeding nights, we

---

[1] The artist and illustrator, best known for his illustrations to *Little Lord Fauntleroy*.   [2] Charles Scribner, Jr., now president of Charles Scribner's Sons.   [3] Henry Seidel Canby, critic and writer.   [4] Harry Hansen, writer and book reviewer.

dined with different people like Stark Young, and lunched with others. I felt homesick for a little work in the office.

Waldo Peirce[1] has been hereabouts lately with plans for trying to do some writing, in which I have little faith — that is, I have little faith in his ever doing the writing, though I think it might well be excellent if he did it. His mother has died and he seems to be heir to a large part of Bangor, Maine, where he now is "established on the back piazza with an antiquated typewriter." He went down to visit Hemingway in Florida and came back with a pocketful of photographs of himself and Hemingway and Dos Passos (who was there too) with fishes almost as big as themselves. He gave us a very fine, simple drawing of Hemingway's head, and promised to do some studies of him.

Scott[2] is now in Paris finishing his novel.[3] He went there for that purpose because of the expense of living in this country, which compelled him many times to drop the novel in order to write short stories for the *Post*. He promises to be back in August with a complete manuscript.

Did I tell you that when John Marquand was last here, some time ago, he was about twenty pounds, or more, heavier than I ever saw him, and had lost much of his nervousness? A doctor had discovered what was really the matter with him, which was not what he had thought, and fixed him up in no time.

. . . I hope I shall hear pretty soon from you about your plans.

Ever yours,

Aug. 28, 1928

Dear ——:

We have read with interest your letter in criticism of "The

[1] The painter. [2] F. Scott Fitzgerald. [3] *Tender Is the Night*, Scribners, 1934.

Great Gatsby" by F. Scott Fitzgerald, and we thank you for it. Probably if you had read the book through, you would not have felt any the less repugnance to it, but you would no doubt have grasped its underlying motive, which is by no means opposed to your own point of view.

The author was prompted to write this book by surveying the tragic situation of many people because of the utter confusion of ideals into which they have fallen, with the result that they cannot distinguish the good from the bad. The author did not look upon these people with anger or contempt so much as with pity. He saw that good was in them, but that it was altogether distorted. He therefore pictured, in the Great Gatsby, a man who showed extraordinary nobility and many fine qualities, and yet who was following an evil course without being aware of it, and indeed was altogether a worshipper of wholly false gods. He showed him in the midst of a society such as certainly exists, of a people who were all worshipping false gods. He wished to present such a society to the American public so that they would realize what a grotesque situation existed, that a man could be a deliberate law-breaker, who thought that the accumulation of vast wealth by any means at all was an admirable thing, and yet could have many fine qualities of character. The author intended the story to be repugnant and he intended to present it so forcefully and realistically that it would impress itself upon people. He wanted to show that this was a horrible, grotesque, and tragic fact of life today. He could not possibly present these people effectively if he refused to face their abhorrent characteristics. One of these was profanity — the total disregard for, or ignorance of, any sense of reverence for a Power outside the physical world. If the author had not presented these abhorrent characteristics, he would not have drawn a true picture of these people, and by drawing a true picture of them he has done something to make them different,

for he has made the public aware of them, and its opinion
generally prevails in the end.

There are, of course, many people who would say that such
people as those in the book should not be written about, because of their repulsive characteristics. Such people maintain
that it would be better not to inform the public about evil or
unpleasantness. Certainly this position has a strong case. There
is, however, the other opinion: vice is attractive when gilded
by the imagination, as it is when it is concealed and only vaguely
known of; but in reality it is horrible and repulsive, and therefore it is well it should be presented as it is so that it may be
so recognized. Then people would hate it, and avoid it, but
otherwise they may well be drawn to it on account of its false
charm.

Very truly yours,

*In September, 1928, Madeleine Boyd, the literary agent, sent
Scribners the manuscript of a novel by Thomas Wolfe, entitled
"O Lost." Wolfe had previously shown the novel to various
publishers, but without success. He had then placed it in the
hands of Mrs. Boyd, as agent, and had gone abroad feeling,
as he afterward explained, that there was little likelihood of
the book finding a publisher. When the manuscript was read,
Perkins, and others on the Scribner editorial staff, recognized
its extraordinary quality. The following letter sent to Wolfe in
Vienna, Austria, is the first of the now historic series that passed
between Thomas Wolfe and Maxwell Perkins. Before publication, the title "O Lost" was abandoned, at the request of the
publishers, and the book was given the title "Look Homeward,
Angel."*

TO THOMAS WOLFE

OCT. 22, 1928

DEAR MR. WOLFE:

Mrs. Ernest Boyd[1] left with us, some weeks ago, the manuscript of your novel, "O Lost."[2] I do not know whether it would be possible to work out a plan by which it might be worked into a form publishable by us, but I do know that, setting the practical aspects of the matter aside, it is a very remarkable thing, and that no editor could read it without being excited by it and filled with admiration by many passages in it and sections of it.

Your letter, that came with it, shows that you realize what difficulties it presents, so that I need not enlarge upon this side of the question. What we should like to know is whether you will be in New York in a fairly near future, when we can see you and discuss the manuscript. We should certainly look forward to such an interview with very great interest.

Ever truly yours,

TO STARK YOUNG

MARCH 15, 1929

DEAR STARK:

You have written beautifully all your books, but certainly you have never done such beautiful writing as in the new one.[3] It is magical in many of its effects — your best book, I think.

We could put it in hand right away, but we must have a title. I think that one would be good which should suggest the difference between the young and old, the inevitable conflict,

---

[1] Madeleine Boyd, literary agent. [2] Original title of *Look Homeward, Angel,* Scribners, 1929. [3] *River House,* Scribners, 1929.

in spite of mutual respect and affection even of the deepest sort.

I think that John requires to be brought out more in his character, by having him say more or do more in little ways, during the earlier part of the book. But if this is true, you could easily amend it in the proof.

Anyhow, we can talk things over whenever you have time.

Ever yours,

Nov. 27, 1929

Dear Sir:

We have received your letter with regard to ——. We are sorry that you feel as you do about the book — it is far from pleasant to us to have given offense to anybody, and in particular to those who belong to your faith, which we respect. At the same time, you seem not to understand the function of a publisher, nor to attach any importance to one of the greatest principles in the whole world — that which upholds free speech for the sake of the freedom of the intellect. According to this principle any serious and careful book upon any person of importance and significance to the general public should find a publisher; and any publisher who refrained from publication, even if he did not agree with the author's conclusions, because of fear of some particular sect, would be untrue to his profession, and indeed to the cause of intellectual freedom.

You assume that this book is manifestly unfair and irresponsible, but not one single reviewer has thought this. The very opposite has been the opinion of all the leading publications which review books, including the greatest newspapers and magazines of the United States.

It is a part of the American philosophy as expressed in the Constitution — that, except in the most extreme cases, people should be allowed to express their opinions, and that the result of this is to stir up thought and controversy, out of which will emerge the Truth. It is only what is false that is killed by discussion, not what is true.

Ever truly yours,

TO JOHN GALSWORTHY

DEC. 13, 1929

DEAR MR. GALSWORTHY:

We will not use the picture with the little O'Riordan boy any more. I am enclosing herewith an advertisement[1] from last Sunday's *Times*, and also a review that came out last week in the *Saturday Review of Literature*. The sale is not what we had hoped, but perhaps we were wrong in expecting a large, rapid sale, for the sale is very steady and "The Forsyte Saga" never sold so very great a number in any season. One always has a tendency — or perhaps I should say I always have — to find an alibi (as we wrongly use the word in the U. S. A.) in case of disappointment. But, anyhow, we plan for a long and steady sale, and shall keep at the advertising without respect to season. To date the sale is 21,500. The sale of the "Saga" is 5,232, of the "Plays"[2] 1,390, and of "Caravan"[3] 635, since the last royalty report. The stock-market crash does not seem to have been as fateful as was generally expected. The watchword in the last campaign was "Hoover and Prosperity" and the Republicans are determined that the partnership shall not be dissolved even if they have to put the party into business. And it seems as if we might avoid reaping the whirlwind, even if we did sow the wind.

We have been having quite an exciting time here with ——.

---

[1] Of his play *The Roof*, Scribners, 1929.   [2] Scribners, 1928.   [3] Scribners, 1925.

We published a book which truly was a genuine and sound contribution to the discussion of a highly significant character, and the —— did what they could to scare us out of it in advance, and they have since done what they could to injure it, and, in fact, us. We thought they were attacking that principle which it was most appropriate a publisher should defend, and we fought them back so far as we could. They certainly have injured the sale of the book, but I believe we are winning the fight on the principle, which is more important. I thought this might interest you, and so I enclose an account of the matter from the *New Republic*.

I wanted to send you a novel we published called, "Look Homeward, Angel," because it seemed to me to be an extraordinary exhibition of varied talents, even though some of them were in the raw. I have not sent it, because the book is extremely long, and I did not know whether you would want to go through it, and also because there are passages in it which are extremely unpleasant. Evans[1] is publishing the book, and I hope he will come out all right with it. We have made a considerable success, and may make a great one. It pleased me in one particular especially — it showed that whatever American life may be in a small city in respect to ethics and culture, it is full of character and color, and not drab as it was represented in Sinclair Lewis's books.

A Captain Cohn,[2] who is a great collector of your first editions, etc., and comes in often to ask questions in connection with them, told me that you regarded "War and Peace" as the greatest novel. I had spoken of it because I was reading it again, to my children. I read it to all of them as they get old enough, and they adore it, and won't permit skipping except those parts that give Tolstoy's theories of war. Every time I

[1] Evans of the firm of William Heinemann, Ltd., English publishers. [2] Louis H. Cohn, rare book collector, with bookshop at West 56th Street, "House of Books."

read it, its dimensions seem to grow larger, and its details to have more meaning. I have always tried to get other people to read it, but they, most of them, trip up on the crowd of characters with unrememberable names, at the beginning.

I shall speak to Mr. Scribner[1] right away about the payment on the Compact Edition — but we shall gladly pay it at any moment.

Wishing you and Mrs. Galsworthy and the Sauters a happy Christmas,

Ever sincerely yours,

TO JAMES BOYD

DEC. 30, 1929

DEAR JIM:

You will have all of chapter ten[2] in your hands within a day or two now (I have the last galley still with me), and the rest of the proof promises to follow shortly. I have now through galley 41. This chapter ten is, of course, of the utmost importance, although to tell you so is presumably superfluous. The reason I speak of it is that I am inclined to think that, if only at the end, it requires intensification. For instance, I think Murfree would have had a much harder time getting past Laura's house. I think he would have suffered badly — well, he does, by implication, but I think perhaps you should enlarge upon it. Then, all these thoughts that go through his head, during the chapter, are excellently given and imply ever so much, but I think one thought that would bother him a great deal would be the grief he is going to inflict upon Laura. He is in one of those situations where a man is taken possession of by something in his nature that makes him act almost against his

---

[1] Charles Scribner, Senior (1854–1930), president of Charles Scribner's Sons.
[2] Of his *Long Hunt*, Scribners, 1930.

conscious will, and I think that the struggle this would mean, and his knowledge of the sorrow he was bringing upon the person he loved, should have more emphasis. It was almost like a man with a passion for drink, who has a most intense desire, and an overwhelming reason for wanting to break it, and yet he ends by going off and drinking. But, before the end, he goes through a great struggle which has even physical manifestations. I have seen a man groan and wring his hands before he gave in. Anyway, I only say this to suggest that this chapter ought to be utterly right and to urge you to scrutinize it most carefully because of its importance. You do not want to overwrite it, of course, but I think it ought to be at a pretty high tension in spots, and especially at the end. He might have a fierce struggle with himself when he passed the house, and yet feel relieved and even light-hearted, once he got past it.

I am enjoying the book extremely in reading it again.

Always yours,

TO ERSKINE CALDWELL

FEB. 26, 1930

DEAR MR. CALDWELL:[1]

I hope you will give us another chance. This story[2] greatly impressed me, as did what you had in *Transition,* in the way it was told, and in the quality of authenticity about it; but in the superficial sense, which we do have to consider, it would seem too much an anecdote, we are afraid. It truly does disclose the nature of the people in it, and of the region, but what happened is of an anecdotal character, and we would much rather

---

[1] Author of *Tobacco Road*. This, and an earlier book, a collection of short stories entitled *American Earth*, were later published by Scribners, the latter in 1931, the former in 1932.   [2] "The Poor Fool."

have a story of which this would not be true. I do hope you will let us see others.

I had not heard at all of the controversy which led you to get out the handbill. Was the book[1] published in Portland? I am asking our bookstore to see if they can get a copy. The trouble is, very few people, even in the least provincial communities, seem to understand that the *motive* for fiction, or the impulse from which it arises, is a serious one. They think of fiction as having no value excepting that of amusing and passing the time; and so it is impossible for them to understand why it could not just as well be pleasant and pretty. They think a writer can write one thing just as well as another, and so he is perverse if he writes about things they do not like to think about. I daresay you know all this, but I have so often argued the case that I can hardly avoid talking about it. Anyhow, I hope you will come out well in this particular matter, and I should think you were bound to come out well in the end.

Ever sincerely yours,

TO LEON TROTSKY

MAY 22, 1930

DEAR MR. TROTSKY:

We enclose a representative selection of reviews of your book.[2] They include cuttings from important metropolitan newspapers and also a number from newspapers in smaller towns, so that you may gain an impression of the way the book has been received throughout the country. It seems to us a very favorable reception. Some of the reviews enclosed show a certain hostility to your ideas, but we feel that you would prefer to see all shades of opinion. And they show a practical unanim-

---

[1] *The Bastard*, by Erskine Caldwell.　[2] *My Life*, Scribners, 1930.

ity of praise of your autobiography as a literary product. The very carefully considered reviews of the various journals of opinion, such as the *Nation* and the *New Republic,* have not yet appeared.

Although we usually accord an author only six copies of a book, in the case of your book we increased this number to twenty, which enabled us to supply the lists given in your two letters, and also to send six copies to the *Militant,* in addition to the six which went to you.

It is gratifying to know that you find the edition satisfactory. The book seems to be very well liked, and we are hopeful of a long-continued sale.

Cordially yours,

TO THOMAS WOLFE

JUNE 3, 1930

DEAR WOLFE:[1]

I was mighty glad to get a letter from you. We all miss you greatly, and I expect to miss you more this summer. There aren't many people who take pleasure in walking, and there are fewer with whom I take pleasure in drinking. Everything is much as usual here except that the fiction market, which was bad enough as things were, has been rendered still worse by the Doubleday announcement that they are to publish new novels at one dollar. I am glad you worked hard and we were able to get out "Look Homeward, Angel" before this collapse came.

When you get down to work, just do the work the best you can. Don't ever think about the public, or the critics, or any of those things. You are a born writer if there ever was one and have no need to worry about whether this new book will be as

[1] Wolfe was in England at the time this letter was written.

good as the "Angel," and that sort of thing. If you simply can get yourself into it, as you can, it *will* be as good. I doubt if you will really think of any of the extrinsic matters when you are at work, but if you did, that might make it less good.

There are two people I hope you may see — Scott Fitzgerald and John Galsworthy. I dare say the Heinemann[1] crowd will see that you see Galsworthy, and I hope you will see that you see Scott. I know you would have a grand time together. I meant to have written him that you were likely to turn up, but never did it. If you need any introduction, you can tell him that I was extremely anxious that you should look him up, but the fact is you won't need any introduction, for he will know all about the "Angel" and will be eager to see you.

I shall write more when there is more to be said.

Ever yours,

Wolfe wrote from Geneva, Switzerland, August 18, 1930: "Will you please have Mr. Darrow[2] send me a statement of whatever money is due me? I shall not write any more books, and since I must begin to make other plans for the future, I should like to know how much money I will have." This was Wolfe's reaction after he had read certain adverse English reviews.

TO THOMAS WOLFE

AUG. 28, 1930

DEAR TOM:

If I really believed you would be able to stand by your decision, your letter would be a great blow to me. I cannot believe

[1] William Heinemann, Ltd., Wolfe's publishers in England. [2] Whitney Darrow, a vice-president of Scribners.

it, though. If anyone were ever destined to write, that one is you. As for the English reviews, I saw one from an important source which was adverse, though it recognized the high talent displayed. It argued that the book[1] was at fault because it was chaotic and that the function of an artist was to impose *order*. That was the only review that could be called unfavorable, and, as I say, it recognized that the book showed great talent. Otherwise the reviews — and I must have seen all the really important ones — were very fine.

For Heaven's sake write me again. I am sending you herewith a royalty report showing the money due.

Always and anxiously yours,

TO THOMAS WOLFE

SEPT. 10, 1930

DEAR TOM:

I wrote you very hurriedly at the end of August: I was then on the edge of a ten days' vacation which is now ended. I hoped when I got back there might be another letter telling me you felt differently than in your last, and I have had that letter on my mind ever since you wrote it. I could not clearly make out why you had come to your decision, and surely you will have to change it; but certainly there never was a man who had made more of an impression on the best judges with a single book, and at so early an age. Certainly you ought not to be affected by a few unfavorable reviews — even apart from the overwhelming number of extremely and excitedly enthusiastic reviews. By the way, Scott Fitzgerald wrote me how much better things were with him now; but most of his letter was taken up with you. I daresay it would be a good thing if

---

[1] *Look Homeward, Angel*, Scribners, 1929.

you could avoid him at present, but he was immensely impressed with you, and with the book, and however you may regard him as a writer, he is certainly a very sensitive and sure judge of writers. Not that there is any further need of confirmation with respect to you. There is no doubt of your very great possibilities — nor, for that matter, of the great accomplishment of the "Angel."

Somewhere, perhaps to Jack,[1] you referred to a young man of our friend Madeleine's[2] having run you down and taken observations. I daresay this was not pleasant, but I have seen the letter he wrote her — she came in with it — and it was extremely interesting. He also has great admiration for you, and he quoted some of your sayings, which I could recognize as authentic, and which were extremely discerning. There was one about Scott.[3]

It seems rather futile to write this letter, in view of your having stopped all communications.[4] I hope somehow it will break through to you. If you do not write me some good news pretty soon, I shall have to start out on a spying expedition myself. You know it has been said before that one has to pay somehow for everything one has or gets, and I can see that among your penalties are attacks of despair, as they have been among the penalties great writers have generally had to pay for their talent.

Please do write me.

Always your friend,

In November, 1930, Wolfe wrote Perkins that two New York dentists were dunning him for $525 for two weeks' work. The letter went on to say, "I left instructions with Mr. Darrow[5] to pay them but, fortunately, told him not to go be-

---

[1] John Hall Wheelock, an editor at Scribners.   [2] Madeleine Boyd, literary agent.
[3] F. Scott Fitzgerald.   [4] Wolfe, at this time, was still abroad.   [5] Whitney Darrow, a vice-president of Scribners.

yond $200, which I thought would leave a big surplus. Now the dentists are threatening ominous things if I do not pay in full at once. I have written them telling them I have not money enough to pay such a bill, and have never had (one of them had just come back from his vacation when I left, business was bad, I think he intended me to pay for it). In letters to Mr. Darrow they are threatening to 'put the matter in the hands of their Paris representative' — why Paris, I don't know; I don't live there and have no connection there. . . ."

And Perkins replied in the letter dated November 12, 1930:

TO THOMAS WOLFE

Nov. 12, 1930

DEAR TOM:

I have your letter about the bill, but don't worry over it. We investigated the party and found that he was supposed to be highly reputable, but very high-priced. But now we are trying to effect some kind of a compromise. But anyhow, you are making too much of it, I think. I do not believe for a moment that they have any Paris representative who could do anything, or any other foreign representative. Let the thing ride if you like, and it will be fixed up, when you get back, some way. Come back with the novel finished and that amount of money will seem trifling. I enclose herewith some remarks about the "Angel"[1] by Mr. Sinclair Lewis, who recently wrote to congratulate us on publishing it. When they interviewed him about getting the Nobel prize, he immediately began to talk about your book, and only mentioned one or two others at all. We put out what he said in an ad.

When are you likely to come back?[2] Everything goes on here

[1] *Look Homeward, Angel*, Scribners, 1929. [2] Wolfe was then still abroad.

well enough in spite of the extremely severe business depression. A man in our cashier's department took away sixty-one thousand of our dollars and lost all of them in the stock market. Ernest Hemingway, motoring in Montana at night, went off the road in the glare of an approaching car and down into a gully, and came out with a very badly broken arm. Dos Passos was with him but not hurt; but Ernest has been suffering a great deal, in a hospital in Billings. I suppose you saw that the election all went the right way in respect to prohibition, and in other respects too, from my point of view.

Always yours,

TO ALLEN TATE

JUNE 27, 1931

DEAR MR. TATE:

I am taking your poems home to read, but I know a number of them already, well, and of course anybody would be proud to publish them. I shall write you more definitely next week, and everything would be very simple indeed if it were not for these detestable practical questions that cannot be eliminated. I am not referring to the mere matter of a contract, for that too would not be difficult, but there is also the serious question of an author dividing his work between two publishers.[1] I think your letter shows that you have considered that, and you would not intend that it should always be divided. And I only raise the question because you should. Our policy has always been definitely to publish for an author rather than to publish individual works, and it has also always been opposed to taking steps to detach an author from another publisher. I am not asking you to discuss these questions with me, but I thought I

---

[1] Putnam and Scribners. Putnam had published Tate.

ought to explain our position, although I do not wish to do that even, in any way that will be embarrassing to you, and I need hardly say that — like any publisher — we should value your name on our list.

I shall write you again next week. It was a pleasure to hear from you, and to receive a manuscript of yours.

Ever sincerely yours,

P.S. I have been trying hard to get proofs of your wife's book.[1] I am pressing the printer for them, and should very soon begin to have them, and then they will go to her rapidly.

TO MORLEY CALLAGHAN

NOVEMBER 16, 1931

DEAR CALLAGHAN:

I distrust the validity of the criticism I am about to make, but I can't shake off the feeling from which it arises. My suspicion of it comes from a fear that this feeling is derived from literary conventions — which both authors and editors should not be ruled by — but I'll give it to you tentatively for you to deal with.

In almost all your writing your characters were the common run of people — people who have not had the chance to develop much, intellectually or emotionally. This has led many readers, even some reviewers, to regard you as a "hard-boiled" writer. But there were reviewers, and some readers, not so utterly dumb: they saw that a very unusual delicacy of perception was one of your most marked and most distinguishing qualities, and that it was expressed with corresponding subtlety in your

---

[1] *Penhally*, by Caroline Gordon, Scribners, 1931.

writing. They should have seen this even in your first book,[1] about a bootlegger.

But you were writing about a bootlegger and you naturally dealt in what I think is called realism. Many unpleasant details had a significance in that narrative and you put them in, and quite rightly. And this was true also in many, perhaps most, of the stories. Your very unusual delicacy in perception and expression did not generally get a fair show, alongside the mean and sordid details which belonged and were there.

In this new story,[2] this delicacy, or subtlety, or whatever, does get its first real show, and it is pervasive, and that is why I said this reveals your talent more fully and satisfyingly than anything you've done. But the mean and sordid details are still here and my feeling — which I can't feel sure is justified — is that they are not compatible with the glamour of this romance, or its tragical conclusion. The story is a tragic idyll, or could be. Sordid detail perhaps doesn't *belong*. And if it doesn't, perhaps you have brought it in because you have become accustomed to using it in stories where it does belong.

All this is based on the assumption that when one writes a story he does not, of course, put everything in, but selects with a view to the motive of the story. Details he takes are those which are significant in the light of the motive. I question whether you have not, in turning to a new sort of story for you — and one which gives you a fine show — selected details partly under the influence of the writing you have done before.

The fact is that in revising the story you have yourself tended to reduce those details which were unpleasant, presumably on this very account — because they were not suitable to the motive of this story. But even so, I think that that element of the rather sordid is still in the story to too great a degree, in the light of its essential character as an ideal.

[1] *Strange Fugitive*, Scribners, 1928.   [2] *A Broken Journey*, Scribners, 1932.

For instance, I think that perhaps the whole physical element of love is over-emphasized. Now, Peter takes up with the other girl only because he considers his love-affair with Marion has concluded, and perhaps too much is made of his relations with the other girl, and he treats her too brutally at the end. Because this story is about the love between Marion and Peter, and it is a different kind of love from the merely physical, and should be so presented. And in the end of the story, where the idyllic qualities are more than ever marked, I do not think that the affair with the guide need be gone into to the degree that it is. The only important thing about it is that it happened, and in circumstances which make it seem inevitable and excusable. In many places through the story there are almost naturalistic details, which do not seem to me to blend with the story's intent and motive. I would even question the incident of the false teeth. That was so horrible and unpleasant, and yet I recognize that it had a great value too.

In fact, the whole difficulty with my position is that none of these things are false in the least, they are all true. But you are writing a story that is almost poetic, and the question is whether they belong. You know, it has been contended that when one writes tragedies the characters should be kings and queens, etc., because they are the most suitable material on account of their lofty position, their high obligations, etc. I don't agree to this, but what justice is in it serves to illustrate a point about the appropriateness of material to theme. A story of tragic love can be told, certainly, about people of any sort who are capable of love; but the few details selected from the thousands available should probably be those most significant in the light of the motive. Other details which would be significant in a plain story of commonplace reality should probably be discarded.

I don't advance this view with much confidence, but I can't shake off the feeling that there is a kind of sordidness in your story which could be in any story but seems to be inappropriate in this.

Ever yours,

TO ERNEST HEMINGWAY

JAN. 14, 1932

DEAR ERNEST:

I wish that manuscript[1] would come — but keep it until it is ready. But I expect to get a lot out of it that will act as a counterbalance for things that one sees on all sides. . . .

The house must be grand, and Key West too. That is the place to forget about the troubles of the world. I have been recommending it to young men out of jobs. If you begin to see strange young men appearing, with enough capital to buy a boat, I'll be to blame, and I can guess what you will say about me. I tell them they ought to go down there and stay until after the depression, and then they will come back fit and happy to start in, instead of all frazzled out.

There is one sentence in your letter that made me think you had sent the manuscript, but I guess not yet. It has not arrived.

I read MacLeish's "Hamlet" and think it grand. It is astonishing that a man can be doing what he is, and not have got across better. But I think the new poem will do it. And Houghton Mifflin seem to be playing him up in their spring announcement as if they meant to play him hard when they publish.

I have heard nothing of Scott[2] except by telegraph, but he is back in Alabama, and is to do an article on "Hollywood Revisited."

You asked about Tom Wolfe. He has accomplished a great volume of work, and what I have seen of it, not much, is as good as it could be. He keeps getting all upset, and he is so

---

[1] *Death in the Afternoon*, published by Scribners in 1932. [2] F. Scott Fitzgerald.

now, and I am to have an evening with him and try to make him think he is some good again. He is good all right.

I wish I were down there with you all. . . .

Always yours,

JULY 22, 1932

DEAR ERNEST:

Everything seems now to be right with the book.[1] And you will see, when we send you the page-proof, what we have done about the words, and it is not so bad. For Heaven's sake get Cape's[2] set off to him as soon as you can, because he will be getting in a jam soon. I have written him about the pictures, which I think he will have to take from us all printed, with captions; and the jacket and the frontispiece. Everything looks altogether to the good about the book in every way — except the bad business conditions — and I believe you will surmount them.

Is there any chance you will be here in October? — Scott[3] and I have got a grand tour of the Virginia battlefields planned, and although I do not see how I could take in more than two, it would be a great time if you were there. It all came from my going down to Baltimore and seeing Gettysburg, and really, Ernest, it was perfectly magnificent: you could understand every move in the whole battle if you had read about it. You could see the whole battlefield plain as day. There is a stone wall, as good as any in Connecticut, about two feet high, on Roundtop, built on the 3rd of July, by some Maine regiments. They knew all about stone walls. It is as good as new today.

---

[1] *Death in the Afternoon*, Scribners, 1932.   [2] Jonathan Cape, publisher of Hemingway in England.   [3] F. Scott Fitzgerald.

Scott and Zelda[1] are living about forty minutes out from Baltimore in a house on a big place that is filled with wonderful old trees. I wanted to walk around and look at the trees, but Scott thought we ought to settle down to gin-rickeys. But you could see the trees from the piazza where we sat, and a little pond there, too. It was really a fine sort of melancholy place . . . Scott did not look so well, but he was in fine spirits, and talked a lot. He told me that if I went to Key West he would certainly go next time. You know he was in Florida, and he began inquiring about the fishing. It seems he caught an amberjack, I think, that weighed about forty pounds. He asked me how big the fish we caught were, and maybe I stretched it a little, but I could see it worried Scott. He said he had had an awful fight with this amberjack. It was mighty good to see him anyhow. I wish you would come and go to Antietam with us. It is beautiful country all around. The depression seems simply silly when you motor all over that country and see the crops and all the rich foliage, and the orchards coming along, and even the villages looking all neat and fresh. It makes you feel as if it were all a lunacy, this depression.

I hope everything is right with you now, and that you won't overdo it for a while.

Since I last wrote you, I saw Archie MacLeish. It was at the Davenports — this Marcia Davenport wrote "Mozart."[2] I like to talk to Archie a lot, but didn't have much chance. He is a Scotchman and I am a Yankee, and there is something in common between the two. Russell Davenport[3] is an awfully good fellow. I know you would like him. Probably Archie has told you about him. These Davenports (I have seen a lot of them on account of her book) have moved up to Windsor and taken a farm there, and their only real farming item is one pig, and

---

[1] Mrs. F. Scott Fitzgerald. [2] Published by Scribners in 1932. [3] Newspaper man, writer and poet.

they named him Max. But I am in hopes it was after Max Foster.

Let me know if you are all right soon. . . .

Always yours,

DEAR CHARD: Nov. 23, 1932

Herewith is a list of the chapters you enumerated in writing about the Book about Poets.[1]

The ones I named in my memorandum are all of them duplicated in your list except "The Quarrels of Poets" and "Poets as Adventurers." But there could be a magnificent, perhaps final, chapter written on "The Deaths of Poets." To name some at random — there was Kit Marlowe stabbed in a speakeasy; Shelley drowned in a storm; and Byron in Missolonghi, with Trelawny (the skunk) uncovering his dead foot to see why he limped; and Keats coughing himself to death (you might even quote from the "Caballa" by Thornton Wilder[2]) ; and Seeger[3] going to meet his rendez-vous; and Burns getting pneumonia when drunk, etc.

There could also be a grand topic in "Poets as Prophets," because they are seers too. You could go easy on Tennyson's "In Memoriam," but Shelley foresaw a great deal.

Ever yours,

DEAR ——— :   JAN. 17, 1933

We were very glad to receive your letter with regard to Mr.

---

[1] *Annals of the Poets* by Chard Powers Smith, Scribners, 1935.   [2] A. & C. Boni, 1926.   [3] Alan Seeger. His famous "I Have a Rendez-vous with Death" appears in his *Poems*, published by Scribners in 1916.

——'s "——" because we are naturally quite aware of your work and position, and respect your judgment. We are certainly very far from regarding your views as old-fashioned: in fact, it is easy for us to sympathize with your objection to the words you refer to.

It seems to us, though, that a publisher — unless he choose to be a purely personal one, and so not to fulfill the larger functions of publishing — must take a very different attitude from that of personal preference or taste; that is, an attitude according to which he may serve as a medium for what is alive and important in the literature of his day. He may, and in fact is sure, sometimes to make a mistake of judgment; but, if he finds that his view is supported by a very important public which includes those who must be recognized as excellent judges, it seems to us that he is fulfilling this function. As a publisher he is not a censor of taste, or of morals, though as a man he is likely to have the common human impulse of wishing that his own ideas of taste could be generally imposed.

The fact that this book has received the support, both in England and in this country, of a very large public composed, to judge by all the available evidence, of those of the higher levels of education and taste, does not prove, of course, that your view of the book is not the right one. But does it not indicate a sufficient body of important opinion on the other side to leave the question open to doubt, and to sustain the publisher in his judgment? After all, it is historically true that the most enlightened ages have been the most free-spoken — that the Eighteenth Century, generally regarded as the greatest of all in taste and intellect, was the very one in which there was the greatest freedom in respect to literary expression.

Your objection is perhaps only to specific words, and we suppose that you would argue that the publisher should simply strike out these words from the text; but the fact is that no genuine writer will allow a publisher to exercise this kind of censorship over him. The true artist has always insisted upon making his work what he wanted it, and it is our opinion that it would be an extremely bad thing for literature if real writers did allow themselves to be censored by their publishers.

You have, of course, every right to question whether Mr. —— is such a writer; but we, as publishers, can hardly question it, in the light of statements concerning him from the highest sources in this country, England, France and Germany: most of the leading critics and writers in those countries have testified to their admiration of him in extreme terms.

In short, we are far from maintaining that your view is not the right one. Our position is that no absolute decision but a purely personal one can be made on that point; and that when a publisher believes in the literary importance of a writer, and finds his belief supported by an imposing body of literary opinion, he is compelled in the exercise of his professional function to publish him to the very best of his powers.

Very truly yours,

JAN. 31, 1933

DEAR ——:

The matter we have been discussing in connection with Mr. ——'s book is a perplexing one, we quite agree, but we are very strongly of the opinion that the intelligent and discriminating public does rule in these matters. It may not do so instantly and despotically, but it does so with reasonable certainty. For instance, if the public will not buy books because they contain such words as these, if they feel them to be offensive, vulgar, etc., and show it by not reading the books that contain them, they will cease to be used. Taste and conduct are governed by public opinion. It is rather our judgment that they cannot be governed by anything else — as is exemplified to a striking degree, by the failure of the Eighteenth Amendment. We hope we are right, because we think that if, in the end, publishers were compelled to assume the functions of censors they would do vastly more harm than they could do good. Certainly every record of such attempted censorship has turned out that way. As a book-lover, you have very likely read, for instance, "The Fear of Books" by Holbrook Jackson — a kind of companion or supplement to the magnificent "Anatomy of Bibliomania" which we had the pleasure of bringing out in this country. This "Fear of Books," which is most excellent reading in itself for one who cares for literature, clearly shows how difficult are attempts to govern writers on the grounds of good taste or morality, and how treacherous are standards adopted by public or self-appointed censors.

It is a difficult question, and I talk of it perhaps too much because it is very much in our minds.

Ever sincerely yours,

TO MARJORIE KINNAN RAWLINGS

OCT. 27, 1933

DEAR MRS. RAWLINGS:

I did not expect you to come back to New York, or understand that you intended to; but I hoped you would and thought you might, because that often happens with people who say they won't. Perhaps you may, too.

As to the book,[1] it is too bad we should be getting into a

[1] *The Yearling*, Scribners, 1938.

tangle about it, because the idea is really perfectly simple to me. I am thinking of a book about a boy, but his age is not important. Every boy between twelve and eighteen who lives an outdoor life is interested in the same things. In a general way (though your book would of course not be supposed to resemble them, and could not resemble all of them because they do not resemble each other), I associate it with such books as "Huckleberry Finn," Kipling's "Kim," David Crockett's Memoirs, "Treasure Island," and "The Hoosier School Boy." All of these books are primarily *for boys*. All of them are read by men, and they are the favorite books of some men. The truth is the best part of a man is a boy. It is subject matter that counts, and the fact that the hero is a boy. I do not know what —— is thinking about, and it does not make much difference, but of course the sales department always want a novel. They want to turn everything into a novel. They would have turned the New Testament into one, if it had come to us for publication, and they could have. But I am right about it, and a book about a boy and the life of the scrub is the thing we want. Anyhow, the thing for you to do is to write it as you feel it and want it, without regard to anybody at all. It is those wonderful river trips, and the hunting, and the dogs and guns, and the companionship of simple people who care about the same things which were included in "South Moon Under"[1] that we are thinking about. It is all simple, not complicated — don't let anything make it complicated to you.

I don't think, though, that you can lift out any of the actual words in "South Moon Under." Probably you did not mean that, you meant to retell the incidents. That you could do, and I do hope you will have something about going down a river, because the rivers there are so good, and the journey element in a narrative is always a fine one, particularly to youth.

[1] An earlier novel by Mrs. Rawlings, published by Scribners in 1933.

There would be no use in doing anything about the illustrations until the manuscript is pretty far on. The first thing would be for the artist to read the manuscript. Wait until I send you the David Crockett pictures, which I will the moment I can get proofs, but not for quite a while. I wish John[1] would go down there. He would enjoy it and, I know, would get the greatest pleasure from talking to you.

The royalties on "South Moon Under" are not strictly due until four months after September first. But I think we could at any time send you payments from them, or even all of them if you wanted.

Sincerely yours,

TO MARJORIE KINNAN RAWLINGS

Nov. 15, 1933

Dear Mrs. Rawlings:

Thanks ever so much for writing me. I think your handwriting is as easy to read as anybody's I ever saw, so don't ever let the absence of a typewriter keep you from writing me if you have the inclination.

I am glad things have worked out the way you want to have them, and I'll say no more about that. If it is all right for you, it is right.

But what is all this mystery about your writing a novel? You wrote one very fine novel, and I know of no reason to feel anxious about another, except that I can understand *your* feeling anxious, because a good writer always does, and ought to. What such a one wants to do is very hard, and perhaps unattainable even, but no one who wrote "South Moon Under" ought to be doubted by other people. Certainly I have no

---

[1] John W. Thomason, Jr.

doubts, and the only reason I favored your doing the boys' book[1] was, first, the fact that the old hunter was available now and might not be later, and then that I do think when one is to do a difficult novel a long period of meditation, mostly unconscious, is helpful. But you have probably had that long period anyway. Of course, all our sales force, etc., etc., would be delighted to have you do the novel first. I would not have wanted to hurry you into the boys' book either, but I thought that having done so well by Lant, and having thought so much about the scrub, and the rivers, and alligators, and all, from the point of view of Lant, you would be pretty well primed for a book about another boy. But it is all right that you should do the way you think best.

I am glad you do not have to come up here to get the five hundred, except that I had hoped we would see you again. Maybe something will bring you. Anyhow, please let me know how things come on.

Always yours,

TO CAROLINE GORDON

JAN. 16, 1934

DEAR MRS. TATE:[2]

I like your outline very much indeed.[3] The information about game and methods of hunting and shooting, etc., does not worry me at all. I think every man is interested in this anyhow, even though he never made use of rod or gun. The idea of this book, the purpose that runs through it, is that it shows how a man saved his independence in spite of everything — at least that is how it seems to me. This is a real and important theme, to

---

[1] *The Yearling*, Scribners, 1938. [2] Caroline Gordon, the novelist, in private life Mrs. Allen Tate. [3] Of her *Aleck Maury, Sportsman,* a novel published by Scribners in 1934.

which anyone could respond. People's lives are unhappy because they do what other people do, or what they think they ought to do. That is the idea, it seems to me. Maury had some instinct that saved him from this, even if it only was due to the strength of a single passion. I think it is a fine theme for a novel. However, it is better if it were unconscious, as it was in a way with Maury.

I am only afraid you may concentrate too deeply upon the sport. One cannot tell from the outline because the emphasis falls upon what is intended to be emphasized in the book, but I think his marriage, and all the other relationships, etc., ought to be given a real show. But in general, I think the book promises to be a very fine one, and we are all for it. Have you a title, and do you want us to make up a contract?

Always yours,

Mrs. Rawlings's letter, telling of the trouble she was having in getting started on her novel, "Golden Apples," drew the following reply:

TO MARJORIE KINNAN RAWLINGS

FEB. 1, 1934

DEAR MRS. RAWLINGS:

I am sure you will do a fine book,[1] and you ought to have trouble in getting under way with a fine book. Incidentally, you once remarked upon my having sent "South Moon"[2] to Scott Fitzgerald as not being very apt because it was not his sort of book. He had never said anything about it to me, but last night, in talking about his own book by long distance, he

---

[1] *Golden Apples*, Scribners, 1935. [2] *South Moon Under* by Marjorie Kinnan Rawlings, Scribners, 1933.

referred to yours, and in the highest terms. It is not his kind of book either, but he knew it was a beautiful book. I shall be patient, but you ought not to get discouraged if it goes hard. I know you won't be.

As for the Prix Femina, I have tried to find out about it, but I do not know how to get hold of the French woman who now and then calls up about it. But apparently it has not been awarded. I do not understand how they do, for I was informed that it lay between your book and one other, a long time ago. But I shall let you know the moment I hear, and I hope things will turn out so that you will come to New York.

I do not want you to be neatly boxed in a workshop at all, and if personal angles seem to you to tend to embarrass me, remember that I am a Yankee on both sides of my family, and I suppose I shall never get over it altogether.

Couldn't you some time do an account of the rattlesnake hunt, for an article?

I am struggling with Tom Wolfe for a couple of hours every night now, and he is going to get his book[1] done for the fall. But it is the most difficult work I was ever engaged in. I feel that Scott having got his done is a good omen, for that seemed perfectly hopeless many times. Now he has done it,[2] and it is a very fine thing, and will restore him to the position he held after "The Great Gatsby,"[3] if not put him in a higher one. I was down with him for three days last week in Baltimore.

If ever you want to show me any fragments of "Hamaca"[4] even, please do it. You must not let my Yankee reticence ever make you feel that there is any book in which I should be so interested.

Always yours,

---

[1] *Of Time and the River*, Scribners, 1935.   [2] *Tender Is the Night* by F. Scott Fitzgerald, Scribners, 1934.   [3] Scribners, 1925.   [4] Published by Scribners in 1935 under the title *Golden Apples*.

JUNE 25, 1934

DEAR JIM:

I read the manuscript[1] again and I think very highly of it and have nothing to add to what you yourself said about developing it (and with which I fully agreed) except this: I think there is a danger that Thomas may appear too weak, too much of a defeatist. There is no reason this should be so. He did accept the conventional views of that time, and he did fall into the groove that his family expected him to fit into. But there was nothing feeble about him in doing this. It was the way people did then and thought they ought to do, but I think unless you have him in some way show more spirit from time to time that there will not be enough sympathy with him and that, in fact, he will not be consistent with your real conception of him. In those days, people thought they ought to do what they thought they ought to do, and it was not weakness to accept the views of those whom they had been led to suppose were right. But I do think it seems so as it stands, and that Thomas ought to show more initiative and more spirit in this part of the book. It is probably only a matter of a number of little incidents. He is too passive. He could be passive in the matter of his work and his marriage, as people then were; but he ought to show that he has something else in him in other ways. It is quite probable that you have this in mind yourself, but I thought I would mention it because I do think it important.

Always yours,

---

[1] *Roll River*, Scribners, 1935.

TO ERNEST HEMINGWAY

JUNE 28, 1934

DEAR ERNEST:

I guess the only way to do is to drop the cheaper edition of "Death in the Afternoon" for the present. It will not work out except in the way we said, and then by only a slight margin. I only thought that it might be well to do it that way, solely for the sake of bringing the book forward again and holding it there. Everything you say is logical, and ought to be sound (probably is sound too), but this cheap edition would not interfere with the Modern Library taking the book, and that would be the best outcome in the end. The regular cheap houses would not take the book because they run entirely to fiction, but the Modern Library does not care what anyone else does. They have a market curiously their own. But I do not like the idea altogether myself, and I guess we had better drop it, for this season anyhow.

I did not hear anything about that sailfish. It sounds wonderful. You never told me if you joined up with that Philadelphia museum. I always hoped you had done it, because not only might it be financially advantageous, but it would give you a chance to enlarge your name as a sportsman, and add a scientific element to it too. I guess even if you have not made any connection this time, you will be likely to do it later with some museum. I suppose the New York one would be better.

I cannot come down now. I cannot leave as long as I can keep Tom[1] going well, as he is doing now. We have over half the book[2] finished, except for a little touching up on another reading. We have got a good system now. We work every evening from 8:30 (or as near as Tom can come to it) until

---

[1] Thomas Wolfe.　[2] *Of Time and the River*, published by Scribners in 1935.

10.30 or 11:00, and Tom does actual writing at times, and does it well, where pieces have to be joined up. We are organizing the book. That is the best part of the work we are doing. It will be pretty well integrated in the end, and vastly more effectively arranged. The fact is, Tom could do the work, but his impulse is all away from the hard detailed revision. He is mighty ingenious at times, when it comes to the organization of material. The scheme is pretty clear in his own head, but he shrinks from the sacrifices, which are really cruel often. A couple of nights ago, I told Tom that a whole lot of fine stuff he had in simply ought to come out because it resulted in blurring a very important effect. Literally, we sat here for an hour thereafter without saying a word, while Tom glowered and pondered and fidgeted in his chair. Then he said, "Well, then will you take the responsibility?" And I said, "I have simply got to take the responsibility. And what's more," I said, "I will be blamed, either way." But he did it, and in the end he knew he was right. We go over to "Chatham Walk,"[1] where you sit in the open, afterwards. Anyhow, we will have this book done by the end of July, if we go on as we are going now.

I am sending you a book I thought you would like, called "Pirate Junk."[2] Evan Shipman[3] said he would have his book done by the end of the summer. He looks as if he knew where he was going much better now, and I am in hopes it will be a fine book. It will be different from any other about horses.

I am awfully glad you have got so far on with that story.

Always yours,

---

[1] Open air restaurant of the Chatham Hotel, 48th Street near Madison Avenue. [2] *Pirate Junk: Five Months Captivity with Manchurian Bandits*, by Clifford Johnson, with an Introduction by Peter Fleming, Scribners, 1934. [3] Author of *Free for All*, Scribners, 1935.

TO MARJORIE KINNAN RAWLINGS

DEAR MRS. RAWLINGS: AUG. 10, 1934

I am sure you need have no anxiety about this second part of the book.[1] I have read it through three times, and each time with greater pleasure. The Englishman is excellent, and there was your only danger. You have done everything that you aimed to do. You have made the hammock seem beautiful, and yet you have made the reader understand how it seems horrible to Tordell. The only criticism that I could make — and I do not do that with any great confidence — is in the matter of timing; the way he takes to drinking is excellent. The widow's visit is a very good scene indeed, and might be lengthened a little with good effect — for you are never in danger of over-stressing, but perhaps just a little bit the other way. When she says, "Don't let him git to Allie," the idea of that element is first introduced. It seems to me that perhaps his beginning to talk about the advantage of being a eunuch in Florida comes a little too quickly after that, and that his stumbling upon Rhea in the woods, when he has fever, comes perhaps too quickly after he has drunkenly talked about the Queen of Sheba. Perhaps you ought to separate these incidents further by developing the intervals between them, or by putting in other incidents, of a different kind. But I think that in every large and serious sense you are absolutely right, and the Englishman is coming out excellently well.

Now from what you tell me of the doctor, and from the general turn the story is to take, I can imagine how beautifully it will go on. The truth is you are a writer, and no one need have any anxiety about what you do. The other story was the first novel[2] you wrote, and it did seem to be wrong in construction

[1] *Golden Apples,* Scribners, 1935.   [2] *South Moon Under,* Scribners, 1933.

in the beginning. But I never saw anybody so quick to understand what a book needed. You have always given me great credit for helping you, but all you needed almost was a hint. I believe now that, having done that one book, you have learned vastly from it, and that everything will go well.

I started marking little trifles, but there were so few that I thought anything like that might wait for proof. I did mark, on page 36, the phrase "in a tone of anxiety." If Luke could hear the tone, would he not also have gained a sense of its foreignness? I know you do not want to, and should not, overstress little English peculiarities like accent, but it must have struck Luke as a strange way of speaking and might be mentioned, that once. I think you have had him use the way of speech of an Englishman always well, without forcing. On page 53, it seemed a little artificial and unnatural when he spoke of the Lancashire Hills and of having been a boy at the time of the Civil War. This is a trifle, but I think it would be better not to fix the time of the story at all. I suppose this would put it in the 80's, but it could as well have been in the 90's, and there is no need of calling attention to the fact that it was a score of years in the past.

I did see a few other little things, but they were so small as not to be worth mentioning, and particularly as you have not revised, and may easily change them. Otherwise, I would leave them to the proof, when one gets a new view of a book anyhow.

I am returning this part of the ms. by registered mail, and with many thanks. I look forward to reading anything you write, and I hope some more may come pretty soon.

Always yours,

P.S. Quite a bit of Tom's book[1] is in proof, and we are having

[1] *Of Time and the River*, by Thomas Wolfe, Scribners, 1935.

a great struggle over it. Stark Young's book[1] is selling astonishingly well for these times.

TO ERNEST HEMINGWAY

OCT. 1, 1934

DEAR ERNEST:

I seem to get busier all the time, and I cannot figure out the reason why it should be so, although business has very distinctly improved, for us anyhow. I think that in an underlying way it has been improving slightly for two years in publishing, almost imperceptibly, but yet really.

I had meant to write you about Bumby,[2] though I suppose the telegram was all you needed. He is a boy who is likely to get ruined by being so remarkably attractive. When we put him on the train to Chicago and I told the porter that there was no one to look after him, and that he must do it, about half the car rushed up to volunteer to do it. I'll bet Bumby had a bad trip, for all the attention he got from old ladies and gentlemen. My son-in-law took him up to the Natural History Museum, but they did not see all the Indians because some of those rooms were still shut off. Then, in the afternoon, Louise[3] took him up to see our grandson in the Doctor's Hospital (he was about a week old then), and Bumby expressed very great, but I suspect polite, interest, and said that he had seen babies before, in Chicago (I guess at the World's Fair), but that they were in incinerators. None of the children were home, but Bumby left his helmet as a gift to our youngest who, we had told him, was about his age. Louise found him most entertaining; he imitated the way Americans talk French, as he said, and the way English boys talked in the school he went to in

---

[1] *So Red the Rose*, Scribners, 1934. [2] Nickname of John Hemingway, eldest son of Ernest Hemingway. [3] Mrs. Maxwell E. Perkins.

France, and he was very enthusiastic about what he got to eat.

People keep asking me what you are doing and I simply tell them that I do not know, and Sidney Franklin[1] did not know either. But I suspect that it is something mighty important and will wait to find out.

I expect to see Scott[2] in about ten days. He has been selling some stories. His novel[3] sold almost exactly 15,000 copies, which was disappointing to me, of course, though it seemed at that time that that was about as far as books were going. It is about as far as any books seemed to go that season, but I guess it must have been because there weren't any books that could go further. Books are doing better now. Stark Young[4] has sold 35,000 almost, in barely more than two months, and other people have books that are selling well. If we knew things wouldn't get worse, there would be plenty of reason to feel much better than in a long time.

Yours,

TO ERNEST HEMINGWAY

NOVEMBER 28, 1934

DEAR ERNEST:

Maybe I might come down to Key West. I would like to do it mighty well. I'd like to spend an afternoon on the dock looking at those lazy turtles swimming around. . . .

Now to take up minor points: I am sending you a couple of clippings from the *Times* and the *Tribune,* and there was a piece in the *Telegram.* Herschel Brickell on the *Post* is going to do one, and there will be others too in less important places. I imagine the Sunday papers had pieces last week, or will this

---

[1] The bull fighter, translator of *Shadows of the Sun* by Alejandro Perez, Scribners, 1934.　[2] F. Scott Fitzgerald.　[3] *Tender Is the Night,* Scribners, 1934.
[4] *So Red the Rose,* Scribners, 1934.

week. I did not see the papers last Sunday because I had to go off for a week-end of talk and drink. But the Art section would cover the issue anyhow. I haven't seen it. I tried to call up the man who runs it, but only got whoever was in charge. They knew we had helped them some, and I suppose gave me the truth, which was that they had sold quite a few, had had a good public, and good expectations. If we can do anything further, tell us. They thought everything was all right.

I do not think I saw all the pieces in *Esquire,* though I must have read eight of them. The truth is I did like them, even including the one about Ring Lardner. I had heard some of them criticized, as that one was. But no one could have admired or been more fond of Ring than I was, and, although knowing you, I may have read something into it, from you, I did like it. Ring was not, strictly speaking, a great writer. The truth is he never regarded himself seriously as a writer. He always thought of himself as a newspaperman, anyhow. He had a sort of provincial scorn of literary people. If he had written much more, he would have been a great writer perhaps, but whatever it was that prevented him from writing more was the thing that prevented him from being a great writer. But he was a great man, and one of immense latent talent which got itself partly expressed. I guess Scott[1] would think much the same way about it.

I think it is magnificent about the story.[2] Couldn't you modify the title (which I am altogether for, in general) to "In the Highlands of Africa"?[3] It would imply something that happened, or things that happened there. Without the "In," as a title alone, it might be what they call a "travel" book. You will suspect that in this suggestion I am thinking of the trade and the wholesale department. I know they would bring the travel

[1] F. Scott Fitzgerald. [2] *Green Hills of Africa,* Scribners, 1935. [3] Published in 1935, by Scribners, as *Green Hills of Africa.*

suggestion up, against the title. But I have not told anyone about this book except Charlie,[1] and he has not told anyone. The title suggests a great deal to me, and all I want to do to it is to get in something that makes it seem as if it were a *story*.

I do not want to put anything so emphatically that it will embarrass you to overrule me if you must, but it is my strong conviction that this story[2] ought to be published by itself. It detracts from a book to add anything else to the same volume. It does not make it more desirable, but less so. This comes partly from the fact that publishers are always padding books, and everybody is on to it. They get a story of 25 or 30 thousand words and it is too short to interest the trade, the price would have to be so low that the margin is too small. The public seems to object to small books, so then they proceed to pad it. Either they pad it by putting in a great many half-titles and some illustrations or, much more often, by asking the author for pieces to add to it, or stories. It is never so good as a complete unit. What is more, I do not think it is so good absolutely. "Spring Freshets" [Turgenev] is really a long story, and should have been published by itself, because it is a masterpiece and ought not to be thought of with anything else but only by itself. If this book[2] were only 40,000 words, I would say, publish it alone. Then, to revert to the purely practical: when the reviewers review the book with the short pieces added, their comments would be somewhat vitiated by being scattered to some extent over the other pieces. I hope you will publish it by itself.

The other possibility was to put it in the lead of "The First Fifty-Seven."[3] That would make a very big book, for one thing. But the chief objections I have to it are the same ones that apply to the addition of the *Esquire* pieces. The reviews then would be of all the stories. I see that you regard this as a story,

---

[1] Charles Scribner, president of Charles Scribner's Sons.   [2] *Green Hills of Africa.*
[3] Published by Scribners in 1938, as *The Fifth Column and the First Forty-Nine.*

not a novel, but that makes no difference. It is a complete unit and considerably longer than would be necessary to make a full book. Besides, with this story you are writing you will have plenty to give "The First Fifty-Seven" the element of new material that is needed, and fine things too. The reason I wrote about the last *Esquire* piece was mostly because of what it said about writing. I thought that was magnificent, and as true as any utterance could be. Old Tom[1] has been trying to change his book into a kind of Marxian argument (having written most of it some years before he ever heard of Marx), and I have been trying to express to him that very thing, that what convictions you hold on economic subjects will be in whatever you write, if they are really deep. So you don't have to drag them in. I thought the whole piece was very interesting, but it was that writing part that particularly got me.

Always yours,

P.S. If you do write me again, tell me if you know a painter named Kuniochi, a Jap—I mean personally. Do you like him himself, not his paintings? I am in hopes of seeing Mike Strater[2] soon.

When the letter which follows was written, Perkins knew that "Of Time and the River" was to be dedicated to him, but he had not yet seen the dedication. The dedication, in its original form, covered three pages in Wolfe's rambling handwriting but, at the suggestion of one of the editors at Scribners, Tom compressed it into the form in which it now stands, eight lines in length.

---

[1] Thomas Wolfe.　[2] A painter.

TO THOMAS WOLFE

JANY 21, 1935

DEAR TOM:

I'm committed to Key West now, however impossible it seems to go, and since, when I return, "Of Time and the River" will be a book, I'm taking this last moment to say what I've long been on the point of saying:

Nothing could give me greater pleasure or greater pride as an editor than that the book of the writer whom I have most greatly admired should be dedicated to me if it were sincerely done. But you cannot, and should not, try to change your conviction that I have deformed your book, or at least prevented it from coming to perfection. It is therefore impossible for you sincerely to dedicate it to me, and it ought not to be done. I know we are truly friends and have gone through much in company, and this matter, for my part, can have nothing to do with that, or ever shall. But this is another matter. I would have said this sooner but for some fear that you would misinterpret me. But the plain truth is that working on your writings, however it has turned out, for good or bad, has been the greatest pleasure, for all its pain, and the most interesting episode of my editorial life. The way in which we are presenting this book must prove our (and my) belief in it. But what I have done has destroyed *your* belief in it and you must not act inconsistently with that fact.

As for your preface, there is this obstacle to it at the start: a reader is meant to enter into a novel as if it were reality, and so to feel it, and a preface tends to break down that illusion and to make him look at it in a literary way. But perhaps that is, in some degree, a literary objection to a preface and when yours began so finely I thought you might be right to have it. But when I read more of it today, it seemed to me you did the very things you meant to avoid doing in the novel: you made the book seem personal and autobiographical, and by showing resentment against those who objected to the apparent reality (as the preface implied) of the characters in the "Angel"[1] you opened yourself to the same charge against *this* book and notified the whole public that it might rightly be brought. And of the whole public not a handful can understand the artist's point of view or the *writer's* conscience. In these, and other ways, I thought, you bared yourself to all the enemies you have and I told you so because I am your friend ——

P.S. I thought that woman looked dangerous!

On February 8, Perkins saw the dedication to him of "Of Time and the River," and, on the same day, he wrote the letter which follows.

TO THOMAS WOLFE

FRIDAY, FEBY 8, 1935

DEAR TOM:

I have seen the dedication in your book and, whatever the degree of justice in what it implies, I can think of nothing that could have made me more happy. I won't go further into what I feel about it: I'm a Yankee and cannot speak what I feel most strongly, well. But I do wish to say that I think it a most generous and noble utterance. Certainly for one who could say that of me I ought to have done all that it says I did do.

I am glad the book is done because now it will be published. But, although I had moments of despair and many hours of

---

[1] *Look Homeward, Angel*, Scribners, 1929.

discouragement over it, I look back upon our struggles with regret that they are over. And, I swear, I believe that in truth the whole episode was a most happy one for me. I like to think we may go through another such war together.

Always yours,

Wolfe had gone abroad, wanting to be out of the country on the day when "Of Time and the River" was published. He was tired, and apprehensive of the effect that adverse reviews might have upon him. He had asked that no mail be forwarded, and no reviews. Perkins, knowing that Tom could only be pleased by the wonderful reception accorded the book, sent him the excerpts from reviews referred to in the letter which follows.

TO THOMAS WOLFE

MARCH 14, 1935

DEAR TOM:

Everybody outside of this house, outside the business, was amazed by the reception of "Of Time and the River." In the business it was expected, but even there the excitement of the reviewers and their enthusiasm were beyond the degree of expectation. You told me not to send you the reviews (I did send you a cable on the 8th which you must have got), but I am sending you herewith the first thing I can lay hands on that gives any kind of summary, excerpts from some of the reviews. The reviews, on the whole, I think, are much better than these excerpts would indicate. They all make parallels with the great writers, except in a few instances where no parallels are made. About the only one that mentions a contemporary is the one by Chamberlain,[1] which mentions Lewis.[2] Honestly, unless you expected no degree of adverse criticism at all, because of course there was that about too great length and the sort of things we all talked of, I cannot imagine why you should have any restraint upon your happiness in this vacation. If any man could rest on his laurels for a bit, the man is you. As for the sale, we cannot tell yet how it will go on, because a large number of copies — some fifteen, seventeen thousand — were distributed to the stores, and it will take a little while for them to sell out. But we are getting some reorders now, and we have printed five editions, 30,000 copies. The *Times, Tribune,* and *Saturday Review* gave you full front pages, and your picture was everywhere. People who went out on Sunday afternoon to teas, etc., as Louise[3] did, and Wheelock,[4] where they were not publishing people but just regular people, said that the book was excitedly talked about. We have a splendid window, of which I have a copy to show you. None of the things you feared about the book were even hinted at, and your position is enormously enhanced in every kind of way. So, for Heaven's sake, forget anxiety, which you haven't the slightest ground for, but every ground for the greatest happiness and confidence, and enjoy yourself.

Always yours,

P.S. A lot of letters have accumulated for you, but I am holding them as you directed. I am just writing this line the moment I got to the office and mailing it immediately so as to get it to you as soon as can be done.

---

[1] John Chamberlain of the New York *Times*. [2] Sinclair Lewis. [3] Mrs. Maxwell E. Perkins. [4] John Hall Wheelock, an editor at Scribners.

APRIL 15, 1935

DEAR MRS. TATE:[1]

I found your last letter very interesting indeed and there is no harm done, I should think, by the delay excepting in disappointing me personally, which is not a matter of importance. But I do get so impatient to see what you're doing and also to see it published. But, anyhow, you have promised to send some manuscript,[2] and while we shall not now make a dummy, I hope you will do it, even if I may only keep it over-night.

I think I understand what your idea is. If Lee had been ruthless in dealing with his subordinates, if he had court-martialed them for delinquency and shot them for disobedience, the end might have been different. In a way, you think that he symbolizes the whole command of the Confederates, or that that weakness of his, which was so lovable and admirable too (but it has no place in war), pervaded the whole thing. I think Freeman[3] shows that failing of Lee. Of course, Stark[4] said it would not have been worthwhile to win on the other basis. But it is true that Jackson was ruthless. He court-martialed and shot. Nobody crossed him with impunity. But however all that may be, I think you have a splendid scheme for a book, so far as you show it, and that Forrest would be a great figure in it. It will certainly interest me intensely, and I am most anxious to see any part of it.

Always yours,

---

[1] Caroline Gordon, in private life Mrs. Allen Tate. [2] *The Garden of Adonis,* Scribners, 1937. [3] Douglas Southall Freeman, in his *Robert E. Lee,* 4 volumes, Scribners, 1934–5. [4] Stark Young.

TO THOMAS WOLFE

Dear Tom: Aug. 30, 1935

I am sending you the very first English review,[1] and you ought to like it. From the *Times*, which is probably the most influential paper, or at least I always thought so, though probably you know more about that than I do. I think it is a good indication of what may come, especially as the English always speak with much greater restraint in praise than we do.

If you can manage to answer any letter, answer that Brooklyn outfit's invitation to speak. They keep calling me up, and I tell them you are way behind in your work and will want to settle right down to it when you get back, but they are very keen to get you and say that they will put your lecture later on, if you will give it. I would like to see you give it, except that I do think you ought to give all you have to your work.

I have been through the stories,[2] and I think they are very fine stories. They show how objective you can be, and how varied you can be, and I was looking at the book from that point of view considerably. It would be an answer to what you have had in adverse criticism. It is a fine book. But I'll wait and argue with you when you come back, over a glass of coca-cola.

I hope you won't quarrel with anyone else but, if you had to quarrel, I would suppose that Mabel Dodge Luhan was the right person to quarrel with. I myself never quarrel except with you, but I think I could always do it with her — and perhaps with Gertrude Stein, if I had the courage.

Everything goes along all right. I had another letter from Fred,[3] and enlarged on my suggestion that he should keep an inn.

Yours,

---

[1] Of *Of Time and the River*, Scribners, 1935.   [2] Published by Scribners in 1935 under the title *From Death to Morning*.   [3] Fred Wolfe, a brother of Thomas Wolfe.

TO HAMILTON BASSO

SEPT. 10, 1935

DEAR HAM:

I am glad to hear the novel[1] is getting on well, for I consider what you report about it to be very favorable. I know all that you say about Swift perfectly well, but I was pointing out the things that are not realized because people judge by "Gulliver's Travels" and his poems. I don't think he ever thought of anyone else reading the "Journal to Stella" but Stella. It has the most freezing contempt for writing with an eye to the future in that intimate way. I almost think that there is no need of any explanation of his relations with women beyond that habit of mind which made him look with scorn upon any kind of yielding to illusions, even to those by which we all have to be governed to some extent, which are prepared by nature. I have read the Ford letters, and almost everything else that Swift ever wrote, and a good deal that was written by other people to him. I have the whole set of his correspondence.

I think probably your book will be all the better for having done it the hard way. I hope you can work it out. I guess you can, if you have got through one bad place.

I suppose you probably feel very sorry about Huey Long, but to lose an old enemy is the next worst thing to losing an old friend. Still, you won't have to consider escaping over the border after the next election.

Always yours,

---

[1] *Courthouse Square*, Scribners, 1936.

SEPT. 16, 1935

DEAR FRERE:[1]

The London *Times* gave Tom's book[2] a very fine review, I thought, but I have seen others that were not good, or only partially so. I hope you will make out well though, and I should think you were bound to in the end.

The situation of the stories[3] is that they were in galley proof before Tom left for a tour of the West, some seven weeks ago. I could not get him to read them then. I therefore corrected them so far as I dared, and returned them to the press to be sent back in revised galleys. The moment Tom gets here, I am going to try to make him read them. If he will not, I shall try to get them away from him and put them into pages, unread. I shall either send you a set of the revised galleys or a set of the pages. I think these stories will make a very favorable impression, because most of them are not autobiographical in the sense in which the novels are, and they are objective, and are relatively free from those extravagant characteristics which are regarded as Tom's defects, particularly, I guess, in England. They make a very fine book of about 95,000 words. I am only afraid that he will now want to add other stories to them, which have yet to be written, but I shall fight hard against this. He seems to feel a certain shame at the idea of turning out a book of reasonable dimensions.

I hope you will be here this winter, but anyhow I shall write you how matters develop with Tom.

Always yours,

---

[1] A. S. Frere-Reeves of William Heinemann, Ltd., Wolfe's publishers in England.
[2] Thomas Wolfe's *Of Time and the River*, Scribners, 1935.   [3] A volume of short stories by Thomas Wolfe, entitled *From Death to Morning*, Scribners, 1935.

JAN. 10, 1936

DEAR ——:

It is hard to be obliged to tell you that "——" does not seem to us acceptable for publication. The fact that we also feel that it is now unlikely that it can be made acceptable compels us to speak plainly about it.

We ought to tell you at the outset that we think you are both creating and writing too hurriedly, which is not fair to your unquestionable talent. Your novel seems to us to show the consequences of this in both conception and execution. We were not disturbed by faults apparent in your original rough draft of the first half, because you told us that it was the product of the time you could spare from income-bringing writing in the course of several weeks only, and we felt that they would be taken care of in a more leisurely rewriting. But the faults, we think, are still there, in the second half of the story as well — which we now read for the first time.

This story still seems superimposed upon its background, and not in any real sense to grow out of it. Many characters are introduced who do not touch the story. It is as if you had carefully gone over the local newspaper files of the eighties, made copious notes, and used this background material valiantly, with the result that much of it seems dragged in, and awkwardly handled. Very often, too, your exposition is disproportionate: things really important to the story are set forth briefly and indirectly, whereas some of the local and political detail, of no real consequence in the novel as such, is given the emphasis of exposition by dialogue.

The fact that we were willing to pay you an advance, provisional upon acceptance, is evidence enough that we believed in your talent. Emphatically, we still do. But we apparently overestimated your faculty for self-criticism. It seems to us now that you must have written this book when you were only half ready to begin it.

If you were to rewrite it now, from stem to stern, we don't think that it would come to life, even though you might succeed in integrating story and background more effectively. Your right course — unless we are wrong in our opinion of this manuscript — seems to us to be to put it aside, take up one of the other novels in the plan you outlined to us, and then write this entirely anew a few years from now. If you write another novel, we believe that you ought to put it away, once you have finished it, until the impulse that led you through it has gone quite cold; then take it up again and see if you are ready yourself to accept it.

All this gives you brutally less than your due; you have created some sympathetic characters, and done much effective writing. But we think that your rapid writing for income has got you into an attitude toward your material that you will have to lose. And, of course, you will want to check our opinion immediately by submitting your manuscript to another publisher. If his decision supports ours, this letter then may be worth an attentive reading. We appreciate the difficulties under which you must work. A novel of this kind should come out of long reflection upon the characters and upon the scene, so that the background and the people and the events all, in the end, become part of a true unit. It is a harder kind of novel to do quickly, perhaps, than any other. You are hard pressed for time because of your circumstances. We greatly hope that you may be one of those to get a Guggenheim Fellowship, which would free you from the necessity of so much rapid writing which develops habits in writing incompatible with the dimensions of such a book as you had designed.

Ever sincerely yours,

MARCH 6, 1936

DEAR ——:

I have read over your "——" several times. I do not think it is successful, but it is very hard to explain to you why, except that it has the technical disadvantage of being told by a character within the story. That always somewhat diminishes the vividness and sense of actuality by removing the reader further from the things recounted. But it is, of course, a method that has often been followed by the best writers. Otherwise, I think the story failed mostly in not giving the reader a keen enough sense of the reality of what happened, so that he is moved in reading. This has nothing to do with technique, or structure, or anything of that kind, but only in the ability of a writer to feel with intensity himself, and then so express himself as to make the reader feel in that way too. If this is the case, I do not know of any way of telling a writer how to get the result. Some men can do it by nature, even though in every technical way they write badly. It has been learned by many, too, who did not seem to have it at first, but they had to teach that to themselves entirely, for it is not at all a technical matter. Many of the very best writers of narrative, such as history, etc., have been unable to succeed with fiction. You write very well, but this story is not successful, in spite of that.

It is also true that it is hardly the material for a short story, from an editor's standpoint, but that has nothing to do with its intrinsic interest.

Ever sincerely yours,

APRIL 3, 1936

DEAR ——:

We have received your letter, written as secretary of the Woman's Club of ——, in protest against certain books. We are the publishers of one you name, "Europa."[1] We are not to be counted among those who pretend to omniscience in the selection of books, and we no doubt often make mistakes. But when a book, upon publication, receives practically the universal praise of the leading reviewers, it is hard not to think that our selection has been vindicated. "Europa" was, for instance, reviewed on the front pages of both the *Times* and *Tribune* literary supplements, and was the leading review in *The Saturday Review of Literature,* and all these reviews by prominent critics were highly laudatory. This is no proof, we fully realize, of the excellence of the book, but it is proof that there is a different opinion of it from yours, and any publisher would assume that the critics were better qualified to judge than people in general.

We are soon to publish a little book called "The Story of a Novel" by Thomas Wolfe[2] which, we think, better than perhaps anything else written in recent times, reveals the point of view of the writer — shows what his nature is, and what he is trying to do. We hope you will accept this little book with our compliments. So wise a man as Plato has argued for censorship, and indeed for the suppression of poetry, because he believed, at least for purposes of argument, that society was happiest if it was not disturbed by new ideas, or by revelations of reality. This is a tenable point of view, but one could hardly expect publishers to hold it.

Ever truly yours,

TO THOMAS WOLFE

DEAR TOM:

APRIL 22, 1936

I am giving directions to reckon your royalties on "The Story of a Novel" at 15% from the start. The difference in what you

---

[1] A novel by Robert Briffault, Scribners, 1935.   [2] Scribners, 1936.

will receive, if 3,000 copies are sold, between the ten and fifteen percent royalty, will be $225.00. We certainly do not think that we should withhold that sum of money if it is going to cause so much resentment and so much loss of time and disquiet for all of us.

I would rather simply agree to do this and say nothing further, but I should not have the right to do it without telling you that the terms, as proposed, on the $1.50 price are just, and that if the matter were to be looked upon merely as business we should not be justified as business men in making this concession. You are under a misapprehension if you think that when we suggested a reduction of royalty — such as in similar cases have been freely made by writers of the highest rank, at least in sales — we were basing the suggestion on the question of price. I do remember that the price of $1.25 was mentioned as a desirable one, or a probable one, but the idea of the royalty was not dependent upon that. We could not, at that time, know what the price would have to be. We found that the price had to be higher, because of the question of basic costs which come into every phase of the handling, advertising, promoting, and making of a book. Many of these basic costs do not vary at all because of the size of the book. We do not want to put our prices any higher than we are compelled to and, in fact, more than most publishers, have tried to keep them low. We put them up only because we have to. The terms we proposed were therefore, in my opinion, just.

You return to the question of the excess corrections,[1] which were, I believe, $1100.00. If I gave you the impression that I thought this was unfair, it came from my dread of the resentment I knew you would feel to have them deducted from your royalties, even though they have always been taken into ac-

---

[1] Corrections or alterations made by the author in excess of a certain percentage of the total cost of composition.

count in every publisher's contract, and generally at only half the percentage that we allow for them. I once said to you in Charles Scribner's presence that you had a good technical argument for not paying these corrections, because you did not make them and therefore could say that they were not author's corrections, but publisher's corrections. This would be true, since you did not read your proof, but, if you had done so, is there any doubt but what these corrections would have been much larger? They were almost wholly unavoidable corrections, like the change from the first to third person, and the changing of names. They were therefore rightly author's corrections, and why should the author not pay for them? I think we began wrong by making no charge, in the case of excess corrections on the "Angel,"[1] which amounted to seven hundred dollars, so that this charge came to you as a surprise. And the truth is that many authors do resent being charged for such corrections, because they cannot be got to consider them in advance. But if the author does not pay for this cost, after the publisher has paid the 20% allowance himself, the publisher will have to pay that too. Why should he have to do it?

As to the other matter you speak of, your freedom to do whatever you think is to your best interests in business, nobody could ever deny it, and I have often said that we did not. I certainly would not wish you to make what you thought was a sacrifice, on my account, and I would know that whatever you did would be sincerely believed to be right by you, as I know that you sincerely believe the contentions you make in this letter to me to be right. I have never doubted your sincerity, and never will. I wish you could have felt that way toward us.

Always yours,

---

[1] *Look Homeward, Angel*, Scribners, 1929.

TO MARJORIE KINNAN RAWLINGS

AUG. 5, 1936

DEAR MARJORIE:

Here is a check for the amount due in royalty according to the last report. We seem to have got into confusion about the boy's book.[1] Those sentences from my letter that you quote are exactly the way I have always thought of it, but when I write in that do-as-it-seems-right-to-you way, it is because it has always been my conviction — and I do not see how anyone could dispute the rightness of it — that a book must be done according to the writer's conception of it, as nearly perfectly as possible, and that the publishing problems begin then. That is, the publisher must not try to get a writer to fit the book to the conditions of the trade, etc. It must be the other way around. I know that you think this yourself. Everything that Herschel[2] said was absolutely true. But I do feel sure that you have the best possible idea of the book, and I do think that the rivers, the hunting adventures, the characters, and the ways of life, ought all to be in. I know that a writer ought not to give summaries of what he means to do and that, with some, even telling the story and talking about it, makes it so that they cannot write it. It is often that way, and it is not hard to see why. But I have the most complete confidence in the quality of this book. I would not be a bit surprised if it were the best book you have done, and it might well be the most successful.

I should love to come to Florida sometime, but it always seems just impossible for me to get away from here. It is not so bad here, either. But if you cannot come here in October, we'll meet somehow.

Always yours,

---

[1] *The Yearling*, Scribners, 1938.   [2] Herschel Brickell, editor, critic and book columnist.

OCT. 7, 1936

DEAR JOHN:

How are things coming? Could you send me a line to say, for instance, when you think the book[1] will be done?

And would such a book as this interest you? It could be a truly great book. To be called, "Tour of the Battlefields." It could be confined to the American battlefields. It could bring out both sides of the question of war, the magnificent in it, and the dreadful, the beauty and the sordidness and horror. In a sense, everything that there is in mankind is involved in war and is shown dramatically in it. It would be, as I thought of it, just such a book as was, for instance, "Don Quixote," for there would be the idealist in company with the realist. I had always thought of an elderly man who never could get to a war because of the circumstances of his life but had always studied it and read about it and thought it glamorous, and finally was able to fulfil his great wish and make his "tour of the battlefields." But a soldier, or an ex-soldier, had always been his friend, with whom he had studied and disputed about war, and this man accompanies him. As they went over the battlefields, and from one to another, they would talk about war and all that there is in war could be brought out in their talks, from the two contending viewpoints. To take an obvious example, the idealist on a battlefield would say, "We are now at the very spot where the recruits from Maine began their heroic charge." And the realist would add, "Yes, this is the hollow where they lay down and would not get up until the veterans in the woods stoned them out." I am giving a most ridiculously obvious kind of example. I mean a much deeper book than just that, but it would be full of amusement. Every-

[1] *Gone to Texas*, Scribners, 1937.

thing about war could be said in such a book and, then, there would also be the narrative of the tour, which could be whatever a writer wanted to make it — the adventures on the road. Does the idea appeal to you? It could be confined to the Civil War, for that matter, and all there was to tell about the battlefields could be given in it.

Always yours,

The letter below was written in long-hand at a time when Wolfe was troubled about his relationship with his publishers; in fact, was planning to make a break. Perkins often wrote by hand where the situation was delicate and it was desirable to give a letter a more personal and intimate touch.

TO THOMAS WOLFE

TUESDAY, NOV 17TH, 36

DEAR TOM:

I haven't time to write today — we have a meeting[1] that often lasts till five and my late P.M. and evening are full too. I can say this though, I never knew a soul with whom I felt I was in such fundamentally complete agreement as you. What's more, and what has to do with it, I know you would not ever do an insincere thing, or anything you did not think was right. I don't fully understand your letter, but I'll answer it as best I can. You must surely know, though, that any publisher would leap at the chance to publish you.

Always yours,

You have with us at present a balance of over $2000, all but about $500 of which is overdue.

---

[1] Monthly meeting of the Board of Directors of Charles Scribner's Sons.

*The following letter, written in long-hand on personal sta-
tionery, was evidently enclosed with the letter of the same date,
which was typed on the Scribner letterhead. Both are in reply
to a letter of Wolfe's written at a time when he was about to
sever connections with Scribners.*

TO THOMAS WOLFE

Nov 18, 1936

DEAR TOM:

With this is a more formal letter which I hope is what you
want. This is to say that on my part there has been no "sever-
ance." I can't express certain kinds of feelings very comfortably,
but you must realize what my feelings are toward you. Ever
since "Look Homeward, Angel" your work has been the foremost interest in my life, and I have never doubted for your
future on any grounds except, at times, on those of your being
able to control the vast mass of material you have accumulated
and have to form into books. You seem to think I have tried
to control you. I only did that when you asked my help and
then I did the best I could. It all seems very confusing to me
but, whatever the result, I hope you don't mean it to keep us
from seeing each other, or that you won't come to our house.

MAX

TO THOMAS WOLFE

Nov. 18, 1936

DEAR TOM:

You ask me to explicitly state the nature of your relations
with Charles Scribner's Sons. To begin with, you have faith-
fully and honorably discharged all obligations to us, and no

further agreement of any sort exists between us with respect to the future. Our relations are simply those of a publisher who profoundly admires the work of an author and takes great pride in publishing whatever he may of that author's writings. They are not such as to give any sort of rights, or anything approaching that, over that author's future work. Contrary to custom, we have not even an option which would give us the privilege of seeing first any new manuscript.

We do not wholly understand parts of your letter, where you speak of us as putting you in a position of denying an obligation that does not exist, for we do not know how we have done that; or where you refer to "exerting control of a man's future," which we have no intention of doing at all, and would not have the power or right to do. There are other phrases, in that part of your letter, that I do not understand, one of which is that which refers to us as being absolved from any commitments of any kind, "should the author fail." If this and these other phrases signify that you think you should have a contract from us if our relations are to continue, you can certainly have one. We should be delighted to have one. You must surely know the faith this house has in you. There are, of course, limits in terms beyond which nobody can go in a contract, but we should expect to make one that would suit you if you told us what was required.

Ever sincerely yours,

TO ERNEST HEMINGWAY

DEC. 9, 1936

DEAR ERNEST:

I have told them to send you the new Mabel Dodge.[1] Were you in it? I shall look and see, but if I had been living in Paris,

[1] *Winter in Taos*, by Mabel Dodge Luhan, Harcourt, Brace & Co., 1935.

and everywhere, the way you did, being me I never would have dared to meet either Mabel or Gertrude.[1] Some instinct would have kept me from it, or maybe just cowardice. I did meet Miss Stein, though, before a dinner, a year or so ago, and thought she looked like a grand old Indian squaw — as if she were very wise too, and had lived, as they say.

I wish you would write a trilogy, but I am glad to see that this is a really big book, not that there is any advantage in largeness, but I expect to have that much more to like to read. . . .

I wish you would give up the idea of Spain. I am sure they will be fighting there for years yet. I think this Rightist general must be good, and perhaps he could take Madrid right now, except that he does not want to waste his few trained men, but even if they did get in, it is hard to think they would stay.

I am enclosing a proof of the black part of the colored jacket of "All Good Americans,"[2] done by Waldo. You will find suggestions of the twins, here and there. It is much better in color. You will catch on easy enough that this is sent partly to suggest that we haven't the Introduction, which I do not doubt you realize. We can use it when you can do it but, God knows, I do not want to interrupt you on the book.

Spent most of yesterday morning downtown at a lawyer's office with Tom Wolfe on account of a $125,000 libel suit[3] he has got us into. That is my way of looking at it. The other night he told me at great length, and overwhelming eloquence, of the injustice done him on all hands in this blank blank country — Germany as white as snow in contrast with it — where the honest men are all robbed and bludgeoned by scoundrels. And it all wound up with, "And now you have got me into a $125,-

---

[1] Gertrude Stein.   [2] By Jerome Bahr, published by Scribners in 1937, with an Introduction by Ernest Hemingway. Waldo Peirce, American painter, designed the jacket.   [3] A suit brought on the allegation that one of the characters in a short story of Wolfe's entitled "No Door," in *From Death to Morning*, was identifiable and that the characterization reflected adversely upon the identifiable individual. The suit was eventually settled out of court.

ooo libel suit." So it is all a matter of the point of view. But Tom had all the legal staff laughing as he told the story, and all for him. He has plenty of humor when the humor gland is functioning.

We have quite a good fishing book here by an Englishman, both about sea fishing and inland fishing, and all over the world. Except that he never fished in Cuba. He does know Bimini. . . .

Always yours,

The "long letter" of Wolfe's referred to in the following hand-written letter was written when he was restless and discontented, and it ran to twenty-eight pages. Perhaps Wolfe felt that the current rumor that he was unable to get his books into final form without the help of Perkins, reflected upon him as a writer. In any case, he was unhappy about the situation, and was inclined to blame Perkins for the extraordinary help Perkins had given him in the organizing and shaping of his material.

TO THOMAS WOLFE

Jan. 13, 37

Dear Tom:

I just got your long letter and have only glanced through it, so that I can't yet properly answer it. The other came yesterday. I am dashing this off now to make clear two things.

My belief is that the one important, supreme object is to advance your work. Anything in furtherance of that is good and anything that impedes it is bad. What impedes it especially is not the great difficulty and pain of doing it — for you are the reverse of lazy, you work furiously — but the harassment, the torment of outside worries. When you spoke to me about the settlement, it was, and had been before, very plain that this suit was such a worry that it was impeding you in your work. It was only because of that that I gave the advice I did.[1] I thought, then get rid of it, forget it, and clear the way for what is really important, supremely. Now this blackmail talk puts a new face on that matter altogether.

As to my own self: I stand ready to help if I can, whenever you want. You asked my help on "Time and the River." I was glad and proud to give it. No understanding person could believe that it affected the book in any serious or important way — that it was much more than mechanical help. It did seem that the book was too enormous to get between covers. That was the first problem. There might be a problem in a book, such as prohibited publication of Joyce for years in this country. If you wished it, we would publish any book by you as written except for such problems as those which prohibit — some can't be avoided but I don't foresee them. Length could be dealt with by publishing in sections. Anyhow, apart from physical or legal limitations not within the possibility of change by us, we will publish anything as you write it.

I simply want to quickly put these points before you. You are not a private character, though. No one whose work has been published, and has roused the interest and admiration of thousands of people, can be that in the sense that a carpenter or truck driver is. To lose that kind of privacy is a consequence of important writing. In this case, the writing is so important that it has to be done, and, I know, at great cost to you.

Yours,

There follows another letter written in long-hand, in answer to the rather bewildering twenty-eight-page letter from Wolfe.

[1] Perkins had advised Wolfe to settle the suit out of court.

TO THOMAS WOLFE

JAN. 14, 1937

DEAR TOM:

I've read your letter[1] carefully. I think it's a wonderful letter. I have no quarrel with any of it, except that you have greatly misunderstood some things I must explain. But what a task you've put me to, to search myself — in whom I'm not so very much interested anymore — and give you an adequate answer. Your position is right. I understand and agree with it.

Always yours,

In his answer to Wolfe's twenty-eight-page letter, Perkins had written, on January 13, that he had as yet only had time to glance through it, and so could not answer it properly. He referred to it again, briefly, in his letter of January 14th. The letter that follows was written after he had read and pondered this long and important document in the Wolfe-Perkins correspondence.

TO THOMAS WOLFE

SATURDAY, JANUARY 16, 1937

DEAR TOM:

In the first place, I completely subscribe to what you say a writer should do, and always have believed it. If it were not true that you, for instance, should write as you see, feel, and think, then a writer would be of no importance, and books merely things for amusement. And since I have always thought

[1] The twenty-eight-page letter previously referred to, and previously answered by Perkins on January 13th.

that there could be nothing so important as a book can be, and some are, I could not help but think as you do. But there are limitations of time, of space, and of human laws which cannot be treated as if they did not exist. I think that a writer should, of course, be the one to make his book what he wants it to be, and that if, because of the laws of space, it must be cut, he should be the one to cut it; and, especially with you, I think the labour and discipline that would come from doing that without help or interference would further the pretty terrible task of mastering the material. But my impression was that you asked my help, that you wanted it. And it is my impression too that changes were not forced on you (you're not very forceable, Tom, nor I very forceful), but were argued over, often for hours. But I agree with you about this too, fully, and unless you want help it will certainly not be thrust upon you. It would be better if you could fight it out alone — better for your work, in the end, certainly; and, what's more, I believe you are now in a position to publish with less regard to any conventions of bookmaking, say a certain number of pages almost, whether or not it had what in a novel is regarded as an ending, or anything else that is commonly expected in a novel. I believe the writer, anyway, should always be the final judge, and I meant you to be so. I have always held to that position and have sometimes seen books hurt thereby, but at least as often helped. "The book belongs to the author."

I certainly do not care — nor does this House — how revolutionary your books are. I did try to keep you from injecting radical, or Marxian, beliefs into "Time and the River," because they were your beliefs in 1934 and 1935, and not those of Eugene in the time of the book. So it did not seem that they could rightly belong in the book. If they could have, then the times could not be rightly pictured, I thought. It must be so. Still, you were then and always conscious of social wrong and

that is plainly in the book as you then saw it. There was the
Astor story. What was told was not heard by Eugene. It was
second-hand, and second-hand material — something told, not
heard and seen — is inferior to first-hand. If cutting had to be
done, ought that not to be cut? I know your memory is a
miracle, but it seems as if you must have forgotten how we
worked and argued. You were never overruled. Do you think
you are clay to be moulded! I never saw anyone less malleable.
And as for publishing what you like, or being prevented from
it, apart from the limitations of space, you have not been, in-
tentionally. Are you thinking of "K 19"?[1] We would have published it if you had said to do it. At the time, I said to Jack:[2]
"Maybe it's the way Tom is. Maybe we should just publish
him as he comes and in the end it will all be right." But if we
had, and the results had been bad at the moment, would you
not have blamed me? Certainly I should have bitterly blamed
myself. I do not want the passage of time to make you cautious
or conservative, but I do want it to give you a full control — as
it has done in the case of great writers in the past — over your
great talent. And if you can stand the struggle, it will. But you
must struggle too, and perhaps even more than in the writing,
in the shaping and revising. That might be the hardest thing
of all, to your nature. You have so much in you, that the need
with you is to get it uttered. Then to go back and polish and
perfect seems petty, and goes against your nature, I guess.

Tom, you ought not to say some of the things you do — that
I find your sufferings amusing and don't take them seriously.
I know something of them. I do try to turn your mind from
them and to arouse your humor, because to spend dreadful
hours brooding over them, and in denunciation and abuse on
account of them, seems to be only to aggravate them. It does

[1] Section of manuscript removed from *Of Time and the River* but never separately published. "K 19" was the name of a locomotive. [2] John Hall Wheelock,
an editor at Scribners.

no good. You have to suffer to write as you do, and the slings and arrows that strike you from outside madden you the more because you instinctively know that all that matters is your work and so why can't you be left to do it. I understand that. Have you seen me amused by other people's sufferings? You know that was unjust.

Then comes the question of your writing about the people here. I don't want to discuss it, because I agree that you have the same right to make use of them as of anyone else in the same way, and if there is an argument on it the whole thing may be bedevilled. . . . But when I spoke of resigning after we published — and the moment I inadvertently said it I told Miss Nowell[1] she must not repeat it, and she said she would not — I did not mean I would be asked or wanted to resign. That would never happen on any such ground. But it isn't the way you think, and it's up to you to write as you think you should. Your plan as outlined seems to me a splendid one too. I hope you will get on with it now.

There remains the question of whether we are in fundamental agreement. But it is no question if you feel it is not so. I have always instinctively felt that it was so, and no one I ever knew has said more of the things that I believed than you. It was so from the moment that I began to read your first book. Nothing else, I would say, could have kept such different people together through such trials. But I believe in democracy and not in dictators; and in government by principles and not by men; and in less government if possible, rather than more; and that power always means injustice and so should be as little concentrated as is compatible with the good of the majority; and that violence breeds more evils than it kills; and that it's better to sizzle in the frying-pan until you're sure your jump won't take you into the fire; and that Erasmus, who begged his

[1] Elizabeth Nowell, literary agent.

friend Luther not to destroy the *good* in the Church because
of the bad in it, which he thought could be forced out with
the spread of education, was right, though not heroic, and the
heroic Luther wrong — and that Europe is the worse for his
impetuosity today. I don't believe that things can't improve.
I believe that the only thing that can prevent improvement is
the ruin of violence, or of reckless finance which will end in
violence. That is why Roosevelt needs an opposition, and it is
the only serious defect in him. I believe that change really
comes from great deep causes too complex for contemporary
men, or any others perhaps, fully to understand, and that when
even great men like Lenin try to make over a whole society
suddenly the end is almost sure to be bad, and that the right
end, the natural one, will come from the efforts of innumerable
people trying to do right, and to understand it, because they
are a part of the natural forces that are set at work by changed
conditions. It is the effort of man to adjust himself to change,
and it has to be led, but the misfortune of man is that strong
will almost always beats down intelligence, and the passionate,
the reasonable. I believe that such as you can help on change,
but that it ought to be by your writings, not by violent acts. I
believe that wealth is bad but that it should not be confiscated,
but reduced by law, and in accordance with a principle, not
arbitrarily and in passion; and if it is done in passion and
violence the result will be a new privileged class made up of
delegates of the man or the oligarchy that has seized the power.
But it may be that the great underlying changes will dictate
Communism as the best society for most people. Then we
ought to have it; but if we can evolve into it gradually how
much better (though I know many on both sides say that is
impossible) than if we go in by revolution and civil war. At
least let us try the way of evolution first. It seems to me that
our Civil War and many of the great convulsions were caused

by extremists on both sides, by those too hot-headed to wait for natural forces to disclose their direction, when the inevitable outcome could no longer be resisted. I do not believe the world can ever be perfect, of course, though it might in a sense approximate a political and economic perfection if conditions ceased from changing so that a long enough time was given to deal with known and permanent factors. But this is getting to be too much of a philosophy of history or something, and I don't think it has anything to do with fundamental agreement. I had always felt it existed — and I don't feel, because you differ with me, however violently, on such things as I've said above, that it does not, necessarily. It is more that I like and admire the same things and despise many of the same things, and the same people too, and think the same things important and unimportant — at least this is the way it has seemed to me.

Anyhow, I don't see why you should have hesitated to write me as you did, or rather to send the letter. There was mighty little of it that I did not wholly accept, and what I did not, I perfectly well understood. There were places in it that made me angry, but it was a fine letter, a fine writer's statement of his beliefs, as fine as any I ever saw, and though I have vanities enough, as many as most, it gave me great pleasure too — that which comes from hearing brave and sincere beliefs uttered with sincerity and nobility.   Always yours,

TO NANCY HALE

JUNE 18, 1937

DEAR MRS. WERTENBAKER:[1]

I got your address from Miss Nowell.[2] I had been asking her about you because I cannot help being impatient to see the

---

[1] Nancy Hale, the novelist.   [2] Elizabeth Nowell, literary agent.

novel done,[1] or even to read some more of it, and yet I do not want to keep bothering you and perhaps worrying you about it. But she thought it would be all right if I wrote you, and she told me you were working well. I am delighted to know this. Writing a novel is a very hard thing to do because it covers so long a space of time, and if you get discouraged it is not a bad sign, but a good one. If you think you are not doing it well, you are thinking the way real novelists do. I never knew one who did not feel greatly discouraged at times, and some get desperate, and I have always found that to be a good symptom. Anyhow, I have seen enough of the novel to have no anxieties about the outcome, but rather the very greatest hopes. I hope you will be able to go on steadily until you get to the end.

I hope when you go through here, in the Fall, on the way back to Virginia, you will give me a chance to see you. Maybe by then you will have the manuscript complete.

Ever sincerely yours,

When Arthur Train was at work on his autobiographical "My Day in Court," he asked Perkins to jot down suggestions, a list of topics that might be covered, or discussed, in the course of the book, and on July 22, Perkins replied as follows:

TO ARTHUR TRAIN

JULY 22, 1937

DEAR ARTHUR:

I have been trying to put down some topics. I'll keep the list by me and add to it whenever I can. I am enclosing herewith an article by Ford Maddox Ford. It might suggest something to you, and it relates to one topic that I think important.

---

[1] *The Prodigal Women*, Scribners, 1942.

While Ford makes some ridiculous misstatements, there is much truth in what he says, that publishing has become a racket, and a mad pursuit of the best-seller. This seems to have happened quickly, in the last six years, say. But I think it is probably due at bottom to the profound changes in ways of life, because it seems also to be true of England. But Ford does overlook one of its chief immediate causes here, the Book of the Month Club. I think that has been very ably managed, and that the man at the head of it feels a public responsibility and intends to serve his subscribers well. He has made something of an institution of the Club. At the same time, its most conspicuous effect on publishing is to concentrate the attention of the entire public on one book a month. I think that this is very harmful, particularly to that very class of craftsmen in writing about whom Ford is especially worried. When people had to find their own books, they followed their own taste, but now, with the American tendency to follow fashion, they satisfy themselves with just the best-sellers. And the newspapers' policy of playing up the best-sellers works in the same way.

Another topic worth discussion is the literary conscience. Mrs. Colum[1] wrote a paper on this called "The Two Consciences." One of them is the one we all have, but the writer, the artist, has another which compels him in the same way not to shrink from revealing life, however unpleasant it is, and however offensive his writing to important elements in the public. He is often looked upon as being immoral on account of the frankness of his expression, or the material he uses, when he would regard himself as immoral if he softened his words or misrepresented his material to conform to the conventions. You may think that the literary conscience is something of an affectation, but it is a good topic anyhow, and leads into a discussion of frankness and the use of unpleasant words, etc.

---

[1] Mary M. Colum, author of *From These Roots*, Scribners, 1937.

You might point out that good writers like Hemingway sacrifice sales by their frankness, and know it.

Another topic should be the economic and literary effects on the writer, of the great popular magazines which are built up on advertising. I think on this you have done some writing.

Your own methods of work, and how you reconcile them with social life, how many hours you write, should be covered. And I think this would be very interesting because, as Kipling did, you got a great deal from talking to people, so that social life has furthered your work instead of hindering it as it does with many writers.

This might lead to a discussion of how a writer gets his characters, to what extent he does or should use real people. In recent years, writers have used real people directly to a much greater degree, I think, than ever was done before — although it is said that almost all of Tolstoi's characters in "War and Peace" were members of his own family, and recognizable. The influence on you of other writers, and which ones, etc., would be interesting. And the writer's relations to his public, and how he can gauge the response to his books, apart from sales. This would bring in what you wrote about fan mail. I read that and thought the letters were excellent for the purpose.

The general scheme of your book[1] is narrative, so that I think it would be better if the topics were worked into the narrative rather than discussed separately.

Always yours,

---

[1] *My Day in Court* (Mr. Train's autobiography), Scribners, 1939.

TO HAMILTON BASSO

AUG. 23, 1937

DEAR HAM:

I was glad to hear about Tom. I took the risk of paying a month's rent on his apartment[1] because the agent has been threatening to dispossess him at any moment, for the last week, and I did not know what in the world would happen if all his manuscripts got thrown out on the sidewalk, or even put up for auction — which I believe the landlord is entitled to do, to the extent of the debt. Miss Nowell[2] has been telegraphing and writing Tom, but has got no answer, and I think this means that he has been away and when he gets back he will send a check. I thought it would do Tom lots of good to get back into the mountains,[3] but perhaps the great fame that he enjoys there, and the happiness of being among his own people, has not enabled him to work properly. It must have done him good in resting him, and I suppose John Barleycorn is not so ubiquitous in that region as in this.

I guess I wrote you that old Scott[4] seems to be on the right road at last, and busy and paying his debts.

I look forward eagerly to seeing both of you.

Always yours,

TO CAROLINE GORDON

SEPT. 7, 1937

DEAR MRS. TATE:[5]

My reading of "The Garden of Adonis"[6] has all been done

---

[1] Thomas Wolfe's apartment at 49th Street and First Avenue.   [2] Miss Elizabeth Nowell, literary agent, a friend of Wolfe's.   [3] Wolfe made a short trip to his home town, Asheville, North Carolina, during August, 1937.   [4] F. Scott Fitzgerald.   [5] Caroline Gordon, in private life Mrs. Allen Tate.   [6] By Caroline Gordon, published by Scribners in 1937.

in sections. I never read it consecutively until just now, in a duplicate set of the galleys. I wanted to tell you that I did it with very great admiration. It seemed to me a most artfully constructed book, and all the characters were alive, and an enormous amount is said in these few pages about the way the South is and the changes that have come, and everything as you had planned it. And I thought the ending extremely moving and fine.

There has always been one thing that worried me a little about the book with the Indian background. The fear you might tend to write it in the way of a chronicle. That was the way you wrote the story — or should it be called an annal? I am not quite sure which, but you will know what I mean. I do not think that method of writing will do today unless varied with other methods, in a full book. It does do in a story. I never understood this, but I always found that, much as one admired that kind of narrative — take, for instance, Defoe's "Memoirs of a Cavalier" — and enjoyed it while reading, one could always lay it down without feeling any particular impulse to take it up again. I know you know more about this than I, but I thought you might feel the temptation to follow that method, and that it would be all right to speak against it. But I think it will be a splendid book.

Ever sincerely yours,

TO WILL JAMES

SEPT. 17, 1937

DEAR BILL:

I have been thinking about a "major" book for you to consider, but without much success so far. It did occur to me, though, that if driving a herd of cattle a long distance, or a

herd of horses, was still done in your time — which I doubt —
it would make a fine basis for a novel. Any book that has in it
a journey during which the plot develops has a strong element
of interest. A march or a journey interests anybody. There is
one trouble, that Phil Rollins used the cattle drive in the '80's
for his "Jinglebob"[1] — but even so, no two cattle drives are alike.
I think driving a herd of horses would be better still, if it was
ever done for long distances, or was within your recollection.
Maybe there is nothing in it, for some such reason as that, but
I thought I would propose it because of the great interest of
the journey element, in fiction, and the opportunity it would
give to bring in all kinds of change and happenings.

Always yours,

*By the time the letter of November 20, 1937, was written,
relations between Wolfe and Scribners were somewhat strained.
Wolfe had left Scribners, and was looking for another publisher. Correspondence between Wolfe and Perkins was now
carried on through an intermediary — in this case probably
Elizabeth Nowell, the literary agent, a friend of Tom's and
of the House, who had the full confidence of both men. This
letter, like some of the others, was written in long-hand.*

[1] Scribners, 1927.

TO THOMAS WOLFE

Nov. 20, 37

DEAR TOM:

I am your friend and always will be, I think, and it grieved me deeply that you should even have transacted the little business that needed to be done, through an intermediary instead of face to face. But it made no difference otherwise and I hope we may soon meet as friends. Of course, I had to tell Fred[1] and others, when they asked me about you, what the situation was. It was humiliating and had to be faced. I could not properly, even by silence, let it be assumed that things were as they had been. I told Fred truly too when I said I did not understand about it. I don't, but that need make no difference between us, and I won't let it on my side. Miss Nowell[2] should never have told you of my concern as to your writing about *us* — it was not *me* — though I think her motive was a kind one. I know the difficulty of your problem and I never meant this point to come up to confuse you. But don't you see that serious injury to this House and to my long-time associates here, for which I was responsible, would make me wish to be elsewhere? I hate to speak about this, but I can't have you misunderstand it.

I've missed you and felt badly about it. I want to hear you tell of all you saw in the South, sometime. I'm sorry about your eyes. Anyone who reads and writes so much must wear glasses, though. The worst thing about them is that they are always getting lost, but in the end one masters even that.

Anyhow, I'm glad to have seen your handwriting again.

Always yours,

---

[1] Fred Wolfe, a brother of Thomas Wolfe. [2] Elizabeth Nowell, literary agent, a friend of Wolfe's.

DEAR HAM: DEC. 7, 1937

I have authorized the acceptance of the proposal for the publication of "Courthouse Square"[1] from Methuen. Methuen is a good publisher, and this will bring the book before the English people and get it reviewed and lay a basis for the future; and it was impossible to delay long enough to consult you,[2] and I felt sure you would accept.

We seem to be having quite a depression here, but there is no use talking about that, and the hopeful ones think it won't last long.

Everything seems to be in the same state, so far as Tom[3] is concerned. He is living at the Chelsea Hotel on 23rd Street, a very nice old place, with large rooms, quiet and pleasant. All the elevator men, etc., have been there for a hundred years, and Edgar Lee Masters[4] is a resident. Tom wrote me a long letter, some time ago, in which he implied that it was not he who had left us, but we who had left him.[5] And the truth is that the story is about that we would not publish him any more, and that several publishers have declined to do it. But it was Tom who put it about, in some strange fashion, and I do not know just how. He was on the point of a contract with some publisher — he told me this in his letter — and had brought all his packing boxes of manuscript around there, and some young man had been assigned to work with him. The publisher himself came in and joked about the size of the manuscripts, and then he handed Tom an envelope. Tom opened it that evening, and found that it said that these manuscripts were left in the

---

[1] Scribners, 1936.   [2] Mr. Basso was abroad at this time, living in St. Paul, France, in the Maritime Alps.   [3] Thomas Wolfe.   [4] American poet, author of *Spoon River Anthology*, Macmillan, 1925.   [5] Wolfe, at this time, had left Scribners but had not yet found another publisher. Harper and Brothers were, later, to become his publishers.

publisher's office at the risk and responsibility of the author. This made Tom so mad that he took them all away the next day. Most of them had been in our offices for several years, without any such notification to Tom, and I am afraid we spoiled him in this respect, and others. Anyhow, we are giving a cocktail party on Friday the 10th, and I sent Tom a card. He and I have exchanged friendly letters, and it is ridiculous of him to refuse to come face to face and forget about all the trouble.

I hope I shall hear from you again soon.

Always yours,

TO MARJORIE KINNAN RAWLINGS

Dec. 13, 1937

Dear Marjorie:

I have read the whole book,[1] and with constantly growing interest, and, taken all in all, I think the last half is better than the first, and that the book gets increasingly good. But the very beginning now is perfect, it seems to me, and of course the father and mother, and all about that life, and Jody's on the island, are as good as can be. When you come to the Forresters, I think there gets into it — especially in that first scene — a slight element of theatricality or romanticism, or something not quite true. Couldn't you make Lem show some of his meanness in that scene even — well, he did in his reference to Oliver — but more of it? They are very tough people, and the toughness ought to be more evident, even though they seemed fine to Jody. And I think you ought to cut out the unseemly performance of the old lady, because there was nothing else in the book like it, and no need to be, and it would prevent the

[1] *The Yearling*, Scribners, 1938.

book from getting a sale that it might easily get, to younger people, in the end, because all the libraries and the schools would object violently to it. I would not suggest taking it out if it were in any way essentially true to the book, but it almost seems to me as if it were a little the reverse.

I think Grandma Hutto is now a first-rate character, but that there does get to be an element of unrealness in everything else when Jody goes to see her. For instance, Oliver never becomes very real — he seems romanticized. He was romantic, of course, to Jody's eyes. But this really is not important, for he is in the book very little as a person, and more as a sort of symbol.

All the hunting, all the nature, is superb, and the whole meaning of people living in that way, with so much to fight; and the development of Jody, and its outcome, is beautifully done. I would only suggest cutting out the next to the last paragraph. I may think of other things to tell you, but the book is ready to go into type, and ought to. It is long — 163,000 words. It might be tightened up some, but whenever I thought of taking out anything, I hated to do it. And I think any such question better wait until we both read it in type and get that new view of it that comes from seeing it in a new form. It is a very beautiful book, and I greatly enjoyed every minute of it. Otherwise I would have read it faster. The better a book is, the slower I go.

Always yours,

TO ROBERT BRIFFAULT

MAY 4, 1938

DEAR MR. BRIFFAULT:

I was extremely glad to hear from you. Of course, I had hoped that you might have got started on a novel, but I know well enough that only those who write as a trade — the manufacturers of so-called literature — can produce at will. The real writer must wait and reflect — and probably most of his work, before actually beginning to set down the words, is largely unconscious. I do hope, though, that nothing will keep you from writing in the end.

I shall look up the charge for corrections on "Europa in Limbo."[1] I do remember that they seemed to me very light indeed, and I shall investigate the question. But we are at the mercy of the Union in respect to what is charged, which is all according to rules and gauged by time. It does seem to me strange, though, that there should have been any charge in this instance.

I have not seen Crichton[2] since last month, when we gave a tea for Marjorie Rawlings. He was in very good spirits that day. The magazine[3] had published her first piece of work when he was on it, and he had always followed her career with great interest. Now she has had a great success. In the Fall, we are to publish a novel which I think would please you. It is called "The Dynasty of Death."[4] It covers about three generations — though always with the same central characters — in the founding of a family on the basis of a great munitions industry, like the Krupps. In a way, it is an exposure, in the Uncle Tom's Cabin manner, of the munitions industry and, to some degree, of any great organized industry tending to monopoly. In fact, what it shows most plainly is the blighting effect of the highly acquisitive and materialistic nature on people, and on places, and everything. It is full of melodrama, but good melodrama. I think we shall have it out while you are still here.

Many thanks for writing.

Ever sincerely yours,

[1] Published by Scribners in 1937. [2] Kyle Crichton, writer and editor. [3] *Scribner's Magazine*. [4] By Taylor Caldwell, Scribners, 1938.

JUNE 21, 1938

DEAR ARTHUR:

I think "My Day in Court"[1] reads very well indeed. One passes easily from the wholly narrative chapters into those in which the practices and ways of writers, etc., are discussed. There is no difficulty on that point, and that was always the point of anxiety with me. That little chapter, "Mea Culpa," I think, ought either to be omitted or to be hitched onto one of the chapters about the criminal courts. It is not of enough importance, it seems to me, to stand alone — the incident is given too much emphasis that way. But I think it could easily be joined on, as a kind of postscript, to what was said before about gambling raids.

I do not think any publisher would agree with you on the subject of advertising. Of course, you might rejoin that authors and publishers never had agreed on that matter, and that is true. Authors generally have a completely unjustifiable faith in what book-advertising can do, and they get it largely from knowing what advertising in general can do. But book-advertising is deprived of the great principle of general advertising — repetition. An advertiser of any other product can go on for several years, and lose money by it, and yet be a great gainer in the end as the result of persistent repetition. But, as each particular book is a separate product, it is impossible to apply to any one, except to a very limited extent, this great fundamental advertising principle. The fact is, as all publishers believe, that advertising will greatly help a selling book, but that it will have no effect, within the time at the disposal of the publisher, on the sale of a book which lacks the mysterious sell-

---

[1] Mr. Train's autobiography, published by Scribners in 1939.

ing qualities. This has been proved over and over. In one case an author of ours, who later had a very great success from the very start in a very bad year, insisted on spending three thousand of his own dollars, on top of about two thousand of ours, because he was certain that his book would sell if advertised enough. It had already sold some four or five thousand copies by the time he put in his money, and it never sold more than three or four hundred beyond that. This is just one instance, but there are thousands of others. I doubt if it often happens that a book with the capacity for success is a failure because the publisher has other leaders on his list to back. But I do think many books fail which would have succeeded two or three years earlier, or two or three years later, because the mood of the public — the directions in which the winds of interest blow — change so rapidly. "The Green Hat"[1] kind of book, for instance, could not succeed now. But then there are certain kinds of books which would succeed at any time, such as "The Yearling."[2]

Always yours,

At the time when the letter of July 25, 1938, was written, Wolfe's brother, Fred Wolfe, had gone to Seattle, Washington, to be with Tom, who had come down with a bad case of pneumonia while visiting the Pacific Coast. Tom, obviously, had not been able to write himself, and the reports that came in about him were alarming. Perkins wrote Fred Wolfe for news.

[1] By Michael Arlen, George H. Doran Co., 1924. [2] By Marjorie Kinnan Rawlings, Scribners, 1938.

JULY 25, 1938

DEAR FRED:

I don't know how things may be, but if you have the time and don't think I am asking too much, I wish you would drop me a letter, or anyhow a postcard about old Tom. I haven't been able to find out anything that one could depend upon, but I know he must have been mighty sick, and maybe still is. Could you let me know? I wanted to write to him, but Miss Nowell[1] thought it would be better not to, that it might bother him. And perhaps he is not in any shape to read letters anyway. I would be ever so grateful to have some word from you. I only know that he has been ill for some time, and with pneumonia, and that a few days ago he was thought to be coming safely out of it. But then, later word from Miss Nowell was much less reassuring. I hope everything will go well.

Always yours,

In spite of the break between Wolfe and his editor at Scribners, Tom never really changed in his feeling of devotion and allegiance to Perkins, of whose selfless and skillful aid he remained keenly aware. Very shortly before his death, in one of the most moving letters ever written, he assured Perkins of this. It is this letter, given in full below — the last that Tom wrote, and written against the advice and orders of his doctors — that is referred to in the answer which follows it.

---

[1] Elizabeth Nowell, literary agent, a friend of Wolfe's.

August 12, 1938

Dear Max:

I'm sneaking this against orders — but "I've got a hunch" — and I wanted to write these words to you.

I've made a long voyage and been to a strange country, and I've seen the dark man very close; and I don't think I was too much afraid of him, but so much of mortality still clings to me — I wanted most desperately to live and still do, and I thought about you all a 1000 times, and wanted to see you all again, and there was the impossible anguish and regret of all the work I had not done, of all the work I had to do — and I know now I'm just a grain of dust, and I feel as if a great window has been opened on life I did not know about before — and if I come through this, I hope to God I am a better man, and in some strange way I can't explain I know I am a deeper and a wiser one — If I get on my feet and out of here, it will be months before I head back, but if I get on my feet, I'll come back.

— Whatever happens — I had this "hunch" and wanted to write you and tell you, no matter what happens or has happened, I shall always think of you and feel about you the way it was that 4th of July day 3 yrs. ago when you met me at the boat, and we went out on the cafe on the river and had a drink and later went on top of the tall building and all the strangeness and the glory and the power of life and of the city was below ——

Yours always,

Tom

TO THOMAS WOLFE

AUG. 19, 1938

DEAR TOM:

I was most happy to get your letter, but don't do it again. That is enough, and will always be valued. And I remember that night as a magical night, and the way the city looked. I always meant to go back there, but maybe it would be better not to, for things are never the same the second time. I tried to find you some good picture books and found three, good in their way. But maybe I shall find something better. I'll keep my eyes open for it.

Everyone hereabouts is greatly concerned over your illness, and that means many people who do not even know you, too. Don't get impatient about loss of time. You don't really lose time, in the ordinary sense. Even six months would not be important. Even if you were really relaxing, as they call it, all that time, you would be getting good from it, even as a writer. I hope you will manage to do it too.

I could send you some good books to read, but I don't think you will want to do any reading for yet a while. What you ought to do is to realize that by really resting now, you are in fact actually gaining time, not losing it.

Always yours,

TO TAYLOR CALDWELL

Nov. 23, 1938

DEAR MRS. REBACK:[1]

I have been very much perplexed about what we should publish next. We ought to be mighty careful not to make a

[1] Taylor Caldwell, in private life Mrs. Marcus Reback.

mistake. I do not think the book should be "There Are No Giants." For one thing, I think you write very much better now than you did when you wrote that, even allowing for the improvements of revision. For another, the book bears, in some respects — in particular in respect to its principal male character — a certain resemblance to the "Dynasty."[1] And, for a third, it is rather a dreary book, and unhappy, not relieved by the gaiety and charm and beauty that there was in the "Dynasty," even though that had always an underlying grimness. Then too, the "Dynasty" was about a class of people who really are more interesting in themselves than as individuals.

Well, then, there are the lesser novels you sent us but, after "Dynasty," they haven't the scope and dimensions that we should put before the public. If one of them were to be published, I think it should be under a different name from Taylor Caldwell, and I always was in hopes we could find one that had more superficially striking qualities to begin a series under another name.

So that leaves us with "My Road to Destiny." I think this last part of it is for the most part excellent, but I really think it is a very dangerous and difficult book. When we first began to read it, it did seem as if we were very probably headed for Fascism, and as if Roosevelt's conduct was such as would lead to it by causing a Fascist revulsion from extreme liberalism, relief, and all that. But now it seems as if the scene has all been changed. Now the middle class has asserted itself in an election, and shown its power, and while this may be only a temporary change, how can we tell? Then, too, there is the big preparedness program, which is undoubtedly going to tend to arouse strong patriotism, even perhaps chauvinism. All that is not inconsistent with approaching Fascism, but it does make it seem much more remote. "My Road to Destiny" is a novel which

[1] *Dynasty of Death,* by Taylor Caldwell, Scribners, 1938.

begins in the past, twenty-four years ago, and then goes on into the future. In other words, you have to gauge the future, and some of that future will have been reached by the time of publication. It is too risky, I am afraid. The future is too uncertain, and the success of the book will depend too much on guessing right. I do not know exactly what could be done about the book but it might in some way be used later, with changes. I think at this critical moment it is too dangerous to use it. The next book is of the utmost importance to your career.

Now it occurred to me that you might have some other material in your mind for a novel. I thought even that it might be drawn in some sense from your own life, from your own family. Could that be? Most novelists draw their best books from experience — as "David Copperfield," "Pendennis," "War and Peace," etc. I am only trying to start you thinking, perhaps, of what you might use, but I cannot help remembering what you told me of your own experience in the Southern mountains.

You have a great gift for unfolding the development and the career of a family, too. Have you anything of that sort in the back of your mind? All this is thrown out by way of suggestion, and for discussion, because I do think it is of the utmost importance that we should turn in the right direction with this next book. I dare to suggest it because you are such a fertile writer, and so rapid a one. But we should not publish another book under the name of Taylor Caldwell for some ten months. Not for less than a year after the appearance of "Dynasty." I have been very much perplexed over this whole thing, and most eagerly wish to do right, and to help you to make a wise decision. Could you think it over and write me fully how it all appears to you?

Ever sincerely yours,

TO NICHOLAS MURRAY BUTLER

DEC. 13, 1938

DEAR PRESIDENT BUTLER:

We are very glad indeed to agree to the publication, in Spanish, of your "The American As He Is,"[1] in accordance with the proposal of the president of the Institute Cultural Argentine Norteamericano at Buenos Aires.

By the way, I had been turning over in my mind the possibility of a book of reminiscences[2] by you which would not be so completely integrated and organized as what you had originally planned, but would be something more in the nature of those political stories which we published in the magazine. That is, it need not be a continuous narrative. After all, the greatest of all biographies is supposed to have been Boswell's *Johnson,* and it was somewhat in that character. The reason I bring up this possibility is that I know how extremely difficult it must be for a man so full of affairs as you to find time for the consecutive steady work which a completely integrated book of reminiscences would require; and I know too that you have — as indeed the political stories showed us — had a system of filing away ideas and experiences. It seemed to me that such a book as I now speak of might be chiefly only a matter of selection. Does this seem to you practicable?

Ever sincerely yours,

TO CHARLES TOWNSEND COPELAND[3]

JULY 17, 1939

DEAR MR. COPELAND:

I wish you could do those introductions at 25¢ a word, for it would help to keep you in the forefront of the battle. But you

---

[1] Published by Scribners in 1908. [2] *Across the Busy Years,* 2 volumes, Scribners, 1939–40. [3] Boylston Professor of Rhetoric at Harvard University, known to undergraduates as "Copey."

never will be forgotten, anyhow. That is the last thing we need consider, really.

I took my youngest daughter[1] to Baltimore with me last week, and to the battlefield of Gettysburg. Also to a roof garden where they had Spanish dancers, and I think she enjoyed that much more. But I enjoyed seeing the battlefield immensely, and especially the Confederate side, which is not defaced with monuments — only one of them near the woods out of which Pickett's men came to line up for the charge, and that a good one too, of Lee. I tried to get Nance to walk across the field diagonally, the way Pickett went. She said she would have done it except that she had on high heels! It was a wonderful day, just such a one as that on which the battle was fought, and you could see exactly how it all was. The Federal position is so much the stronger though, with the round tops and the width of the ridge it was on, that it is a wonder the Confederates ever thought they could win. I went there partly because of a novel we are publishing called, "Artillery of Time,"[2] of which the war is a part, and in which Gettysburg figures. It shows the Yankee side of it better, I guess, than ever has been done.

I suppose it won't be long now — for in two months we'll have cool weather — before you will begin actually to write on the reminiscences, and I am looking forward eagerly to when you do. I wish I could see any fraction of the book, however small, when there is one.

Always your friend,

TO WALDO PEIRCE

DEAR WALDO: JULY 26, 1939

Don't let any of the daughters of the Confederacy see that snapshot or they will get you petrified and put you up on their

_____

[1] Nancy G. Perkins.   [2] By Chard Powers Smith, Scribners, 1939.

side of the lines, where statues are few. I once saw a portrait —
I think it was a photograph too — of that son of Napoleon and
the Polish countess. He looked more like Napoleon than Napoleon did himself, and you look more like a great general of
the sixties than any of them unless it was Stonewall. I did think
the haycocks looked a little European. I would like to see that
Waterloo cyclorama if it is still there.

Binns[1] got back, and very excited about his trip, and they
had had a fine time with you. He thought he had got what he
needed up there, from a writing standpoint too.

I suppose the book[2] may be something of a scrap-book. I have
often tried to think how you would organize it. But they say
that the best biography is that by Boswell, and that is something
of a scrap-book certainly — that is, it is mainly a collection of
illuminating anecdotes arranged in chronological order.

I am mighty glad you are doing so much, and thinking so
much, about it. You will work it out for sure. You have got
to find some method, but it does not make much difference
whether it is like any other that was ever used — only whether
it works for you.

Yours,

TO ALLEN TATE

AUGUST 15, 1939

DEAR ALLEN:

I'd love to be a trout fisherman, but I'm not. My distinction
is as a deep-sea fisherman and when next you go to Cherio's[3]
you will see upon the wall a magnificent sailfish which my wife
could not endure to see in the house any longer and presented
there. But the truth is it took the vigorous and almost abusive

[1] Archie Binns, the novelist.   [2] Waldo Peirce's autobiography, as yet unwritten.
[3] Restaurant at 46 East 53rd Street, where Perkins lunched almost daily.

coaching of Mr. E. Hemingway, fisherman extraordinary, to land that trophy. As a fresh-water fisherman I never succeeded in doing any better than hooking a punkinseed (*i.e.,* sunfish), and that excited me so much that I swung him up into a tree and had to leave him there. But I would have loved to accompany you, if it were possible, for everything about trout streams appeals to me except the trout. Don't tell this to Caroline,[1] because she will despise me. The fact is I can't get away. So many other people have. Jack Wheelock[2] had to go over to London for a longer vacation than usual.

Many thanks for your letter about the "Songs and Ballads," which are now here. Anyhow, I'll see you in some six or eight weeks. I can't get away until after the 15th of September on any account, because some settlement must then be made of Tom Wolfe's Estate[3] and there are a lot of accounts to be fixed up, etc.

                                        Always yours,

                    TO WARD DORRANCE

                                        AUGUST 28, 1939

DEAR MR. DORRANCE:

I don't like to say, "Put not your trust in publishers," and I do not believe an author should distrust them either. But I do think that a true writer should trust most of all his own instinct. Just the same, I should think that this novel you have written — and let me tell you I delighted in the few pages you sent, which I return — ought at any rate not to be written, at the start. And I am inclined to think that a first novel, in which a man tries out his abilities and often learns a great deal, should

---

[1] Caroline Gordon (Mrs. Allen Tate)   [2] John Hall Wheelock, an editor at Scribners.   [3] Of which Perkins had been appointed executor by Wolfe in his last will and testament.

be drawn — if any of his novels are to be — from his own experience and observation, and that therefore the one that you say might turn out to be some kind of a Missouri "Maria Chapdelaine,"[1] if these various subjects that you name appeal to you more or less equally, would be the one to begin with. But I should say, most of all, because of my belief that you are a true writer, that you should trust your own instinct.

I have talked to Burke[2] about your first plan and found him in agreement with me, but editors and publishers are too prone to take conventional views. Nevertheless, I do hope that you will think you can turn to the other subject, which I can see is so rich in character and background and in emotion.

Ever sincerely yours,

TO CHARLES TOWNSEND COPELAND

JAN. 3, 1940

DEAR MR. COPELAND:[3]

I'll be there[4] in May, for sure, whatever the rate per word. I always did mean to make the autumn visit, and I kept putting it off under pressure of work, until the autumn was gone, and what I humorously call the holidays had come. Somehow, the New York authors expect an editor to do vastly more than they used to. Now you have to go for "tea" in the afternoon, which lengthens the day to six o'clock or so. There are some you even have to dine with, in their studios, in order to work with them later. ——'s "studio" is a full-sized apartment, about three blocks away from her husband's (and her own) magnificent apartment. She is writing a very lively and very intelligent

---

[1] Novel by Louis Hémon, Macmillan, 1938. [2] W. J. Burke, at that time an editor at Scribners. [3] Boylston Professor of Rhetoric at Harvard University, known to undergraduates as "Copey." [4] Cambridge, Mass.

book, and I am working with her. But she has such fine dinners, and is so lively to talk with, that we generally don't get much accomplished. We have political and economic discussions — for she is a radical and believes in a classless society. She was telling me that over the coffee the other night, when the maid was washing the dishes, and interrupted herself to fling over her right shoulder: "God damn it, Kate, stop rattling those dishes." (This is profoundly confidential.)

Lady writers expect you to do many things for them apart from their books. One of them called up in tears to say, "My cat, John Keats, is dying." I said I was mighty sorry. She said, "But you must send a veterinary." I said I didn't know much about veterinaries, and couldn't she get one in her neighborhood? She said, "But will you pay for it?" And I did. (You may be sorry to learn that the cat came back.)

Business was very bad in the summer, during the war-scare period, but somehow or other, when war itself came, it got better and has been quite lively through the holiday season, and looks promising now.

I hope May may come soon. Winter is certainly here now and so it can't be far behind.

Always yours,

TO MARJORIE KINNAN RAWLINGS

JAN. 5, 1940

DEAR MARJORIE:

Although I suppose you must manage the dialect[1] — though it is hardly that — according to some general principles of your own, I put in a plea for "sich." Everyone is familiar with that word in that spelling, and will have no difficulty with it at all.

[1] In *When the Whippoorwill*, Scribners, 1940.

I do think there are people who might trip on as obvious a spelling as "keer," though.

It is good to know that you got through the flu comfortably. So many people do not, that I am always worried to hear of people having it.

The only time I ever shot ducks was with Hem,[1] during a week on the White River in Missouri, just before Christmas. I spent some of the coldest hours of my life in doing it, but yet had a mighty good time of it too. My first surprise was to be awakened in the pitch dark by Hem, who had told me when we went to bed that we must get up at daybreak. I always supposed the sun got up at daybreak, and tried to argue that with Hem, but to no avail. It was still at its darkest when we headed up the river. I never said anything more about it to Hem, because he is not the man to argue such matters with, but it seemed to me that we got just as many birds at high noon, in fact more, and that we might just as well have slept what I call the night out. But it was on that river toward evening, once, that we heard a great uproar around the curve, and suddenly a regular old Huckleberry Finn steamboat, with the two parallel funnels and the side-wheels, came down toward us. It was much smaller than the old Mississippi steamboat, of course, but everything otherwise was exactly of that time, even the clothes of the captain and the crew.

By the way, did you ever return to me the Ellen Glasgow prefaces?[2] And if not, can you? I think I could get them back for you later on, if you will want them, but I promised Brace,[3] of Harcourt, Brace, who publish her now, to try to make them available for him, without expense. He proposed to buy the entire limited set, and I suppose I ought to have let him.

Always yours,

---

[1] Ernest Hemingway.   [2] Prefaces written by Ellen Glasgow for the Virginia Edition of her works published by Scribners in 12 volumes in 1938.   [3] Donald Brace.

TO ERNEST HEMINGWAY

JAN. 19, 1940

DEAR ERNEST:

I cabled you the morning after I read what you sent of the ms.[1] The impressions made by it are even stronger after the lapse of time. The scenes are more vivid and real than in the reading. This has always happened to me after reading your novels, and it is true of mighty few writers. That Chapter Eight is terrific, and as one gets further away from it the characters of those different men when they came out to be killed, and the way they took it, seem as if one had seen it all, and had known them. It is truly wonderful, the way the temper of the people changed as things went on and they got drunk with killing, and with liquor too. The first chapter, or the first eight pages, had the old magic. Last night, I had to talk about forthcoming books to the people in the bookstore,[2] and I ended by saying what a simple thing it was to be a real writer, the easiest thing in the world, and I was going to give them an example to show it, how anybody could do it, and then I read them, without saying who had written it, the first three pages, through the point where Jordan gets his glasses adjusted, and sees the mill and the waterfall and all. Having him do that makes the whole scene jump out at you as real as real. I said, "Why couldn't any of us do that? It's perfectly simple." But of course nobody can do it. Then I did tell them that they were the first pages of a novel by you, but I told them nothing else about it. You could see how even that little bit impressed them all. Well, of course, I am mighty impatient to see more.

I did not put in about depositing the check for $250 for the sake of keeping the cable short — Yankee frugality.

[1] *For Whom the Bell Tolls*, Scribners, 1940.   [2] The Scribner Bookstore.

I had lunch with Waldo[1] yesterday, and he was in fine form, and talked awfully well, and so we were much longer at it than we should have been. But as we went out, we met a man who looked exactly like he ought to, which does not often happen. That was Sweeny,[2] the soldier, who said he had had a letter from you, and took it out of his pocket, but didn't read it to us. I was mighty glad to see Sweeny, and to see what he looked like.

Anyhow, I think this book will be magnificent.

Always yours,

TO ERNEST HEMINGWAY

FEBRUARY 14, 1940

DEAR ERNEST:

We have a couple of good books coming next week. I haven't been able to find much of anything worthwhile yet, except the General Marbot.[3] Maybe you have read it before. It is really a grand book. It is a man's book, though, and we did not do very well with Thomason's edition. But my grandson of five pores over the pictures. Of course, I am prejudiced in his favor as a judge of pictures because he says that I "draw better than anybody in the whole world." Elsewhere, my drawing has always been regarded humorously. But, speaking of Thomason, I am quoting something from a letter I just had which is interesting:

"I am told Spike[4] has gone to Russia, which will not add to the tranquility in that quarter. Col. Sweeny[5] I have never met, but I have heard much of him. One item being that he gets along prosperously without either liver or kidneys.

---

[1] Waldo Peirce, the painter, a friend of Hemingway and of Perkins.   [2] Colonel Charles Sweeny, soldier and writer, author of *Moment of Truth*, Scribners, 1943. [3] *Adventures of General Marbot*, selected from his memoirs, and illustrated by John W. Thomason, Scribners, 1935.   [4] Frazier Hunt, author of *MacArthur and the War Against Japan*, Scribners, 1944.   [5] Colonel Charles Sweeny, author of *Moment of Truth*, Scribners, 1943.

"I was mightily tempted by both Spain and Finland — but it seems to me my job, as long as I have anything to contribute, is with my own people. However, unless there is a war, I shan't stay much longer in the service. I'm 47 this month, and I have put in 23 years. That's nearly long enough. And unless everybody goes totally crazy in this country, I don't see an immediate likelihood of fighting. Not right away. Yet, we are quietly but definitely mobilizing in the Pacific, right now. The cruiser force that went to Honolulu last year is being about doubled by detachments from the Fleet, and Honolulu is named — for the first time — as the permanent base of important increments of the Fleet. I think it possible that we will shortly see some capital ships shifted out there. Our new Defence Battalions — they are really very powerful artillery regiments — are designed for service in the Pacific Islands, and the first of them has its preliminary orders. We'll be garrisoning Midway, Wake, Johnston Island, French Frigate shoals, very soon. In all of which lie the seeds of war. That is, it amounts to the shifting of our offensive strength some 2500 miles westward. We'll still have a prohibitive distance between our fleet bases and the potential area of decision — but it's a step in that direction."

In the letter before this one, which you may not remember since you described it as a hang-over letter, you spoke of not being "a Catholic writer, nor a party writer . . . not even an American writer. Just a writer." I don't see how anyone can think that this is not as it should be — but an awful lot of these fellows do, even ones of true ability sometimes seem to. I don't think Bessie[1] thinks so himself. I do not think his ideas would prevent his fiction from being that of a real writer. Another thing: I always understood your problem about the old four-letter words. One time — in fact the last time I ever saw him — Owen Wister came in here to talk about this. And, of course, those words always worried him. I don't think he exactly objected himself so much, but he did think them completely un-

---

[1] Alvah Bessie, novelist, author of *Dwell in the Wilderness, Men in Battle,* etc.

necessary, and that they aroused prejudice. That time, he began telling me how magnificently Homer wrote of the Trojan war, and Tolstoi of war and peace. No four-letter words. He didn't seem to see, though, that any circumlocutions, etc., would be inconsistent with the way you write. I tried to explain this, but I really never fully grasped how you do write, so I couldn't very well. But I pointed out as an instance that you almost never even used a simile. It is a different way of writing. I always knew it wasn't just a simple matter of not using words — that it really did mean a deviation from your style or method or whatever, to avoid them. I knew it was a serious matter. I don't know exactly why I am saying all this, but many people never understood this, and it is hard to explain.

I got very worried about Sweeny,[1] who did not show up for a week, because I didn't know but what your letter might be exceedingly important. But he did show up one afternoon when Waldo[2] was here — told Waldo, who was smoking a cigar, that he looked more and more like General Grant all the time. The two of them went out for a drink, and I wish I could have gone too but had to meet somebody too soon afterward.

I sent Bumby[3] that falconry book,[4] but I could not do it immediately because it was too long before publication.

I am enclosing the royalty report.

Always yours,

The following letter to Ernest Hemingway convincingly records how one sensitive and highly critical reader felt after his first reading of the manuscript of a book which has since become a classic.

---

[1] Colonel Charles Sweeny, author of *Moment of Truth*, Scribners, 1943. [2] Waldo Peirce, the painter. [3] Ernest Hemingway's eldest son, John Hemingway. [4] *Falconry*, by William F. Russell and William D. Sargent, Scribners, 1940.

APRIL 24, 1940

DEAR ERNEST:

I am just sending you a line to say that I have read all of the manuscript[1] there is here, and am still in a kind of daze, half in that land, and half in this — which has happened to me twice before in reading your manuscripts. I think this book has greater power, and larger dimensions, greater emotional force, than anything you have done, and I would not have supposed you could exceed what you had done before. It is a surprising book too. You know right off that you are in Spain, and in the war, and then you expect something so different from what you get. You just naturally expect what you do conventionally get in a book that is in a war, what they call battle pieces, and all. Well, by God, that fight piece, where El Sordo dies, is a wonder. That surprises you, and you know for dead sure that that is the way it would be. The nearest thing I ever saw to that fight was perhaps one or two pieces in Tolstoi, one in a book that was called, I think, "The Thistle." You might not have seen it. But the way you write about war — nobody will ever forget the apparition of the cavalryman, his horse stepping along in the snow, and not seeing Robert until too late — all seems strange. And then you realize that that is because it is so utterly real. If the function of a writer is to reveal reality, no one ever so completely performed it. It was wonderful, too, to give this war — though of course that is not the point of the book — in the way you did, with these partisans, all extraordinarily solid people. A reader feels that it gives you the people of Spain, as the war was to them, in a more real way than if it had been about the actual enlisted men. There isn't a person in it that

---

[1] Of *For Whom the Bell Tolls*, Scribners, 1940.

anyone would ever forget, including old Golta, the general. As for the girl, she is lovely, and as if one had known her.

Anyhow, reading it is an experience, that's all. Even now it has got so these things go through my head as if I had seen them. It is truly amazing. Well, I'll read it in proof, and I know I'll find greater depths in it the second time. It has them. All the memories that go through Jordan's head, which nobody can equal you in giving anyhow, are beautiful. It is an astonishing achievement. You are always in suspense because of the frame of the story.

As to the title, I don't believe you can possibly improve it, and I almost hope you won't try to — and especially when you read that passage. Now the book has the spirit of that passage in it. I never read that before. But nobody who ever did would ever forget that, either.

Cape[1] is coming over here to look at it. He wanted to take it away for forty-eight hours, but I didn't like to let it go out of the office. Weber[2] wanted to too. I did take it away, but I was with it every minute and got it back safely. I was afraid that you had no real copy.

Yours,

P.S. I happened to meet Waldo[3] and Charles Sweeny[4] on the street, and told them about it. But you don't have to worry about me being indiscreet, at least I don't think you do. I would never be such a fool as to show it to ——. In fact, I wouldn't think I had any right to show it to anyone, unless you told me I could. I never did show any of your manuscripts to anyone except to Louise,[5] "The Sun Also Rises," when I was there with her. I didn't mind your saying that, but I just want to reassure you.

---

[1] Jonathan Cape, Hemingway's publisher in England. [2] William C. Weber, at that time head of Scribner's Advertising Department. [3] Waldo Peirce, the painter. [4] Captain Sweeny, soldier and writer. [5] Mrs. Maxwell E. Perkins.

Scott Fitzgerald had written Perkins on April 19:

"You remember a couple of weeks ago I asked you to mail a letter for me in New York. To explain: it was the answer to a dun for some money which I do not owe. The claimant is, of all things, an undertaker. Not that I owe him for a corpse, but for an ambulance which he claims that I ordered. In any case, he now writes me threatening to serve me with a summons and complaint. Now you will notice that this letter is headed by date only. Actually, I am leaving my old address and I have no new one as yet. This is an actual fact. Also I have a new agent here, whose name you do not know, so if this man tries to serve a summons and complaint on me through Scribners, you can conscientiously and truly tell him that you don't know whether I'm in New Orleans or at the North Pole."

This explains the reference in the first paragraph of the letter which follows.

TO F. SCOTT FITZGERALD

MAY 22, 1940

DEAR SCOTT:

I am mighty glad to have an address again. I wanted to write you. I could not make head or tail of that undertaker episode, but I never would let an undertaker take me alive, in any kind of vehicle. I would think it too much of a temptation to him. But you came through.

Your letter sounds sombre but good. There are a few straws of good news in the paper today to grasp at. I am terribly pessimistic, and I think I am naturally an optimist. Anyway, they give me a little cheer to work with. As for your position, it is a mighty high one. I never see an editor or writer, hardly, but they ask about you. It shows what you did, for think of all the writers who were thought to be notable, and whose output has been much larger, who have simply vanished without a trace. But we know the "Gatsby"[1] was a truly great book. I don't think there is much use in the 25¢ publishing though. You know that you are in almost all the school anthologies. I hope you are able to press on with this book, which begins with such promise.

Ernest[2] is still finishing a novel,[3] but he is to be up here on the 10th of June. Ernest's "Fifth Column" was a notable success in its revised form — I suppose you have heard about all that. And now, I understand, there is to be a sale of movie rights at any moment.

As for Elizabeth,[4] I just this morning got a letter from her. She lives in that Church house, as they call it, which she has fixed up and is very happy in, it seems. She will be here Friday, and I'll see her that afternoon, and she will want to know whatever I can tell her about you. It must be mighty interesting, and a happy event, to work on the production of your own story in a movie. Of course you couldn't be one of the regular hacks, and you don't want to become a professional at it.

At the "sales conference"[5] about the fall books, the salesmen were all anxious to know what you were doing.

Always yours,

TO HAMILTON BASSO

DEAR HAM:

JULY 18, 1940

To begin with, I don't think you ever wrote even as well.[6] These pages you sent me are most promising, and I think you give the New England scene and the New England character admirably. I really am delighted with what I have seen.

[1] *The Great Gatsby*, Scribners, 1925.   [2] Ernest Hemingway.   [3] *For Whom the Bell Tolls*, Scribners, 1940.   [4] Elizabeth Lemmon, of Middleburg, Va.   [5] Semi-annual discussion of forthcoming publications, in which the Scribner editorial staff, advertising department and sales force take part.   [6] *Wine of the Country*, Scribners, 1941.

There is, though, this one curious difficulty. I cannot for the life of me understand how Ellen got to be ostracized or, at any rate, looked upon with suspicion and disapproval, just because her fiancé seduced a maid. I do see how that ended the engagement, and I could easily imagine that it might have made her character what it is excellently pictured as being. I do not think that, in the most Victorian England, anybody would be déclassée because of what her fiancé did. Or did you mean that the fact of the engagement being broken had been thought of as discreditable? I don't think that has been true for many, many decades. I think you will have to change the story to make her situation more plausible.

There is just one little point where I think Ellen, in calling on her aunt, departed from the New England way. Even though she had known the maid since infancy, she would either ask where Miss Wyndham was or else she would have asked, "Where is *my* Aunt Abiah?" But this is a trifle.

Now there is another serious question about Ellen. You represent her as despising Kenneth O'Kelley. She could despise him and yet go on this trip with him, but I do not see how she could possibly do it if she found him physically repugnant. When he kisses her, she feels disgust. Well, nobody is going off on such a trip as that with a person that they feel physical repugnance to. This must be somehow clarified. But that is all I have to say in criticism. I think these pages are extraordinarily promising.

Always yours,

TO CHARLES TOWNSEND COPELAND

DEAR MR. COPELAND:[1]   JULY 18, 1940

I was mighty glad to get a letter from you. I had often been

[1] Boylston Professor of Rhetoric at Harvard University, known to undergraduates as "Copey."

on the point of writing you, twice even by hand. But there was nothing but gloom to put on the paper with the ink. I had been afraid when you were supposed to come down here in April, and then didn't, that something might have been wrong, but then I saw Paul Hollister[1] in the Ritz restaurant and he knew all the news and sent me some clippings about your birthday. So I knew everything was right, in that way.

As for Churchill, I never saw a man whom I liked better in the instant of meeting him. We published his magnificent histories of the war, the best of which is "The Unknown War,"[2] the Eastern sphere of the World War. Then we published several smaller volumes, including "A Roving Commission,"[3] an account of his earlier life, which is excellent reading, and then his truly great biography of the Duke of Marlborough.[4] It would have been a little better if he had not been somewhat partisan as a descendant.

When Churchill came here, some six or seven years ago, Charles Scribner and I had quite a talk with him. He is much more like an American than an Englishman. He got up and walked around the office with his cigar sticking straight out from his mouth, and talking. I suggested to him then that he do a history of the British Empire. It was then that he got up and began walking about rapidly, and it seemed as if at that moment he hit upon a project — a history of the English race, which was to include us. He must truly have thought of it previously, but it was as if he took the idea from the Empire and immediately enlarged and changed it. In an introduction to one of his histories of the war, he has likened it to some degree to Defoe's "Memoirs of a Cavalier," and I told him I thought he would have made a much closer comparison if he had spoken of Lord Clarendon's "History of the Rebellion in England."

[1] A radio executive, executive vice-president of R. H. Macy & Co. when this letter was written. [2] Scribners, 1931. [3] Scribners, 1930. [4] Scribners, 1933–38.

Before that, I had heard him speak, by sheer luck, in the House of Commons. Of course, I did know that his mother was an American, and perhaps that is why it seemed to me that he was so American even there — in fact, even more there, it seemed, in contrast to the others. He was vibrant with life, although the topic was something about finance, not a lively topic. I have always been for him. I talked so much about the importance of his being made Prime Minister at the beginning of this war, and even before it, that I almost felt partly responsible. But then things worked out in this way: instead of publishing in the usual fashion, by making his own contracts, he would project a book and sell it for a huge sum to an English publisher. That he did with the scheme for a history of the English race. Then the English publisher would offer it around to American publishers, for the highest price he could get. Well, we had come out so badly, at that time, that putting up thirty or forty thousand dollars for a book not even on paper did not seem practicable, and Dodd Mead got the English race. I have thought these speeches,[1] too, were what you say of them, as good as Pericles. But there is no way of rounding them up into a unit, and presumably they are not in copyright. But I'll talk it over with Charlie.[2]

I believe, as I guess you do, that this country will have to fight in this present war if England holds out long enough to enable us to — and that otherwise we shall have to fight alone, within at latest the next two or three years. So I am all for the American Defense people, and any other organization that is working to get us aroused and prepared.

Hemingway is on the point of completing what I believe will be far beyond anything he has done, a truly deep and beautiful book, "For Whom the Bell Tolls."[3] I did not know whether you

[1] Published by Putnam in 1941 under the title *Blood, Sweat and Tears.*   [2] Mr. Charles Scribner, president of Charles Scribner's Sons.   [3] Scribners, 1940.

would have the heart to read it, or wanted to think about Paris now but, in case you did, I sent you that copy of "Paris France" by Gertrude Stein. I was afraid, since it came out after the fall of Paris, that people would shrink from it, but they have not.

Always yours,

TO MARJORIE KINNAN RAWLINGS

JULY 26, 1940

DEAR MARJORIE:

I must say I myself feel desperate about democracy. You cannot have it without a very strong sense of the thing now detested, "duty," and a sense that material success is a lower form than that of service. These things got to be regarded as hypocrisy, and I suppose the truth is people became hypocritical about them. But they were not that in my boyhood. The Yankees really believed them. We always were taught that, in a community like Windsor, the truly important men were the school-teacher, the newspaper editor, and the clergyman. The doctor, too, was more respected than the business man. These people were supposed to have made a sacrifice because they cared more to serve their professions, and what they meant, than for money. I know that my father, who practised in New York and never made more than a good living for a big family out of it, nor left a penny, always thought that he was doing something more important than that, that he was advancing the idea of justice. And I know that when I was in college and saw so many old Boston people that were friends of my grandparents — and I admit there was some element of unconscious hypocrisy about them — they were obviously somewhat ashamed of wealth, and acted as if they did not have it, in a way. For instance, hardly any of them had men servants. They all had middle-aged, aproned maids with pompadours, who had been in the family from early youth. They soft-pedalled wealth. They didn't think that was supposed to be the point. And business men, who were presumably working only for wealth, were looked down upon, though not their grandchildren! But, anyhow, it certainly is true that we cannot have what we meant to have without a different point of view from the present one, without a deep sense of responsibility.

I am delighted that some of "Cross Creek"[1] will come soon. It cannot come too soon. A large part of yesterday I spent reading the last third of Ernest Hemingway's novel.[2] To prove to you how deeply absorbing and how large it is in meaning, I'll tell you that I read it with great concentration, even though most of the time Ernest was standing behind my chair and reading it over my shoulder. But I think I have told you what the nature of it was, already.

I think the piece you did for the syndicate[3] was admirable, and so did John Farrar.[4]

Always yours,

TO DAWN POWELL

AUGUST 7, 1940

DEAR DAWN:

That was a splendid letter you wrote on August 4th, and you will have to forgive me for not answering it. Because when Ernest[5] comes it is like a hurricane going through town. He left last night by plane. I get to living like one of your characters when he is around, sort of floating on a racing tide and not knowing where it is going to lead. He did wonders though,

---

[1] Published by Scribners in 1942.   [2] *For Whom the Bell Tolls*, Scribners, 1940.   [3] A series of articles entitled, "Why I Am an American." Struthers Burt, Arthur Train, Marjorie Rawlings, and others, were contributors.   [4] The writer and publisher.   [5] Ernest Hemingway.

working all the time with a room generally full of soldiers, adventurers, newspapermen.

You have done what you aimed to do.[1] Anyone would know these people. The note in our list is not really right, but it is written for booksellers and salesmen.

As for the dedication,[2] I could not tell you how much it pleased me.

Always yours,

P.S. The cat books went to you as soon as your letter came. I hope "The Practical Cat Book"[3] will show you how to bring your cat about. Cats seem to be getting into my life too. One was brought into the house by the cook, because we do have rats. Now she is going to have kittens. Then I am going to have a tomcat, a tiger cat, whatever that is. An authoress, who has not yet produced a book, is determined that I shall accept him.

The following was in answer to a letter from Sherwood Anderson in which he indicated that he did not think Perkins, and Scribners, were greatly interested in publishing him since he had not received from Perkins the urgent letters that he had come to expect from other publishers. He was also, it seems, a bit troubled by the fact that Perkins, in his letters to him, was so fond of discussing the work of other writers. Perkins' answer follows.

TO SHERWOOD ANDERSON

AUGUST 12, 1940

DEAR SHERWOOD:

I hope it isn't going to be that way. It all came only from my feeling that you knew so very well indeed what you were about,

---

[1] In her *Angels on Toast*, Scribners, 1940. [2] *Angels on Toast* is dedicated to Perkins. [3] *The Practical Cat Book*, by Ida M. Mellen, Scribners, 1939.

and had so much your own way of doing things, that it would be almost an impertinence for me to question you, or urge you, or certainly to try to direct you. I had looked upon you for so long as a master, and as the father of so many of these other people who became notable, that I could not help talking to you about them — for my own enlightenment largely. But then I was disappointed that we did not do better with "Kit Brandon,"[1] which had such extraordinarily memorable things in it that I remember as if they were things I had experienced, but since we didn't, that also kept me from pressing you. Of course, the times were against us then, but they haven't been too good since. But I always have thought with the greatest eagerness of when you would be willing to let me see that book out of your memories and experiences.[2] I haven't the slightest doubt that it would be a great book, and might well be the most successful you ever did, too, in point of sales. But, as you said, it seems as though one could sometimes do better financially by writing articles, and there is the great gamble of writing a book, and I didn't like to urge your giving up everything to it, with the possibility of disappointment — though I do not believe there would be any disappointment with respect to that book. I had always thought that you would in the end bring in a great deal of manuscript, and that it might easily result, even with what lies behind, in the finest thing you ever did. It just seemed to me, from what you told me of it, that it was one of those things that had to grow naturally, and not be hurried. I wish it might be that way, and I would certainly be willing, and so would we, to give everything possible to bring it to the right outcome. I am sure no publisher could do more than we would, certainly not more than I would — only I do feel that you, of course, are far wiser than I possibly could be.

Always yours,

---

[1] Published by Scribners in 1936.   [2] A book of reminiscences, published by Harcourt, Brace & Co. in 1942 under the title *Memoirs*.

P.S. I sent the piece you sent,[1] which I thought was excellent and quite different from any other that I have seen, right over to the syndicate. I wish they would begin to publish, but apparently it takes time to organize such features. Anyhow, it is very good.

TO SHERWOOD ANDERSON

AUGUST 21, 1940

DEAR SHERWOOD:

The only conceivable reason why you wouldn't have mighty good offers on the book[2] you are doing, from all publishers, would be the old-fashioned prejudice in some quarters against trying to detach an author from the publisher he already has. Some publishers still hold to that, but any that did not would be likely to make a strong effort to get this book. I remember when Louise Silcox[3] came to see us about making a contract, and we arranged one, that she told me you had said (I suppose, humorously), "Well, there is one publisher that still wants to publish me." As a matter of fact, all that had kept me from making the first advance, when Liveright failed, was the supposition of sharp competition, and I suppose at that bad time it was that way with the other publishers too.

But as to this book, I knew it had to be a long time growing, that it was that kind of book; and I didn't think I had any right to be impatient about it or that anything but harm could come from urgency. But "Kit Brandon" was published in 1936, four years ago, and if there is to be an interval of two years more I can easily see how difficult the situation may be from a practical point of view.

We don't want to lose this book. For several years I've known

---

[1] For the "Why I Am an American" series. [2] His *Memoirs,* Harcourt, Brace & Co., 1942. [3] Of the Authors' League of America.

of it and told people here about it and everyone has thought it would be very noteworthy, to say the least of it. I agree with what you say about *selling* in this country. I think, though, the trouble with Ben[1] was that he didn't have enough of a sales force to distribute properly. He was almost all by himself. In a sense, that is the way it ought to be with publishers, but it couldn't be today. As to the advertising, publishers all think the same way about it. It is like getting a stationary automobile into motion. The advertising is like a man pushing it. If he can get it to move, the more he pushes the faster it will move and the more easily. But if he cannot get it to move, he can push till he drops dead and it will stand still.

At any rate, I wanted to put the matter before you and to show you how we stand and what we intend.

Always yours,

TO DIXON WECTER

AUGUST 23, 1940

DEAR MR. WECTER:

I think your estimates in the book[2] are remarkably good, including that of T. R. and that of Bryan, both of whom I remember very well. Roosevelt I met some seven or eight times and talked to on several occasions in connection with his writings. He was supposed to have that marvelous memory for faces and I was always deeply hurt because he never once remembered mine. I helped to cover Bryan's last speech in Madison Square Garden, as a cub. If it hadn't been that one sensed the demagogue, the phony, in him, one couldn't but have thought of him as a magnificent man. As they said of Webster, nobody

[1] Benjamin W. Huebsch, the publisher. [2] *The Hero in America,* Scribners, 1941.

could have been as great as he looked — so it was with Bryan.
I thought it was rather touching, in the first volume of Butler's
"Busy Years,"[1] when he said to Butler, in Washington, "The
matter with you, Butler, is that you will not take me seriously."
I think he was always conscious a little of being a phony. Anyhow, I greatly enjoyed the chapters. I hope soon to send you a
plan of illustrations.

Always yours,

TO RAY STANNARD BAKER

AUG. 30, 1940

DEAR MR. BAKER:

I delayed writing you a couple of days to await the return of
my secretary, for we are in the thick of the vacation season —
but I now enclose quite a long memorandum, which I am afraid
is truly superfluous anyhow. I realize that all that could be
useful to you is merely the impression of a reader sympathetic
to the book,[2] who would presumably see it more objectively than
the author.

If you had not suggested it, I would hardly have thought of
making so many comments, but they are all in the same direction, merely to reinforce and expand what the book does. Its
meaning begins to come to one, emotionally, from the start. It
is only toward strengthening and developing it, and giving one
more of what is so appealing, that I have said anything.

I know, of course, that the most important change would be
carrying the story somewhat further, until the boy had entered
upon a career and gone into the turbulence of active writing
work.

You asked me about the sale. An editor gets mighty careful

---

[1] *Across the Busy Years*, by Nicholas Murray Butler, 2 vols., Scribners, 1940.
[2] His autobiography, *Native American*, Scribners, 1941.

to avoid prophecies. I think there are very considerable possibilities. I think that there should certainly be a long sale, and that as the next volume and the one after that, if there were to be three, came on, the sale would be accumulative. Then the three could be gathered together in one volume, with larger possibilities still.

There are various points, such as what name should be used for the author, etc., but perhaps matters better stand as they are, for the moment. But I do want to make it plain that we are prepared instantly to draw up a contract and that the possible changes have, of course, nothing whatever to do with that. They are merely for you to consider and adopt, or reject or modify, or whatever. The book is a very unusual one in quality, and any publisher should be proud to add it to his list.

Ever sincerely yours,

P.S. I had a note from Edward Weeks of the *Atlantic Monthly* saying that he would be in here on the 5th or 6th. Unless you tell me otherwise, I thought I would speak to him about this book. It could only arouse his interest and, of course, I should be telling him of it as simply a book I knew of which might be very much to the taste of his magazine.

In the pages that follow, there will occur from time to time, as here, a letter or memorandum embodying detailed suggestions with regard to a manuscript, its material and organization. Perkins wrote many such letters or memoranda. His comments were always offered as suggestions merely, in the hope that they might "suggest" to a writer his own solution of the problem involved. The memorandum which follows has been selected as representative from the large number addressed to various writers, some eminent, some unknown, who welcomed such perceptive comment.

Memorandum of possible changes and additions
in the final version of "The Book of My Youth"[1]

Chapter I, which is somewhat introductory, seems to me to be all that anyone could possibly wish for as an opening, but it does seem to me that if it were possible to insert a chapter before Chapter III, or to begin Chapter III differently, in such a way as to present at the start more of a picture of the principal characters in the family — not so much the father, who comes out so fully as one goes on, but the mother and the aunts, especially Aunt Hill – it would be a great advantage to the reader.

Now one comes to hear about the Indians and the river men, and then, in Chapter III, of the author's trip with his father. As to all this part, I know that the reader, just because it is so suggestive of rich material, would want more. I think that if the Indians could be made more of and the way their camps were, and little things that happened, and then that if the life of the river men and experiences with them, and how they handled the logs and all, and the river drives, and some of the not too ribald songs, could be added in part, the reader would be delighted for the enlargement of the picture. I do realize that this book, and those that will follow, are intended more to express a philosophy or a point of view and feeling about life than to record any events on their own account. But this early life was part of what developed this boy into what he became, of course, and the material is so good and interesting in itself that it seems to me the additions would be desirable and valuable, and certainly most interesting. Besides, I do not think that

[1] First volume of Ray Stannard Baker's autobiography, published by Scribners in 1941 under the title *Native American*.

as you write, whereby so much is implied in no great space, the additions would need to be very lengthy.

I know that the author, of course, best knows his book and that suggestions can only be valuable to him as showing how a reader, if he understands the author's purpose, reacts to it. We do not intend that this should be a book of incidents and facts. Just the same, when one reads, on page 14, about the author and his father working along the shore of a wild northern lake, one would like to have that more developed, perhaps, and also the meeting with the Indians. Not greatly, but somewhat.

As I said, in our conversation, one of the very best things in the whole book, one that makes the reader happy with the boy, is the visit to Erickson's. If it were possible at times to put in other incidents, in that degree of development, it is certain that the reader would be pleased. In Chapter VII, the text refers to the boy as being motherless. But it wasn't until very considerably later that the mother's death, which is extremely effective, is given. I think, therefore, that although this book is not chronological, is discursive (which is all to its advantage), it would be better in this instance not to anticipate the mother's death. To do so somewhat reduces its effectiveness, perhaps.

Of course, it is always better to give a little less than the reader wants, than more. My great-grandfather said one should always leave the dinner table a little hungry. But I cannot help suggesting enlargements because, for instance, in "My Father's Stories" — of course that is a grand story about the boats — two or three more would certainly be appreciated, and they would tend to develop further the realization of the father.

The anecdote about the lumberjack in Chapter IX is excellent. People of this kind were all about, and it seems to me that the way they affect the life of the boy should be made more of, for they certainly did affect it. Perhaps additions will previously have been made, to this end, but one would welcome more of a presentation of these men, even if only as part of that frontier landscape.

Chapter XI. Aunt Hill is grand. One could hardly have too much of her. Of course, she comes out beautifully in the play chapter, but perhaps she and the others could be developed long before that, even if it meant the interpolation of a chapter.

The matter of enlargement could really apply to the school days too, though I realize I may well be pressing the point too far. You will know, though, that one reader who greatly enjoyed the whole book as it is wanted to have more of it.

Anyhow, I do wish that Miss Gwynne and Miss Mary Field could be given a little of that novel that they deserve. I feel sure, from the sense one gets of them, that while they might be even possibly a little bit comic, they would be lovable. And just such people do seem so to represent that period. Couldn't an incident or two about them be interpolated?

Chapter XIV is the one where you go out into that wild gorge. I do think this should be more developed. It must have been romantic and exciting to find that man, and in that wild gorge. I know that this might imply rewriting and enlarging of this chapter, but it seems to me such an adventure for a boy that it should be done. It is all suggested, in a way, but how the gorge was, and coming upon the man and the revelation that it amounted to for the boy, could be made more of and be memorable.

Chapter XVIII. I did think, in reading this chapter, which refers to the way the pioneers were, with boundless hopes and faith, that that theme might well be developed. I think perhaps people do not realize how different it was then, and that was such a wonderful thing about life at that time. Perhaps it could be enlarged without great difficulty by inserting illustrations of the quality in people.

Now when we get on to the college and school teaching, I

think that too could be enlarged by working in incidents which would serve as illustrations. Very little is told about the life in that college, for instance, and there must have been some important friendships. At any rate, what I am saying here is all in line with what I thought about the whole book, that one wanted to have more of it.

I was delighted that you thought this, after realizing that what the boy wanted was to write. You could go on further and show how he got to doing that, as a reporter. That would launch him in a career. Then the next book could begin at that point.

As to length, the book is not much more than 60,000 words, and if it were two thirds longer, it would in truth gain advantage from it. That is, a book of 100,000 words is regarded more favorably by the trade and, in fact, by the public.

TO ERNEST HEMINGWAY

SEPT. 20, 1940

DEAR ERNEST:

Now that everything is done that can be done, and done magnificently on your part, I just want to say that I think that to have written this book[1] in fifteen months' time was miraculous. This hardly need be said, but you seemed to think that you had taken a very long time to it. If you had taken five years to such a book, nobody could have thought it was a long time — apart from the fact that there isn't anybody alive who could have written such a book anyhow. It may be silly to say this, but you several times spoke of the time taken, as if it worried you. Of course, in a practical sense it might have worried you temporarily, but the fact of having done it in that space was a great feat.

[1] *For Whom the Bell Tolls*, Scribners, 1940.

Now I am looking out for books for you, since you at last have leisure. I'll send you Dawn Powell's[1] early next week. I did send you one about a judge,[2] which makes good and easy reading and tells some interesting things about criminals, etc.

Always yours,

TO MARJORIE KINNAN RAWLINGS

SEPT. 20, 1940

DEAR MARJORIE:

What you say of the style is true — though there is in nothing you send me any condescension, of which I think you are incapable — but it will all come right if you will look at the book[3] as a whole, as a unit. Then the tone of what you do, or the style, will fall into that conception and take care of itself — and, anyhow, there are beautiful pieces here, like "The Storm," and "The Pecan Tree," which, developed, are in the right tone.

But in writing you how I think it should be I must be cautious, and you still more so. For you only can write the book, and you must — and I know you will — do only what you are convinced of; and what I say must be no more than suggestion and just "for example."

I think the book must give the neighborhood and its characters so that it will have a kind of completeness. And the material to do that is here, or is implied. But none of it is sufficiently developed.

I don't think the book should be episodic in the sense of being just a series of episodes in chronological or some other order, but it could, and even must, be organized about episodes, which should be developed to stand out as the big events in a novel

---

[1] *Angels on Toast*, Scribners, 1940. [2] John C. Knox, *A Judge Comes of Age*, Scribners, 1940. [3] *Cross Creek*, Scribners, 1942.

do. And all these episodes should also serve to develop a sense of the community, to contribute to building up a total picture of the scene. And this really is not difficult. It is only a matter of your attitude toward the material. I think that the book should be a narrative, varied somewhat by description and by reflection — to use a figure, it should be a single piece of string, with knots in it, the knots being the episodes, but each connected with the other by the incidents, etc. I think you could use the talk of your negroes largely to make the connection and to prepare for the incidents in a natural way. No one does negroes so sympathetically and so well, themselves and their talk.

Take an example at random, or perhaps more because I liked the character and his possibilities so much: Mr. Marsh Tucker. He's grand. He was part of that community, a live and picturesque figure. But the reader should have known about him as on the landscape before these things happened, and in a way to be made curious about him, maybe only by your passing him on the road and by someone telling of him — for instance, Martha. Who was she? Did she work for you? Those negresses should be used more to prepare for events, and for their own sake too. Like Adrina. She was in your household and should figure as a person, before that fine incident of the storm.

Or take "The Pig Is Paid For." Wonderful. But how much intensified in its qualities if both Mr. Martin and Mr. Higginbotham had been seen long before, or heard of from Adrina or someone, just incidentally. Perhaps just as a figure on the large scene, in Martin's case. Anyhow, it seems to me that there ought to be some characters that recur a good many times in the course of the narrative, and that the reader ought to look forward to seeing them again.

Now, taking up these different pieces you have sent, some

are episodes and should be developed as such, and some are just incidents and should only fill out the general scene and contribute to the total effect. I think "The Pig Is Paid For" should be one of the knots — but we have spoken of that. The adventure in the mist is another — but oughtn't you to give more about Uncle Barney and old Cab Long, especially old Cab Long? Perhaps you plan for that. It seems to me that you should have a real hunt in this book, because I know you were in them and it was part of the life. And I know old Cab Long was a grand character. You couldn't develop the hunt part of this particular piece without destroying the effect you want, which is about the mist, but I think you could develop the piece into more of a knot on the string. Another of the knots could be Mr. Marsh Tucker. I am only giving these as examples, but if they were the ones that most was made of — and all could be developed — I think that the characters in them should have been known of by the reader before they appear, for that would strengthen the effect of the action in these pieces.

Then there are the incidental pieces, such as that of "The Pound Party." The Townsends are grand and they themselves could be made more of at that party. But couldn't you have something said there about someone or something which was to form one of the knots in the string and so arouse the reader's expectation and prepare him?

Take, as a similar instance, "The Catch Dog." It can be made a first-rate little piece, part of the atmosphere and quality of it all, and yet a sort of story in itself, but couldn't it somehow connect itself with something that follows? "The Dime" is a good incident, but Bernie Bass ought to be somewhere in the book in other places, and it would have been better to have had her in earlier, just so people would know she existed and something about what she was like. And this is true too of the incident of old Boss. Old Jim should have been hanging around on the scene before you developed him to the point you do in the piece of that name, and so should old Joe, the mule, before he died. And who was Snow? If Willie Higgins appeared, he should perhaps be just seen and say what he did, on the road, as you passed him in going somewhere.

Then, there are the other pieces, which you do most beautifully, about the sound of the frogs and the insects, and all that, and such as in "The Pecan Tree," and one could hardly have too much of that kind of writing. But I have a possible suggestion that will bear on that kind of thing later. As matters stand, there aren't enough knots for the string. But what about "Cracker Chidlings"? You meant to get them in, and they ought to be in. And what of that most lovely "Hyacinth Drift"? It was part of that world. Maybe it isn't strictly "Cross Creek," but you don't have to be too rigidly geographical. I swear, I think you ought to have that in the book.

As to the beginning, it is on the right lines, in my opinion. I don't think it should be more than eight or ten pages long, and it seems to me that the little piece, "The Road," could be in it, and that walking along that road could enable you in the most natural way to give, at the start, a conception of the neighborhood.

I have not spoken about everything, of course, but I am afraid even now I may have spoken too definitely. I am always frightened to death of doing that. You must not take what I say as definite at all ever, but all as by way of example only. The whole thing might perhaps be done in some quite different way, and what I say are only suggestions toward the final effect. The ways and means to it may be different from what I have used to illustrate.

Now there is another possibility, and I think it ought to be considered. You are taking a reader into a place, and you want him to get all its qualities, and to know the people. You write most beautifully of nature and of the changes of the seasons.

Suppose you divided this book into four groups — Spring, Summer, Autumn and Winter? The material would be the same as if you didn't do that, or almost the same, but the ordering of it would be different. The knots in the string would each fall into a part, according to the season they came into. And you could lead into each section by telling what the season was like and how it came, in the beautiful language you use.

I could go into all of this at greater length, but it is better not to do it. I am almost afraid I have said too much, and may tend to throw you off the track instead of putting you on it. But I am sure it ought to be one thing, that the characters should, to some degree anyhow, reappear. It can make a beautiful book.

There are very few true writers, and they vary widely, but I have at last discovered that those few share one trait. You would never suspect it, you would think they would be the very ones with supreme confidence. In fact, they do have a subconscious confidence, I think. But when they begin a big piece of work they have vastly less confidence than these men who just follow the trade of writing and who always know just where they are going and go there like business men — those that we publish to keep the business going, because the real ones are so few. I think, in truth, all you lack at this moment in regard to this book is confidence. I wish I could give you that, for I am sure you could make it a lovely book, and one full of the truth of life. One of these pieces began by saying that you sometimes felt as if you should be using your talent for the issues of the day. Sometime your talent might have occasion to fit into some issue. But unless that happened, I would forget about the day. In this depression, men have gone to ruin because they were so tempted to forget their vocation and turn their material to an immediate purpose. In a way, that was one of the issues between me and Tom,[1] and I kept

[1] Thomas Wolfe.

telling him that what he felt would come through his writing, even though not specifically stated. And yet he wanted at that time to be a Communist, the last thing that he truly was, as his last book shows. With you too, what you mean comes through your writing, and don't let anything tempt you into the lists of controversy. I don't know who these people are who talk to you, but there are lots of people of high intelligence, who respond to literature too, and yet haven't the faculty of exactly understanding where it comes from. They just think a writer who is good can turn any way he is asked to. It isn't true, and we know it. You, as well as I. But there is this pressure, and I hope you will resist it. And as for what I have said in this letter, I only hope for it that it may give you an idea, and not that you will follow it closely, but that it will suggest a way.

Always yours,

P.S. If you adopt the seasonal arrangement, which is in no way artificial or forced in this particular book but quite natural to it, you could open each part in a way that would make the reader feel the coming of the new season. All that about frogs and all (Marjorie, I wasn't really able, in the over-worked state of my eyes, to read much of "Toady-Frogs, Snakes, Varmints and Antses," because of the pale copy, as it seemed to me) could be worked in beautifully at the beginning, or near it, of each section. You have plenty of that.

TO JOHN W. THOMASON, JR.

Oct. 14, 1940

DEAR JOHN:

I suppose you read Bob Sherwood's preface[1] too, in which he tells of his evolution in respect to war. Various people have

[1] To his play, *There Shall Be No Night*, Scribners, 1940.

criticized the writers of the last twenty years, on the ground that they impaired the morale of youth. But, in fact, there were many books such as your own,[1] and Winston Churchill's,[2] and others, which went the other way. You know, it used to be said that in former wars, such as the Napoleonic, the pose of the young officer was that of fearlessness; but that in this war it was the reverse almost. And so it may be that for some reason the soldiers themselves, when they came back, emphasized all that was unpleasant about it, rather than anything else. Of course, Dos Passos probably did have a great influence and gave a totally representative picture of the A. E. F. in "Three Soldiers,"[3] but any intelligent reader must have known that his three soldiers were handpicked for the purposes of the author. I think that the state of morale of youth, and indeed of most people in the world, must have some deeper cause. For instance, here is old Somerset Maugham suddenly discovering that loyalty, fortitude, and honour were the only important things, and that people were pretty nice in the face of trouble. He ought to have been born knowing that and, if he had been, he would have been a great writer in more than just the technical sense. And then old H. G. Wells, at the age of ninety, makes much the same discovery. So they too suffered from the malaise that is still infecting us all, though not so deeply as it did. Anyhow, writers should express what they feel, like other artists. Otherwise we could have no Goya. But, as a matter of fact, my own point of view is very much yours.

As ever,

---

[1] *Fix Bayonets*, Scribners, 1925. [2] *A Roving Commission*, Scribners, 1930.
[3] George H. Doran, 1921.

Dear Mr. Wecter:

DEC. 4, 1940

Maybe I once mentioned this completely undeveloped idea to you as the possible subject of a book. It could be called "The Trouble Makers," perhaps, or something meaning that, of more force and dignity, and it might be confined to our own history, although I had always thought of it in universal terms. It would be a historical narrative to show how intelligence, in times of crisis, is almost always overcome and, tragically, by emotion — that the men of good-will, detachment, far-sightedness, and intellect, are overborne by the men of powerful emotions, violence, and strong will. The most obvious example of this, perhaps, is the instance of Erasmus and Luther. Luther was a man of great intellect too, but he was a man of violence and impetuosity. Erasmus tried to keep him from breaking up Christendom, believing that the Church could be reformed gradually, without destruction. I am putting this in a very simplified way, of course, but Erasmus did represent the man of cool intelligence, and Luther the impetuous and intense one. This goes all through history. It could be applied remarkably to our Civil War. The South became impetuous and saw red under the onslaughts of the early Abolitionists. The theme is obvious enough, I guess, but a book on this subject would involve extremely interesting studies of character and of conflicting natures, and would make a valuable argument. A weakness in it is, of course, that, as I have come to believe, no progress would be made, perhaps, without the impetuous ones. They do give the impulse which makes things move, even if through destruction. Anyhow, it is an idea, and seems to me to have possibilities of development into something unusual. Perhaps I once spoke to you about it, for I remember thinking it was

something you might turn your hand to. It has its literary implications too, through such people as Rousseau, for instance.
The proof[1] is coming along well now.

Always yours,

TO WILLIAM B. WISDOM

DEC. 16, 1940

DEAR MR. WISDOM:

I am glad to say that we are already in cooperation with Mr. Malone, and the broadcast[2] is scheduled for sometime early in the year. We have done everything we can to enable him to make it effective. But as to advertising on "The Angel"[3] and "Time and the River,"[4] we cannot do it without entering into competition with Harpers[5] at present, and we ought not to do that. And it is also true that we can hardly ever accomplish anything by advertising any books but new ones. The problem of book advertising is a very difficult one. It often seems as if it were stupidly handled but, so far, neither we nor any other publisher have been able to make it very effective. It does lack one of the principal elements of regular advertising, continuity through a long period.

I was thinking last night that Tom's books, which have never sold in very great numbers — "Of Time and the River" sold about 40,000 in its first season, and so did "The Web and the Rock"[6] — appeal to those with a true sense of literature, and then to those with a true sense of life who are ordinarily not readers of books, I should think, to any great extent. Of course, one cannot separate these two elements, but the ordinary book-buying public is not made up of people with a true sense of either,

---

[1] Of *The Hero in America* by Dixon Wecter, Scribners, 1941. [2] On Thomas Wolfe. [3] *Look Homeward, Angel,* Scribners, 1929. [4] *Of Time and the River,* Scribners, 1935. [5] Who had recently published Wolfe's *You Can't Go Home Again.* [6] Harpers, 1939.

I think, for it is composed of the upper economic levels, the fairly successful people. The ones in the lower economic level have a much truer sense of life. They are not simply concerned with getting on and all that. They know reality and understand when it is revealed. But they cannot afford to buy books much. It is a fact, apparently, that Tom's books are read all to pieces in the libraries. The sales do not measure anything like the strength of his following. It has occurred to me that some day a complete set might be made of all his works. But as I have thought of it, it would be a very great task to do. And I do not know whether it would be justifiable to do it. I'll tell you about it sometime, since anyway it could not be done for several years, I should suppose.

In view of your interest in Tom, I thought you might like to see a letter which I believe fundamentally explains why he left us.

Ever sincerely yours,

The individual to whom the letter that follows is addressed was a writer of distinction obliged at the time, for reasons of health, to give up work and take a complete rest. Perkins evidently sensed keenly the hardship this would impose, and, in his letter, points out that the best part of a writer's work is often achieved during periods of apparent idleness.

MARCH 11, 1941

DEAR ——:

Just for luck, I am sending you "The Hero in America."[1] It is all about America, and America is something that you are interested in. It is good, too. I really think that if you come out of Saranac in fine health, as you will, you will have lost nothing

---

[1] By Dixon Wecter, published by Scribners in 1941.

whatever by this enforced rest. You won't even have lost time, for the rest will have made you younger, so to speak. And turning things over in your mind, and reflecting upon them and all, is something that a writer ought to have to do in quiet circumstances once in a while. That is one of the troubles with writers today, that they cannot get a chance, or cannot endure to do this. Galsworthy, who never over-rated himself as a writer, but was one of great note in fact, always said that the most fruitful thing for a writer to do was quiet brooding. I am going to get you a copy of Barrie's Plays. If you are interested in him, I can send you later a very fine biography that we are soon to bring out.[1]

As for your plan for trying short pieces, I think that is an excellent one for the present. The decision on which novel and when, can wait for a while. As for missing things in being more or less out of the world for the time being, I think you are plain lucky, as the world now stands.

Ever sincerely yours,

TO JAMES TRUSLOW ADAMS

AUGUST 8, 1941

DEAR MR. ADAMS:

It seems to me from your introduction and outlines of chapters[2] that your book is very well planned indeed. I do think you needn't regard nearly as much as you seem to do what you have written in other books, for whatever there was of a certain degree of repetition in narrative would not be really repetition, or repetition in effect. The whole scene in this book would be viewed from another angle. I only mention this because nar-

---

[1] Denis Mackail, *Barrie, the Story of J. M. B.*, Scribners, 1941. [2] For his *The American*, Scribners, 1942.

rative, being the pleasantest form of reading to most people and the most interesting way of conveying information and supporting ideas, I would dislike to see you sacrifice it because of the fact that you had used it with some of the same material in the earlier books. This book would be something new, in any case.

When it comes to particular topics, I do think that one of the important ones would be the position and influence of women here, which is so different from in other countries. When I was a boy in Vermont, I used to see the middle-aged and old men going to church, not with their wives, not in front of their wives, but about fifteen or twenty feet behind them. I remember commenting on it to my mother and her saying, with a laugh, that it was supposed to be the New England way. It was never the way, in any other country. The American attitude toward woman is curious and has never been fully explained.

You also mentioned the topic of the tendency of Americans to be joiners. That is very characteristic of Americans, though I suppose the reason for it is fairly obvious — that so many of us have for so long been lonely people on frontiers. But it is a point.

There is also the remarkable tendency in Americans, which I think you set forth somewhere with great effect, to have a rebirth of democracy such as that which Jefferson gave us, and then Jackson, and which in some sense we are getting now from Roosevelt. It does seem as though we had an instinct to go back to our original idea of equality. But I needn't go into this.

Perhaps in some degree related to that is the disillusionment that was inevitable in a new land which became extremely prosperous. The people were virtually all countrymen at the beginning, and then as they spread Westward they lived hard lives. It was natural that they should have the illusion that wealth and material comfort would make them all happy and the ensuing disillusionment, such as we have just gone through, was inevitable. But such disillusionments would bring us back to a belief in our original conceptions — at least, I think that this recent one will, ultimately.

I think all of these are rather obvious ideas, and in fact are mostly suggested in your list of topics, but merely setting down anything that occurs to one might, if taken hold of by you, become something well worthwhile.

Anyhow, I am looking forward eagerly to seeing the book as it goes forward, for I think it is a splendid subject, and one designed for your hand to form.

Always sincerely yours,

TO WILLIAM B. WISDOM

AUGUST 19, 1941

DEAR MR. WISDOM:

What has kept me from writing you so long was this terrible season of vacations. For one thing, I want to ask you if you could send me a copy, typed or photostated, of the first page of Tom's "Mannerhouse."[1] I got Mrs. Bernstein's[2] copy, but the first page was missing. There's a chance of its being produced in Kenyon,[3] and that might eventually result in a professional production. I have had all but that first page.

I did send you that material of Tom's, and I skimmed through it but missed what you told about.

I have destroyed nothing that Tom wrote, and never shall. There will, no doubt, be found among his letters other sheets of manuscript. I have destroyed some six or seven letters from indiscreet females which really had no value but were com-

---

[1] A play by Thomas Wolfe, published in 1948 by Harper & Bros.   [2] Aline Bernstein, the stage designer.   [3] Kenyon College, Gambier, Ohio.

promising. I hope that you will protect anyone that may be compromised by what you found — in fact, I know you will and I should not ask it.

As to what Joseph Warren Beach wrote,[1] I have only read excerpts quoted in reviews and I thought them mighty good. But I thought highly of Beach more than twenty years ago, when I read a critical book of his, and often wondered into what obscurity he had sunk. I thought, from what I saw of this book, that it was amazing a man of his age should be so aware of contemporary values. As to Bunny Wilson,[2] whom I do think perhaps the best critical writer there is, he is not without great regard for Tom, but Tom is not his kind of writer. He was one of the three judges who gave Tom and John Bishop,[3] to divide, the prize in the *Scribner's Magazine* competition for a short novel. But he calls Tom "verbose," and that turns him off. Wasn't Dickens "verbose"? You ought to read "The Wound and the Bow."[4] All of it is fascinating, even if it is wrong. But here's somebody to watch for — Maxwell Geismar. He has written a book, which ought to be put out in early 1942, called "Writers in Crisis."[5] Tom is one of the giants among them and, though I saw his piece in a preliminary form, I think it will be about the best that has been written. On account of a most curious confusion of situations, I had to lose this book — but watch for it and keep an eye on him. Bunny's criticism is always somewhat personal. Geismar is detached and yet alive with the enthusiasm that comes from perception of talent.

I should have been able to send you more letters too. We have a lot more ready for Terry[6] but I must first get back the ones he has. I have only been delayed because of my secretary's[7] vacation, which ends Monday. Publishing people ought to take

---

[1] In *American Fiction 1920–1940*, Macmillan, 1941.   [2] Edmund Wilson.   [3] John Peale Bishop.   [4] A collection of essays by Edmund Wilson, Houghton Mifflin, 1941. [5] Published by Houghton Mifflin, 1942.   [6] John Terry, friend and biographer of Thomas Wolfe.   [7] Irma Wyckoff (Mrs. Osmer F. Muench).

their vacations in the winter. The preparations for the fall publishing season are the most exacting by far. It's the hardest time of the year, and yet all the gals have to scamper off.

Do protect any indiscreet ladies. Surely, a damnyankee should not say that to a Southern gentleman.

Ever sincerely yours,

TO CHARLES TOWNSEND COPELAND

Sept. 3, 1941

Dear Mr. Copeland:[1]

I certainly, myself, completely agree with Bishop Lawrence.[2] I think the situation is extremely dangerous, and since we are destined for a very serious economic situation when the war ends, a Hitler victory or compromise is still more dangerous — for if Hitler should not be beaten we, in a new depression, would be as vulnerable as France.

As for Harvard men, though, in this region I think they would agree with Bishop Lawrence to the extent of at least 80%, perhaps more. I do know some who are strong isolationists — several of them are active in the America First organization, one is its secretary. His view is that a Hitler victory would be no worse for us than a British victory, and might even be better. But there are very few of that kind, I should think.

I have been hoping to get up to Cambridge, and I have thought of you every day, but I have been terribly busy.

By the way: you probably read how our London representative, Carter,[3] presented Winston Churchill with the original of Clough's poem, "Say not the struggle nought availeth," on

---

[1] Boylston Professor of Rhetoric at Harvard University, affectionately known as "Copey." [2] William Lawrence, Bishop of Massachusetts, 1893–1926. [3] John Carter, head of Scribner's London office.

our behalf. Carter was delighted at the opportunity to interview Churchill, who, as the newspapers told, received him graciously, and was grateful for the gift. It was not told in the story, though, that the last thing Churchill said was, "Well now, tell me, is this presentation made on the principle of the Lend Lease Bill? Do I have to return the manuscript after the war?" I told this to Phelps,[1] and he wanted to print it, but I thought people might not take it in the humorous way in which it was meant, and advised against it.

Always yours,

TO JAMES TRUSLOW ADAMS

SEPT. 26, 1941

DEAR MR. ADAMS:

In reading your first two chapters,[2] which I greatly enjoyed and thought rightly done, including the presence of the personal element at the start, an idea occurred to me that might have some pertinence.

It was Barrett Wendell's[3] theory that the Americans had certain qualities of adventurousness and hopefulness and robustness that were not so much to be found in the British today. This he accounted for by saying that we were children of Elizabethan England when those qualities were so pronounced in the English. But then they had to go through the terrible years of the Civil War, with all the disillusionment and tragedy, and it left a mark on their character which we escaped. This has always seemed an interesting idea.

Then, when you told of the kind of people the English who came here at the beginning were, I remembered an incident in

---

[1] William Lyon Phelps. [2] Of his forthcoming book *The American*, Scribners, 1942. [3] Professor of English at Harvard University, 1898–1917, author of several books published by Scribners.

Harvard. Professor Copeland ("Copey") gave a very large and popular course in English literature. I can't remember exactly what the occasion for the remark was, but in the midst of one of these lectures, he said: "But *we* are all middle-class." There was a kind of resentful rustle throughout the lecture-room, which interrupted Copey, who had gone on with his talk. He lifted his head, and said with great emphasis, "No, gentlemen, there is no use disputing it, we are *all* middle-class."

But I do think that the Barrett Wendell idea might have some real value.

Ever sincerely yours,

TO NANCY HALE

Nov. 19, 1941

DEAR NANCY:

You cannot worry me about your novel.[1] I remember so well the quality of all that I saw of it, and I know that you have a rich and sensitive mind and memory. In fact, I would be much more concerned if you did not have to go through periods of despair and anxiety and dissatisfaction. It is true that a good many novelists do not, but I think the best ones truly do, and I do not see how it could be otherwise. It is awfully hard work, writing of the kind you do.

I, myself, feel certain that it will end very well indeed, if you can endure the struggle. The struggle is part of the process. There is no sign that Jane Austen had any trouble at all, but I am sure Charlotte Brontë must have had, and almost all of the really good ones except Jane, who is good as gold, of course.

I sent you a copy of Scott Fitzgerald's book[2] just because I thought you would be interested to see how he worked out a thing. It shows especially in the notes at the end of "The Last

[1] *The Prodigal Women,* Scribners, 1942.   [2] *The Last Tycoon,* Scribners, 1941.

Tycoon." I didn't send it with any idea at all that you should follow his method, because each real writer has his own method, and sometimes nobody can define it, not even the writer himself.

If you ever feel inclined to show me anything, I would be always delighted to see it. And I am glad you got the Charlottesville matter fixed up more favorably.

Always yours,

TO ANNIE LAURIE ETCHISON

DECEMBER 12, 1941

DEAR MISS ETCHISON:

I'll answer your questions with regard to titles in the order in which you ask them.

Almost all manuscripts do come to us with a title but, more often than not, the title is changed before publication. The title is extremely important, and since there is no logical process by which one may be discovered, it often presents great difficulties. It is hard to say to what degree the title does contribute to the success of a book, but it is important. For instance, we think that Dr. Fairchild's book, which was a distinct success, might never have got to its public except for the very effective title which rightly described it, "The World Was My Garden."[1]

We think that one of the most successful titles, as such, which struck exactly the right note at the moment, and helped the book to its instantaneous success, was "So Red the Rose."[2] Stark Young, the author, thought of that as one of a number of titles, but we immediately said that that was the right one. Perhaps the book would have sold as many copies in the end with another title, but we think that its immediate success was due considerably to the quality of this one.

[1] By David Fairchild, Scribners, 1938.   [2] By Stark Young, Scribners, 1934.

In the same way, Ernest Hemingway thought of a number of titles for his novel, but the first one he named to us was "For Whom the Bell Tolls,"[1] and we immediately took it, thinking it could not be improved upon. It was his title, and it was right. This was true also of his "A Farewell to Arms."[2] He had other titles, but there was no use even looking at them, for that one was so good.

Marjorie Rawlings at first named her book of stories, "When the Whippoorwill Calls."[3] It was on the suggestion of Carl Brandt[4] that the word "Calls" was omitted, and we think that made this title still more suggestive, and that it was an admirable title. That book had a notable sale, for a volume of stories, but, after the great success of "The Yearling"[5] and in view of the quality of the stories, it could hardly have turned out otherwise, whatever the title. But we think that "The Yearling" was a very fine title, and yet there was a good deal of question about it. Many people said to the author that it suggested a yearling calf, etc., and that it was a bad title. We believed it was the right title, covering as it did both the boy Jody and the fawn, and having the spirit of youngness in it. Whether the book would have sold less with another title, is hard to say.

I could think of many anecdotes, if you were hereabouts and we had a talk, but it is hard to do it in the rush of business, and war. But, in fact, I do not know whether it is not almost more true that the book makes the title than that the title makes the book. We have often had great struggles over a title, and thought it might be a bad one. Then the book has succeeded supremely, and it seemed the only title that was conceivable for it. The title came to fit the book. It came to be thought good because the book had been so successful.

[1] Scribners, 1940. [2] Scribners, 1929. [3] Scribners, 1940. [4] Head of Brandt & Brandt, literary agents. [5] Scribners, 1938.

If you ask me any other specific questions, I should be glad to answer them. Of course, some titles are just naturally repugnant to the public. For instance, we have a book now which the author wishes to call "The Egotists." The book is about egotists, but it is amazingly interesting when you come to read it, even so. But the title is the first thing people know of a book, and they do not want to read about unpleasant people, and "egotists" suggests that that is what the book is about. To a great extent it is, too, but a reader would find these egotists so extremely interesting, in a kind of Jamesian way, as to compensate for that. We are therefore urging her to change that title. The title should give the quality of the book, if possible — or else it should be appealing, and should reflect the quality of the book after one has read it.

Ever truly yours,

TO CHARD POWERS SMITH

JAN. 29, 1942

DEAR CHARD:

When we were talking the other day, I did not make myself clear in the matter of background and atmosphere as revealing a time, and the danger of overdoing it. When one writes about the distant past, having studied it up, and having a strong feeling about it and knowing how everything was done in those days, and believing that most people do not know, there is a great temptation to overdo the detail. And there is a great temptation for an editor to hate to see such valuable work cut from a manuscript altogether. Perhaps you did — as the reviews often assumed — overdo the detail in "Artillery"[1] and somewhat so in "Ladies' Day."[2] But when a writer is writing of his

---

[1] *Artillery of Time*, Scribners, 1939.   [2] Published by Scribners in 1941.

own time, which is also the time of a large part of the people now living, there is not that temptation. You realize the way it was from such books as "The Cloister and the Hearth" and some of the novels of Scott. The authors could not help putting in much more of the detail of the life of long ago than they need have done to make the reader feel the time. But contrast that with Jane Austen's novels. She was writing about her own time. There was no temptation to her to overdo it, and yet to us no novels could possibly give the tone and quality of a time better than hers did. I therefore was arguing that in writing this new book, if you regard the criticism that applied to the others as to detail, as applying to this one, I believe you would make a mistake. In this one you would not run the risk of over-doing the detail, but would just necessarily give the quality and tone of the period. In other words, I am afraid that you may not give enough of the background and atmosphere of the times if you have the criticism on that point too much in mind.

Always yours,

DEAR ——:

We thank you very much indeed for your letter of the 12th speaking so frankly with regard to several of our publications.

As to the two books you name, we should feel that we were disloyal to our profession if we refused to publish the works of distinguished writers because we realized that they would arouse hostility; for it seems to us to be the function of a publisher to put before the public whatever utterances are important, whether he agrees with them or not. James Truslow Adams has a right to express his opinions[1] on the basis of his record as a scholar, a historian, and a publicist. So, it seems to

---

[1] *Empire on the Seven Seas*, by James Truslow Adams, Scribners, 1940.

us, has Herbert Hoover,[1] a former President of the United States, whose loyalty to the country and whose integrity cannot be questioned. And, as the regular publishers for both these gentlemen, it seemed to us our plain duty, whatever our own personal views, to coöperate with them.

After all, we are not a nation of children. Our citizens are presumed to be able to judge for themselves, to draw their own conclusions from what they read. Certainly, ex-President Hoover's experience in the Peace Conference is of great importance, and the ways in which that Conference went wrong, as we agree with you that it did, should be examined with a view to seeing that the next conference goes right. An American citizen can judge of these matters and yet not be transformed into an isolationist by the fact that, as is inferable from the book, the writer of it favored that policy.

But the main point we should like to make is that in a republic people are entitled to express their opinions if those opinions are worth consideration, and it is the duty of a publisher, when it is practically possible, to enable them to do it.

Ever sincerely yours,

TO MARCIA DAVENPORT

MARCH 30, 1942

DEAR MARCIA:

I really think that the great difficulty in bringing "The Valley of Decision" into final shape is the old one of not being able to see the forest for the trees. There are such a great number of trees. We must somehow bring the underlying scheme or pattern of the book into emphasis, so that the reader will be able to see the forest in spite of the many trees. And that will

---

[1] *The Problems of Lasting Peace*, by Herbert Hoover, Scribners, 1942.

mean reducing the number of trees, if we can possibly manage it — though, so far, I haven't found that easy. For instance, I thought for a time we might eliminate Elizabeth, but I don't know that that could be done, because of her necessary off-spring.

The two great defects are that Louise, so very important a character, is not nearly enough to the fore, is not early enough realized (this you know, as your notations show, and incidentally I think your own criticisms attached to the various chapters are all of them in the right direction), and that Part Six, although well prepared for in the earlier development of the very successful character of Claire, does seem to me to have a different quality and to go out of the novel. I think Mary must be made the protagonist of that last part, that she must be much more the active power which saves the company from serving the Nazis, etc. She must act through Claire, and indeed she does somewhat, but she must be the compelling force to a greater degree than she now is.

But you have been very successful in many fundamental ways. Almost all the characters have reality, even though in many cases they do not seem sufficiently developed until you get deep into the book. Perhaps this is because you did not have a firm grip upon them when you first began to write, and some of them changed. Even Paul seems like a weak man, at first, but he was really a strong man. He is good, though, and his father is, and Clarice is — though she is rather shadowy in the early parts of the book. Mary is perfectly consistent as a character, but I do think you must find some way of giving her more individuality as a figure. For instance, if you had her lose her brogue but still speak in a characteristic way derived from her early life, her Irishness. She is really always herself, but she should be more physically visible and palpable. I should think you could make her so. Both Claire and Mère Constance are extremely good characters. And so is James.

The book should have a unity, by its very nature, because the steel mills and their influence run all the way through it, and so do Mary and her influence. And we should be able to bring it this unity by pulling it together. I am still baffled, especially about that last part, which is so much taken up with the coming of the European crisis that the reader is carried away from these two influences, which he should always feel.

Apart from the way you have divided the story into books, it has three definite parts. The first is from the start to the death of William Scott; the second is the whole period through which Paul is at the head of the mills; and the third centers around Mary, who must become more markedly a protagonist, from the death of Paul to the end of the book. I think if you agree to this, and the revision is made on the principle of these three figures who, of course, are all interwoven with one another until after Paul's death, it will greatly help. I mean that the revision will be made with the consciousness that in each case one person should be thought of as central. And in each case that person will be working for the company and struggling to maintain its character and integrity. I never, before yesterday, read in its present form the meeting in which William Scott forced his son's father-in-law to relinquish his stock. That is well done, and so indeed are all the meetings, at any rate fundamentally.

There are a great many instances where it seems to me there is too much melodrama and too much coincidence. For instance, there is the coincidence of Paul dying on Armistice night. But I think that is good if it were the only one, but then there is the double coincidence of Constance arriving on the night her mother dies, and of Louise giving birth to twins that same night. We have to talk over all such matters, if you are willing — but I wanted to set down a general impression first. If you agree in principle, then I can take up the whole first part of the book, looking at it in the large sense, that being the one where William Scott is the prevailing influence, and suggest ways of organizing it better. Even if what I suggest does not seem right to you, it may result in your finding ways and means which are more effective. But after you have read this letter, if you think the general idea is sound, we had better first of all have a talk.

Always yours,

TO ANN CHIDESTER

MAY 26, 1942

DEAR ANN:

Marion Saunders[1] kept me informed and I was delighted, and greatly relieved, to know that all had gone well with you. I am one of those New Englanders who always expect things to turn out badly, or else it is a kind of cowardly superstition that makes me pretend that I do, in the subconscious idea that then they will turn out the other way. Anyhow, it was a great relief to know about it, and I hope you will soon be out of the hospital and may come back to this region. You should try to do that, anyway, by the time the book[2] is published.

The chapter divison will be effective in emphasizing the development of the story, and it will read even better as a final book than it did in the proof. By the way, that picture agent, Friede,[3] called me up today and spoke with very great enthusiasm, comparing it to other books which represented the use of what we now call generations, though they seem only to come about ten years apart, greatly to the advantage of yours.

I am certainly mighty proud to have you dedicate the book[4] to me, but I do think that just to say "To," and then my name,

---

[1] The literary agent. [2] *Young Pandora* by Ann Chidester, Scribners, 1942.
[3] Donald Friede. [4] *Young Pandora*, Scribners, 1942.

says everything. I think that it would not be wise in the interests of the book to add what you have set down, although it is hard for me to explain that to you; and, besides, I don't think that I am the things you think. Now, you know that vastly too generous dedication that Thomas Wolfe gave me for "Of Time and the River"[1] — I never saw that until the book was printed. I knew that he was dedicating it to me, but if I had known what he was going to say — if he had shown it to me — I would have said exactly what I have to you. Everything was said by just "To" and my name afterward. So, if you are willing, I'll set it up that way.

Always yours,

TO ERNEST HEMINGWAY

Dear Ernest:　　　　　　　　　　　　　JUNE 8, 1942

I hope my cable from Baltimore made some sense. I know it won't help you much, anyway. I couldn't answer your letter properly from there, but I wanted you to understand that publication of your stories early in the year will be presumably as good as to do it now, and that my only disappointment is because I would like to see them out, for the fun of it, and to read them, and all. Otherwise there isn't any harm whatever in the delay, and I rather inferred that they would have to be delayed. I think it is a miracle that anyone can do any sort of work now, outside the Army and Navy, except the kind I do, where there is a compulsion upon you. I understand exactly your position with regard to the advertisement, and that was why I just posted it to you without any particular comment. And it is easy to settle on that.

[1] Scribners, 1935.

As to the anthology,[1] I only saw the contents briefly, and I made hardly any comments then. I know that the Empey, Hilton and O. Henry should come out. The others you name I have not read. I am not sure whether he had in one very good story by Stephen Crane which tells of a sergeant taking out a squad on an autumn day down a country road, and how one of the men persuades the sergeant to let him climb a fence to get some fine apples, and then they go on and take up an outpost position in an abandoned farmhouse, and then comes the fighting, and it is a hell of a fight. I don't remember the name of that story, so I am not sure he has got it. He should have it.

The other things I spoke about particularly were the obvious "Incident at Owl Creek."[2] And Winston Churchill's cavalry charge at Omdurman (of course there was no reason in the world for his putting in that biographical sketch by Dick Davis).

The rear-guard action in the early part of "War and Peace," where Andrei joins Bagration and acts as an aide, is one of the finest "battle pieces" in the world, partly because it gives you a complete little battle that anyone can comprehend, and then partly because of the way that battery commander fought his guns, and then the way it all turned out to be so different from what Andrei thought it was going to be, his first battle.

Then, there is the episode of the Russian partisan band's pursuit of the French in the rain, and their attack the next day: the boy Petya brings a message to the band from a German general and then, when he finds there is going to be an attack on the French, he persuades the leaders to let him stay and be in it, and then of course gets himself killed through recklessness.

Those two Tolstoi pieces have almost perfect unity, and

[1] An anthology of war stories entitled *Men at War,* edited with an Introduction by Ernest Hemingway, Crown Publishers, 1942.   [2] By Ambrose Bierce.

Borodino, grand as it is, hasn't the same completeness, and is rather confusing, I should think, taken all by itself.

I did also suggest a story called "The Thistle" by Tolstoi, but I don't really think it should be in, because it is perhaps about war on too small a scale. No use talking about that.

I suggested "The Burial of the Guns,"[1] mostly because it does show what must be true — the attachment men get to their weapons, and I should think especially to cannon, and how they individually take on a personality of their own. And, as compared to anything else of Page's, it is told in a very straightaway manner. It does have some of the defects of the time but, for the most part, what you feel does come from a direct recording of the facts. But don't you put it in, if you do not like it. It is mostly that I know of no other story that does do that thing.

I'll write to both Charlie Sweeny[2] and John Thomason.[3]

As a matter of fact, I think perhaps we shall do better if we publish the stories early in the year, before the market is crowded, possibly even in January.

Always yours,

P.S. A Princeton boy — a friend of Charlie, Jr.[4] — came in today in the hope that he could get some unpublished "fragment" to print in a number, devoted to you, of the Princeton *Lit*. I could not help him, of course, but I did say I thought it would be all right if he wrote you, and I told him that the only thing I could think of, and the thing I never forgot, was that fragment about the cornfields you took out of "Death in the Afternoon" and that I had kept in proof until about a year

[1] By Thomas Nelson Page, Scribners, 1894. [2] Col. Charles Sweeny, author of *Moment of Truth*, Scribners, 1943. [3] Col. John Thomason, Jr., author of Marine stories. [4] Charles Scribner, Jr., son of the president of Charles Scribner's Sons.

ago, when you asked me to send it back. I thought this number of the *Lit.* would be a good thing, because it goes to the young.

We are planning an anthology here, to be called something like, "The American Scene,"[1] without any political things in it, or history, but just the way it is in the U. S., and what the manners and customs have been, etc. I was going to try to get you to let us use that piece in it.

TO ERNEST HEMINGWAY

DEAR ERNEST: AUG. 13, 1942

I am enclosing your royalty report, but there isn't very much difference between it and the one I sent you some few weeks ago. I hope you are not having a bad time, working with all the pressure that thoughts of the war must put you under. I have heard from Wartels[2] off and on, and I did make him one more suggestion, apologetically, because the date is late for it. There is one stretch in "Through the Wheat"[3] that has five or six fine little spots in it, and has a kind of unity. It begins with an attack — I think it must have been Soissons — and the marines got to a point where they could not advance. Hicks, lying on the ground, looks at the insects going around, as if they were not in a battle. Then he looks around and sees the long-legged, black-faced Senegalese striding along. They go through the American lines, steady and looking like murder, and Hicks is surprised that when one gets hit he merely claps his hand to the wound and turns back without a word — if he can walk. Hicks remembers that an American always cries out with such words as "My God, I'm hit." Then the marines are withdrawn into a wonderfully peaceful forest, and the end of the section is when suddenly the stillness is broken by the fall-

---

[1] This project was later abandoned.   [2] Nat Wartels, of Crown Publishers.   [3] By Thomas Boyd, Scribners, 1923.

ing of a great branch. The heavy end strikes a sleeping marine on the head and kills him, and this to Hicks seemed obscene, and a dreadful betrayal, in these woods, after the fighting.

I am trying to read proofs on Alden's[1] book, and it is most interesting. It is certain, to my mind, that the man Shakespeare was not the author of what we consider Shakespeare's works.

Always yours,

TO ERNEST HEMINGWAY

SEPTEMBER 4, 1942

DEAR ERNEST:

Of course I greatly wished we were doing that anthology,[2] after you got into it. But the truth is, if we had been the ones to plan it, I would never have proposed to you to edit it, or even to write an Introduction. I would have thought it wrong to try to divert you from your main work, your own writing, and when you got in so deep and gave so much of your time — even though I had become very much interested myself — I was sorry about it. But when I read that Introduction,[3] I was mighty glad of it. I can't forget it. It raised my own morale a good many points, and it would make any soldier feel good.

I have the book you recommended, "West with the Night,"[4] and it certainly does look good, from a glance here and there in it, and, on the strength of what you said of it, I sent a copy also to Arthur Train,[5] who is in the Massachusetts General after an operation.

I had stopped sending you books except occasionally, because I had got the idea that all transportation between here and

---

[1] Alden Brooks's *Will Shakspere and the Dyer's Hand,* Scribners, 1943.   [2] An anthology of war stories published by Crown Publishers in 1942, called *Men at War.*   [3] Ernest Hemingway wrote the Introduction to *Men at War.*   [4] By B. Markham, published in 1942 by Houghton Mifflin.   [5] Author of *His Children's Children, High Winds, Yankee Lawyer,* the Mr. Tutt stories, etc.

Cuba was terrifically crowded. I'll have two very fine books for you in a short time — one of them the first volume of "Lee's Lieutenants,"[1] which I told you of. I am dead sure you will like it. Wilcox[2] sent those you ordered.

By the way, when the selection for the war anthology was going on, I all but suggested a story that is certainly very interesting in several ways. But I wasn't sure how good it was. I am not, of course, suggesting it now, but I wonder what you would think of it. "A Son of the Gods," by Ambrose Bierce. One way in which it is good as a war story is in telling very simply how an army acts when following a retreat and halted by ignorance as to whether the enemy is behind those stone walls, a mile away, on the summit of sloping fields. The pursuing army has advanced to the edge of woods and, as it is an old army, everybody knows what is going to happen. The foremost men on the edge of the woods keep looking back at the General and his staff for the expected order to advance as skirmishers. Then, of course, if the enemy is behind those walls several hundred of them may be killed before they know his strength. And then will come the old familiar operation of flanking him out.

But suddenly laughter comes down the line, and everyone looking there sees a handsome young popinjay, all dressed up, on a snow-white horse, with a scarlet saddlecloth, ambling along toward the General. The laughter is derisive, for only a fool would ride a white horse with a scarlet saddlecloth in battle. Now there may be something phony about that in itself, and perhaps it is superheroism in the young officer. For what he does is to persuade the General, who at first frowns and finally gives in. Then the officer rides at a walk through the woods to the open, and then out into the meadows and right

---

[1] By Douglas S. Freeman, published in three volumes by Scribners, 1942 and 1944.   [2] Charles Wilcox, a salesman in the Scribner Bookstore.

straight up toward the wall. Everyone gets the idea. Why not save a few hundred lives for one? His manœuvres, as he rides this way, that way, and finally, by making as if to ride straight up to the wall and jump it, brings the enemy to fire, are watched with utter fascination. He then turns and races back toward the woods, and the whole enemy's line is now firing. Yet he makes a great part of the distance before his horse falls. He rises, draws his sabre facing his own men, and salutes, and then goes down. Then Bierce says something like: "Couldn't the Supreme Ruler of the universe permit one perfect act?" for the soldiers in the woods have been so enthralled by all this that they rush wildly out, without orders for the attack. They are recalled, but not until a good many have been uselessly killed.

Now there is something phony about this young officer, and the whole thing, and what he does, and yet he is supposed to be unreal and god-like, but, anyhow, what always interested me about the story is that it is one of those rare ones in which the reader is not identified with the actor, but with the spectators. He reads with the psychology of one of the soldiers in the wood and, what is still more interesting, I believe that because he feels himself to be among a great number of people watching, the emotions he feels are increased, as they would be if you were in a crowd watching something. And whatever the story does amount to, if I were a teacher in those useless courses in composition which they give — which were better abolished — I would prescribe this story for those technical reasons. Did you ever read it?

I had not heard anything at all about Mike Strater,[1] but I'll try to find out. Haven't seen Waldo[2] for five or six weeks, though he is generally around at this time of year. A Mrs. Slater Brown told me that she had seen Evan[3] here on leave last week, and that he was in very good shape.

[1] The painter.　[2] Waldo Peirce, the painter.　[3] Evan Shipman, author of *Free for All*, Scribners, 1935.

I'll follow all instructions in your letter with regard to the movie production, and the cheap edition, and the deposit when payment is made by the Modern Library. Everyone was greatly pleased by the news that Ingrid Bergman was going to play Maria.[1]

Always yours,

TO WILLIAM LYON PHELPS

SEPT. 21, 1942

DEAR MR. PHELPS:

I am returning the clippings on J. M. Barrie, which I read with a great deal of interest, and to a great extent agree with. I think, though, that it is unfortunate he has come to be thought of only as a playwright. Highly as I regard some of his plays, including "The Old Lady," I truly believe that the most important of his work, and that in which he showed his greatest talent, was in his early fiction, even especially his stories. And I believe everyone would think this except for the very difficult dialect. If it were not for that, they would appear in all the anthologies.

As for his revival, I think we have a right to hope for it. Kipling had something of a renascence. We have sent to England for a copy of the Plays,[2] and if we do not undertake it, we'll see that you get it.

I never talked to Barrie but once. That was in London. I am one of the few people of our time who had, and still have to a great extent, an enthusiasm for Thomas Carlyle. By some chance, Barrie, in telling how things were when he first came to London, stated that he used to see Thomas Carlyle walking along the street in a broad-brimmed hat, with a thick stick. He

[1] In the motion picture production of *For Whom the Bell Tolls.*   [2] By Barrie.

didn't make any description of him or say anything brilliant. He just stated the fact, or so it seemed. And the effect upon me was exactly that which made Browning write his poem, "And did you once see Shelley plain?" Carlyle was always more visible to me after that, and realer. Possibly there was something in Barrie's voice that conveyed what a vivid description might have, though I don't think he had any particular admiration for Carlyle but perhaps a sympathy for him as another Scotchman who came to London poor, to make his way.

Many thanks for putting me in touch with the Yale Librarian, Mr. Knollenberg, from whom I received a very welcome letter.

Always yours,

Oct. 13, 1942

Dear ——:

You wished us to acknowledge your attack on Nancy Hale's "The Prodigal Women," and we do so hereby. In the early days of our publication of John Galsworthy we received similar letters, as we did when we first published Thomas Wolfe, who is now regarded as one of America's greatest writers, and as we did when we brought out the various books of Ernest Hemingway, who is now thought to be America's foremost writer of fiction, and whose stories will be found in innumerable high-school and college anthologies. We are publishers, and therefore interested in writing, and there is no question about it but that Miss Hale has very extraordinary talents as a writer. As for her patriotism, nobody could possibly doubt it, nor that of any of her family. Nathan Hale was her great-great-uncle, Edward Everett Hale, the author of "The Man Without a Country," her grandfather, and Lucretia Hale, author of the classic, "The Peterkin Papers," her great-aunt. She is proving her patriotism by giving a large part of her time to real professional work for the Treasury Department of the United States.

Respectfully yours,

TO NANCY HALE

Oct. 21, 1942

Dear Nancy:

I am trying to get hold of Van Gelder[1] to see what he has written, but I don't believe you said foolish things.[2] You don't do it. But whatever is printed of what you did say we shall publish, because we are to do a book from all those pieces that Van Gelder has written.[3] I always liked him, at first because he wrote much the best piece, and in the right vein, about the Eastman-Hemingway[4] fight. He did refer to me as "the *pacific* Mr. Perkins," about the last adjective any male would wish to have applied to himself. Almost as bad as having a favorite authoress say that she couldn't imagine your having been a bad boy.

As to that information you gave me, I shall forget it, and I am discreet. Don't think of it again.

I am glad you had such a fine time in New York. I think your book[5] is really much bigger and better than even the best reviewers realized. It tells much that never was before revealed. And the business of literature is to reveal life. Not, of course, in just the realistic sense, for it is done by the poets too, and in fact what underlies your writing is a poet. But still, I do know that you can do even better. I know that this book was a very hard book, for specific reasons, and that it was one of those books that a writer must get out and get through with before

---

[1] Robert Van Gelder, author and critic. [2] In the newspaper interview she gave Mr. Van Gelder. [3] *Writing and Writers*, Scribners, 1945. [4] Max Eastman and Ernest Hemingway. [5] *The Prodigal Women*, Scribners, 1942.

she can go on. But I am getting more satisfaction, and just as much pleasure from your triumph, even upon egoistic grounds alone — for, from the very beginning, I believed in you and said so, and while I don't believe that sales are in themselves a proof, they are the only proof and the irrefutable proof to a lot of people to whom I have to say things — booksellers and such. So don't thank me for any pleasure. It is I who must thank you.

The stories[1] have not come yet, but I'll wait patiently until they do. What you have told me about your well-named friend gives me great confidence in him.

Always yours,

DEAR ——:   NOVEMBER 2, 1942

Chapters 12 and 13 do constitute a problem, and a serious one. We published what I thought was a very interesting book by John Cudahy,[2] which contained a magnificent interview with Hitler — magnificent especially because of the portrait of Hitler it gave. It did show suspicion of England, and fear that we were being their monkey's paw, etc. And what was the result? It was almost completely ignored by the reviewers and never got around the corner. That was also true about another good book we published — and one of the great reviewers, who always prides himself on being all for freedom of speech and against tyranny, called up and said he regarded it as German propaganda. I wish he had said it to me. But the truth is that in saying what you want to say in these two chapters you must not arouse that kind of hostility, for the sake of the distribution of your book. You may not care so much whether it sells, but you do care whether it is read. It must have readers.

---

[1] By Nancy Hale, published by Scribners in 1943 under the title *Between the Dark and the Daylight*.   [2] *The Armies March*, Scribners, 1941.

What is said in these two chapters is not very essential to the main argument: what the book does is to show us what we are up against, and then how we must meet it. There is no sense in throwing all that away for the sake of saying some things that will turn people against you, if you can say them in effect in ways which would not turn people against you.

Take the chapter on England. As it stands, it would undoubtedly tend to foment discord between two nations who simply must stick together, although it must be we who finally do the directing, because their view is prejudiced by the position of England, and by their obsession over the Empire. It is true they should be willing to give up England if necessary, and let us hope that if that point comes a great prime minister will arise who will do it. But it is terribly dangerous to spread the idea we are so willing to accept, that England always lets someone else do their fighting. You say what great people they were in the crisis, but that when we came in they thought, "Here are the ones who will do our fighting." I don't know whether it wasn't, with the people, just that they relaxed a little at having a great ally.

As to Churchill, it may be his day is over, and that he has done his work. But — and here is my prejudice, and this is just an interpolation and don't get mad — you attack him on account of Antwerp and Gallipoli. You were a soldier, and it is ridiculous for me to oppose my opinion to yours on such matters but, just the same, wasn't he looking for a flank, and who else was? Not even the Frenchman you quote, von Schlieffen. Wasn't he following his principles there? And he barely missed at Gallipoli. But maybe I am wrong on all that. I couldn't know as much about it as you do, of course, but didn't he almost save England by mobilizing the fleet? Still, all that is just by the way. I only think that you should not castigate him, in the circumstances, because he is so popular. Argument can never be separated from persuasion. If you make your audience mad, it doesn't make any difference how cogent is your reasoning.

As to India: don't you too easily dismiss all that? What can England do? Can they just toss it out? I doubt it. It is true that Singapore, Burma, etc., were disgracefully lost by the old-school-tie boys. But it was to such places that they sent the old-school-tie boys.

And then Egypt. Napoleon thought that the strategic center of the world. And has England lost control of the Mediterranean for good? Isn't it possible that they will defeat Rommel, and will get back true control? This book can't be published until February, I should say. Will Russia by then have gone beyond the Urals? In two weeks, the fighting will have to die out at Stalingrad, won't it? And then, that which you say about Hitler leaving England in tranquillity. But two nights ago he raided Canterbury — I doubt if he has quit on England. Wait for the winter. If he hasn't, and you have statements like that in the book, it arouses doubts about everything else in it. ——, I only want to have this book achieve the purposes you want and tell the truth in such ways that the truth will reach people. And, if you seem to be prejudiced, it won't.

Then take Chapter 13, which begins and ends so beautifully. I sent you what Charles Scribner[1] said about the planes. It is terribly hard in these times, with all the confusion there is, to get things dead-sure right. But you must not risk anything you are not positive about, in a chapter like this. Why shouldn't the general argument of the part of this chapter that is about the administration be: that a democracy like this always goes through an amateur stage; that a president can never completely forget politics; that Lincoln could not until things got desperate, and the war was carried on politically until it was

[1] President of Charles Scribner's Sons.

evident that only the military control could win; and that Roosevelt knows this himself, but cannot escape from it, and that in truth a powerful opposition would truly help him. I am entirely in sympathy with what you think about him and the administration, but I think that the way you tell it will arouse such tremendous hostility as to defeat your own purpose, if it stands as it now is. I think you should try to say it all in a different way — even what you say about Nelson[1] and Knudsen.[2] They in fact were not politicians, though I do know what you mean, and think it most probably true. But don't defeat the main thesis of the book because of your *saeva indignatio*. I don't think you should say contemptuously — though by God I share the contempt — we'll give him a fourth term if he will let the professionals run the war. You are defeating what you want to do.

I don't know whether all this will help you, but I know it is right in principle. You can't make people mad and convince them. If they are mad, no amount of argument will do anything at all. You have been a soldier, and have been able to *tell* them. That is different. You can't do it, in war-time, in books. If you antagonize them in little things, you lose all the big things as well.

But you said you had thought these chapters over, and all I thought is that my views about them wouldn't do damage — and might perhaps help. Anyhow, we are losing no time, because the book is at the press to be figured out by the printers, and we can go ahead even though these two chapters are not yet in.

Yours,

---

[1] Donald M. Nelson.   [2] William S. Knudsen.

DEAR ALDEN:

DECEMBER 2, 1942

The moment the index and front matter[1] come back from you, we'll go to press. If you haven't sent them by the time you get this letter, do so by airmail.

Corinne[2] told me that you are planning to do a mystery story. You certainly showed talent in detection in preparing the book we are about to publish. Maybe you could do something so distinctive as to change the rather monotonous course detective stories have followed ever since S. S. Van Dine[3] brought them back to popularity.

You may not have been among his admirers — did you know him in Harvard? He planned his campaign very carefully — before he wrote his first story, he had outlined the plots of three. We took him up on the outline and paid advances. He was the kind of man who never did anything but that he did it thoroughly, thoughtfully and well. He thought the first might sell very little but by the time the three came out he would be successful and then the other two would be picked up. As a matter of fact, even the first volume sold remarkably well for a detective story in those days and, by the time the third came, he'd reached 100,000 in the *original* edition. And he kept that up for several more. He gave the mystery novel a new twist and then had a lot of details that added interest, such as footnotes. People here disliked Philo Vance[4] and his mannerisms and so I argued that matter with him, though I felt somewhat differently myself. He said the point was not whether people liked Vance but to make him distinctive, so that they could not forget him.

---

[1] Of *Will Shakspere and the Dyer's Hand*, Scribners, 1943. [2] Daughter of Alden Brooks. [3] Pen name of Willard Huntington Wright. [4] The detective in the S. S. Van Dine detective stories, all of which were published by Scribners.

I don't exactly know why I am saying all this except that I have a feeling that you might well be the man to do the thing anew, to write an *original,* and that therefore the practical experience of Willard Huntington Wright might have some pertinence, whether or not you thought well of his work.

Always yours,

TO RAYMOND THOMPSON

FEB. 18, 1943

DEAR MR. THOMPSON:

I hope I'll see you then, and your wife. I am delighted that John Thomason was a help.

Terry[1] has turned in his Introduction, and it is good, and if you are hereabouts when it gets into proof, I'll let you see it.

I should like to have you explain all of this Tugwell matter to me. I do not understand it, and am not qualified to, for lack of information. I know everybody likes Tugwell, even those who are bitterly opposed to him. I know that he is a man of the best will in the world — but I have come around to the opinion that the good, well-meaning people do more damage than the bad. For one thing, they are so convinced that they are working with God that they think they can do no wrong. You remember that George III, a most conscientious man, once said, "My intentions are good, and therefore those who oppose me are scoundrels." It is mighty easy to think that way. What's more, after some twenty years of observing them with great interest, I have little faith in economic planning. The intricacies of the problems are too great for men to cope with in that way. They must leave something to God, just as in the natural physical world. I think these extreme New Dealers are

[1] John Terry, a friend of Thomas Wolfe; he wrote the Introduction for *Thomas Wolfe's Letters to His Mother* published by Scribners in 1943.

for the most part men of the best intentions, but that if they have their way it will inevitably lead to the concentration of all capital, and all power, in the hands of a government, and that that government must then necessarily become a dictatorship, whether it will or not. And then it will rule the nation through a bureaucracy which will become, as has happened in Russia, a kind of aristocracy, a privileged class. The only hope for man is in the diffusion of power. If it ever gets into the hands of any single group we are done for in every way excepting, conceivably, a material one. Everyone might get enough to eat, etc., but he would have no freedom. But then, on the other hand, it may be that capitalism cannot function any longer, and that we shall have to acquiesce to communism. That is where I am always stumped, for perhaps it is true.

Hoping soon to see you, I am,

Always yours,

TO BETTY GRACE BOYD

MARCH 10, 1943

DEAR MISS BOYD:

I am sending you two pictures of your father,[1] around the time when we first knew him here. The smaller one may have been while he was still in the marine corps. The larger one is a much better likeness, except that one would think it must have been touched up. It makes him almost pretty, which he was not. He was very masculine-looking, and even somewhat rugged. But, on the whole, that large picture is a very good likeness, and can tell you more than any description I could give. I can't tell you what color his eyes were, but I should

[1] Thomas Boyd, author of *Through the Wheat*, Scribners, 1923, and of other books published by Scribners.

think gray. And his hair was light brown, and wavy. He was not much below six feet, strongly built but rather slender — not spare. In his manner he was quiet until one knew him well, almost shy — not one of those who put themselves forward in a conversation, especially when a number of people were present. But he was sympathetic, and made friends easily, even with those with whom he did not agree. He seemed to have no resentments against anyone, and I cannot remember his ever speaking badly of a person unless for reasons that nobody could dispute about. And yet he had strong feelings too, as a great deal of "Through the Wheat" will show — for instance, in the presentation of the General making the speech. And you can see that he was capable of great admiration for the simple, manly virtues of courage and leadership, in what he tells of his Major in that book.

In the first years that I knew him he was thinking mostly of literature, as in fact he always was. That was his first interest. But he also talked a great deal about the economic situation and the injustices of capitalism. He was apparently in favor of some very considerable degree of socialism, though I don't think he would ever have called himself a socialist.

"Through the Wheat" was a very distinct success, and its influence and reputation were all out of proportion to its sale, which was never very large — 12,032 copies in the regular edition, and 1,390 copies in the edition illustrated by Lieut.-Col. John W. Thomason, Jr., who was a great admirer of the book. He, also, was in the marine corps, but never knew your father.

If you wish to ask me any further questions, I should be very glad to try to answer them.

Ever sincerely yours,

TO WILLIAM LYON PHELPS

APRIL 1, 1943

DEAR MR. PHELPS:

Although we were very small boys indeed, and perhaps I was only four and my brother Edward a little short of six, my Aunt Mary,[1] who kept house for her father and mother, was determined that we should not lose the opportunity to see Washington while our grandfather[2] was still in the Senate. And so we went from Plainfield, N. J., with our governess, who was to leave us there, on the Royal Blue. Parlor cars in those days were in very bad taste, and not nearly so comfortable as now, but they were much more gaudy and magnificent, and we were greatly impressed — most especially, though, with the two colored maids who sat in beautiful white aprons, with their hands folded, on a kind of sofa at the end of the car, looking toward the passengers. They did nothing, so far as I could see, during the whole trip, but they were most ornamental. They were luxuries that we did not have even in the booming twenties. Aunt Mary was all for educating us and, in real truth, we went through many boring experiences, one of which was to listen to Grandpa make a speech in the Senate. There wasn't any particular novelty in this for us. He looked and talked just as he always did and, although we meant to behave rightly and keep still, we fidgeted around so much and kicked the railing of the balcony involuntarily so often that we were finally taken out.

But then we had the one great experience. We were playing in the drawing-room in the front of the house right off the hall, and there was no escape from it except through the hall. The

[1] Miss Mary Evarts.   [2] William Maxwell Evarts (1818–1901), United States Senator and one-time Secretary of State.

doorbell rang. We thought it safer to be out of sight, and crawled under a table and lay low. The door was opened by a colored maid, and a very spare, erect man in a frock coat that was buttoned up, and so emphasized his angularity, stepped in. He asked for my grandfather, but my Aunt Mary came down the stairs quickly and greeted him warmly, and said that he was not there. He was about to go, when she said, "Oh, General Sherman, I want you to see my sister Betty's boys." So he turned back quickly. Everything was quick about him. And then she said, "Where can they be — Edward! Maxwell!" and she peered into the drawing-room. We tried to lie low but, of course, we began to giggle and General Sherman stooped down and saw us under the table. He said, "If you two young rascals don't come out from under that table, I'll send for one of my big guns and blow you out." And so we came out, and we shook hands, and how we liked him. I remember looking up at him and thinking that his white beard, which was like the beard of a man who had not shaved for four or five days, so close cut, looked exactly like pin feathers on a chicken. And then he followed up what he had said about the big gun by telling Aunt Mary with great vivacity about some wonderful new ordnance the Army had just acquired.

Well, that's all there was to it, but I named a lead soldier for General Sherman and, one night, I don't know how much later on, when I was in bed and my mother was just going down to dinner, there was telephoning and I heard excited voices, and then my mother came into the room and told me General Sherman was dead. And I felt very sorry about it for about five minutes before I went to sleep.

Always yours,

TO WILLIAM LYON PHELPS

APRIL 8, 1943

DEAR MR. PHELPS:

My grandfather,[1] not long after his marriage, which was one hundred years ago next August, bought a large house in Windsor, Vermont. But it wasn't so many years before it was too small for the family, which ended up with twelve children, and so he bought the house next to it. And then the house next to that, and in the end there were five houses in a row, with open country behind them, and a lake. By then his sons and daughters had families of their own, and so there were many cousins there every summer. My mother[2] had one of these houses, and my father[3] was one of the original Mugwumps and, as my grandfather was one of the original Republicans, it was natural that all his own children should have been violently Republican when Benjamin Harrison was President, and that his other sons-in-law should have been. And so my brother Edward and I felt a certain disapproval among the older people. We were not outcasts, but we were, it seemed to us, under a slight suspicion.

I don't know why Benjamin Harrison came, but I suppose he was on some political tour, and it is a curious thing that he took all us children completely by surprise. Although my grandfather's career had made presidents, and other high officials, of less importance than they would have been to the average American, the entertainment of the President and his whole entourage must have been talked about for days. But children have that curious life of their own, by which they hear only what they want to. Perhaps it was just that we were not much interested in seeing the President — and perhaps we didn't realize that his appearance meant also a grand buffet luncheon,

[1] William Maxwell Evarts. [2] Elizabeth Hoar (Evarts) Perkins. [3] Edward Clifford Perkins.

which would have interested us profoundly. Anyhow, when we went up to our grandfather's house, where the members of the family had all gathered, and saw the long line of carriages drive in, with many stately men in black frock coats and silk hats, we realized so little what it was all about that one of my cousins, William Evarts, who was then three, said, "It looks like a funeral." His father was a clergyman.

Edward and I saw the President come in, but he interested us very little indeed. We knew how to make the most of an occasion like that, and were soon at the tables where the caterer's men were working, and making the most of our opportunity. But eventually Aunt Mary, who had a different idea of our opportunities, and wanted also to make the most of them, ran us down and herded us through a forest of legs and skirts, for a long distance, until we came into a little clearing where the President stood. He was a short man with a remarkably large round chest, like a barrel, and a white beard, which rested upon it. He was surrounded by all sorts of great Republicans. Aunt Mary said, "Mr. President, may I present my sister Betty's children?" And the President laughed and shook our hands, and said in a remarkably deep, booming voice, "Well, I suppose you boys are good Republicans too." There was silence all around the President, of course, when he was speaking, and there we stood in the silence. I didn't know what to do. It was quite awful. For one thing, it seemed dreadful to offend the President to his very face, and then, too, I felt like something of a black sheep. There was a long silence — and then my brother Edward spoke up loudly and defiantly: "No, we are not. We are Democrats." There was a great burst of laughter, to which the President himself contributed. I think he felt rather embarrassed on our account.

Years later, only a few years ago, I said to my mother, "I really think that was a magnificent thing that Edward did. It was truly brave of him," but my mother, after thinking it over for a minute or two, said, "Yes, but it would have been different if you had been the one to do it. Edward always did like to stir up the animals."

Always yours,

TO MAXWELL GEISMAR

APRIL 12, 1943

DEAR MR. GEISMAR:

I liked the reviews you gave me very much and wish I had time now to read some of the book.[1] I thought you showed great ingenuity in bringing all that miscellaneous group into a unified article, so that the discussion of each book led naturally into the next.

I thought of a story I once told in a letter about Scott.[2] It shows how perceptive he was of other people's feelings. I only wish I could give it the way he did, because it was most effective. This very charming woman[3] was motoring us from Washington down to Middleburg to dine at the house her family had lived in for a very long time. Its members were very deep in the Civil War. I once asked her to go to see the field of Gettysburg with me, and she said, "Do you think I would like to see the scene of my country's defeat?" In a rough way, and on a small scale, the house rather resembles Mt. Vernon. It was built some time considerably before the beginning of the Civil War. There is a cannon ball half-submerged in the wall of one of the stables. Quite a long avenue leads into it, through an untended lawn. There are the Civil War portraits, and older ones too. We passed all kinds of bronze tablets on the road, put there in commemoration of battles and incidents of the war. Scott and I, both being Yankees — though that lady who

[1] *Writers in Crisis* by Maxwell Geismar, Houghton Mifflin Co., 1942. [2] F. Scott Fitzgerald. [3] Miss Elizabeth Lemmon of Middleburg, Virginia.

was hanged in connection with the assassination of Lincoln was a relative of his — took a kind of interest in all this, which Scott, who was very sensitive, perceived was not considerate of our companion's feelings. So he suddenly launched into an account of the surrender at Appomattox. "Well," he said, "it was all a great mistake, the surrender. The facts never got out. The camera men flashed the pictures at the wrong moment, and then it couldn't be changed to the truth. For the truth was that when Lee handed Grant the written terms in that farmhouse, Grant said, 'General Lee, there is no pen here. May I borrow your sword to sign with?' For Grant, of course, had no side-arms, as history records. And in the moment when Lee courteously handed him his sword for that purpose the press pictures were taken." This doesn't sound like much when written, but Scott in all his high spirits made a fine thing of it. He was fascinated with the quality of that place, and thought the house was haunted with the old South, and once tried to do a story about it, but it did not turn out well.

Always yours,

TO WILLIAM B. WISDOM

JUNE 14, 1943

DEAR MR. WISDOM:

I am returning the pictures, with envy and covetousness. I think your daughter is a most charming-looking girl, and one could see right off that she is unusual in imagination and intelligence. As for the boy, I won't mention him. I think you know that we have five girls. It just seemed incredible to me that I should have any girls at all, and I always thought there would be a boy. But in the end I got to telling people that we always drowned the boys. It is too bad you have to be in the Army, though that is the place I think a man unquestionably ought to be if he can.

I am also returning your excellent review of "The Shock of Recognition."[1] I had just got the book — it was lying on my desk — when your letter came. Didn't they make a really beautiful book of it? A man who loves books would buy it for its physical qualities alone. I have only read Sherwood's[2] letters to Van Wyck Brooks, but they are very fine and revealing. In some ways, they make me think more highly of Sherwood than he himself did. It is a curious fact that he was disappointed in the end in both Waldo Frank and Van Wyck. In the case of Van Wyck, he was unjustly disappointed. Van Wyck is not a fighting man. That isn't what he is about, or should be about. Sherwood thought that he ought to become the aggressive leader of the movement. It was not in his nature to do that. He is rather an Erasmus, not a Luther. People must be what they are, or they will be nothing. I should have liked to send your review to Bunny,[3] but he will see it in the end anyway, and I thought you might want it for purposes of record. I think I'll copy that book, in an anthology we are to have of Russian fiction.

We may be getting into the odd situation where our letters keep crossing, for you will probably now write to tell me that you got the one I wrote in which I told you that everything was right with Aline.[4] It is completely so. And you will hear from her about Tom's[5] letters, and I hope you will get them.

I have made some progress with John Terry[6] too. He now only asks that he be given a chance to see what there is here, only to scan, and not to copy. He admits he has been doing the work too thoroughly, as I have been telling him all along he was.

I hope your brother may come. I look forward to seeing him.

By the way, long ago — as you probably know — Padraic

---

[1] By Edmund Wilson, published by Doubleday & Co., 1943. [2] Sherwood Anderson. [3] Edmund Wilson. [4] Aline Bernstein, theatrical designer, a friend of Thomas Wolfe. [5] Thomas Wolfe. [6] Friend and biographer of Thomas Wolfe.

Colum did a version of Homer which was, I think, called "The Children's Homer"[1] and there were excellent illustrations by Pogany.[2] You know how wretched most such books are, but that really caught the spirit, or so it seemed to me. I am sending a copy to my grandson. Some years after that was published, Padraic was invited to Hawaii at the expense of some Hawaiian society. He wondered why he should be so lionized as he was. It seemed a little too much, even if he was a poet of note. And then at a dinner he found himself introduced, on account of this "Children's Homer," as the author of the Iliad and the Odyssey.

Neither shall I sleep easily until you have all the letters.[3] The whole thing has been a great anxiety to me, and I was nearly frightened to death about it a few days ago. We have been keeping the letters in a locked room to which only certain people in the store, such as Randall,[4] had access. I, also, had a key. When I concluded that we must wind the matter up, I went up there to see just about how much was still on hand — and there was nothing. There was only an empty suitcase. A great many boxes of books and bookcases, etc., had been moved in. Everything was changed. The one thing sure was that the letters were all gone. I sent for a man from the store, who said he did not know what had happened, but perhaps Randall did. Randall was out, and I remained in a state of terror for an hour until he returned and coolly informed me that he had removed the letters to his department because the room was to be used for other purposes. I could have hugged him, though Miss Wyckoff[5] said I should have been angry that he had not told me.

Always yours,

---

[1] Published by the Macmillan Co., in 1925.   [2] "Willy" (William Andrew) Pogany.   [3] Letters of Thomas Wolfe, now in the Wisdom Collection at Harvard University.   [4] David Randall, head of the Rare Book Department of the Scribner Bookstore.   [5] Irma Wyckoff (Mrs. Osmer Muench), secretary to Perkins for twenty-seven years up to the date of his death.

The letter of June 17, 1943, which follows, was written after Perkins had received, and read, a book on writing and publishing which, in the course of an attack on editors and publishers in general, alleged that Thomas Wolfe had been the helpless victim of his editors, who had cut and mangled his work in such a way as to do him, and it, serious injury. Perkins resented these allegations, not only as regarding himself — for he had been Wolfe's principal editor and had sacrificed time and health in an effort to help him — but as regarding editors in general. As Perkins points out, Wolfe's own letters give the lie to these allegations.

JUNE 17, 1943

DEAR ——:

I got a copy of your "——" because I heard it contained a furious attack upon me. It does, and one that is plainly libellous, as Thomas Wolfe's own letters alone will show. But I found the book such good reading, upon the whole, that I suppose I now shall read it through. And I'll enjoy it, for the most part. But I am the slowest reader in the world, and so hardly ever get to read anything but what we are publishing. Which is a very bad thing in an editor.

But then I found your chapter called, "——," and I thought you should hear a few facts which are at complete variance with what you say. One thing you say is that if a manuscript of a novel "did not come in through one of the big agents" it is condemned "to cursory and dilatory reading." When we take on a new novelist we advise him to get an agent for the sake of magazine, dramatic, radio and movie rights. These he owns, and they must be skillfully handled. But here are a few of the authors that came to us on their own and got thorough, deeply interested, and immediate readings:

Struthers Burt	Christine Weston
Scott Fitzgerald	Nancy Hale
S. S. Van Dine	Arthur Train
Robert Briffault	John Thomason
Ernest Hemingway	Will James
Marjorie Rawlings	Taylor Caldwell
Marcia Davenport	

Most of them still have no agents in connection with book publication, but only for these other rights.

Then you come to tell how ninety percent of the novels published bear "bruises and slashes" from editors. I should say that ninety percent of them are barely touched, and then only in view of such matters as libel and other legal points. The publisher has to take some care in those regards, of course. Even so, I should say that ninety percent of our novels were very slightly changed, and that if they were changed it was because the author asked for help, even demanded it, even thought he or she was neglected if it were not given. When it is given, it is given very reluctantly and fearfully because, as you say, the book can only come out of the man. Editors know that mighty well, at least those I am acquainted with.

As for the greater part of Thomas Wolfe's manuscripts being torn out and thrown into the waste-basket, it is not true. Not a page was thrown into the waste-basket. A good deal of what was in "The Angel"[1] was removed, and a great deal of that was used in "Of Time and the River."[2] A great deal was removed from "Of Time and the River" and was used in the two later novels[3] which Harpers published. Almost nothing of what Tom wrote failed to appear in print except much that was so unfinished, as he himself thought, that it could not be published. But that too would have been revised by Tom and

---

[1] *Look Homeward, Angel*, Scribners, 1929. [2] Scribners, 1935. [3] *The Web and the Rock*, Harpers, 1939; *You Can't Go Home Again*, Harpers, 1940.

would have appeared, if Tom had lived.

As for Tom not being in a position to resist sabotage, why not? He had a contract. We were bound to publish everything he wrote except what was libellous and obscene — what would have endangered him with the law. The truth is that nothing was ever taken from Tom's writings without his full consent. When he could go no further with "Of Time and the River," he brought it to me and asked me to help him, and I did it with very great reluctance and anxiety. Tom *demanded* help. He *had* to have it. No one who did not know him could possibly understand it, but he would get into a state of such desperation that one realized that if he were not enabled to complete his book soon, something very serious would happen to him. He intended to proceed in the same way with Harpers. He called his book, which they made into two books,[1] "finished," when it was not at all. And he knew that, and he expected to work with Edward Aswell[2] as he had with me. What's more, I know Aswell's feeling about the matter, one of great anxiety for fear he would do damage. You seem to know only one kind of editor, and it is not the kind that I know. Certain authors absolutely demand help, and if it is not given them they will go to another publisher to get it. But most real writers do not. Most of them know what they want to do, and do it. Nobody ever edited Hemingway, beyond excising a line or two for fear of libel or other legal dangers.

Then you speak of fun being poked at Tom because of the hugeness of his manuscripts — because he delivered a packing-case from a truck. In fact, it was a taxicab. You say he was ridiculed. To my knowledge, he was not. He was admired. This peculiarity of his genius was interesting and was told about for that reason, just as such peculiarities as that of De Quincey,

[1] *The Web and the Rock* and *You Can't Go Home Again.* [2] The editor at Harper and Bros. who was in charge of the publication of Thomas Wolfe's books after he had left Scribners.

in working in a room until it was so full of papers and books, etc., that there was no room for him and so he locked it up and got another, were told about. It was not ridicule. It was affectionate admiring surprise. When Tom's book[1] came here, it was instantly recognized as a work of genius, and we were all excited about it, and it was read in sections by three of us at once. It was too long, and there was one big cut[2] of about 70 pages at the beginning, concerned with events which did not seem to come within the scope of Eugene's story, for they related to things before Eugene's birth, and remote from Altamont. Tom fully agreed that this cut should be made. I have a wonderful letter he wrote to his old teacher,[3] telling how he came here, and when we mentioned certain passages that were pretty rough he said he would take them out, and we said, by God he wouldn't, that they were among the best things in the book. You don't know what you are talking about. Even a good deal of that first part got into the later books in improved form. It is a long and complicated story. It may not interest you, but you have absolutely misrepresented the situation.

As for Henry Miller, I haven't read enough of him perhaps to be a qualified judge, but from what I have read, I should fully agree with you and Bunny Wilson.[4] But I suspect that the reason he cannot get published is that he does not sell. Publishers do have to think about that. It is like a law of nature. They would have to do it even under communism.

Anyhow, from what I have read of the rest of your book, which is a good deal, you have said many right and true things that have not been said before. Editors aren't much, and can't be. They can only help a writer realize himself, and they can

---

[1] *Look Homeward, Angel*, Scribners, 1929. [2] There were many other deletions of material used elsewhere in later books. This one cut may, in parts, have been lost to print — but not the best of it. [3] Margaret Roberts (Mrs. J. M. Roberts) of Asheville, N. C. Excerpts from Wolfe's letters to her were published in the *Atlantic Monthly* during 1946–1947. [4] Edmund Wilson had expressed admiration for the writing of Henry Miller.

ruin him if he's pliable, as Tom was not. That is why the editors I know shrink from tampering with a manuscript and do it only when it is required of them by the author, as it was by Tom. When an editor gets to think differently from that, to think he knows more about a writer's book than the writer — and some do — he is dead, done for, and dangerous. When he thinks he is a discoverer because he doesn't fail to recognize talent — was a jeweler ever praised because he knew a diamond from a lump of glass? — he is a stuffed shirt, and through. But I've known it to happen.

As to libel, I shall look up the law. But I think suit can be brought until one year after the sale of a book has ceased. But my suit would ask no more compensation than would meet the expense, since the purpose would be only to show that what you said was grossly untrue, ignorant, and injurious. On the other hand, from what else I've read of your book — such as that refutation of those silly so-called laws or rules of fiction, since genius can break any law and indeed always does — I think you spoke from misinformation and irresponsibility, and so I should prefer to let the matter lie until — if there is a chance of that — you come to New York and will give me an interview. I don't like quarrels, and I hate the law, but I can't by silence seem to acquiesce in what you have written, for if you now think it is the truth, you will then have grounds to assume that it is.

Ever truly yours,

TO EDITH POPE

Dear Mrs. Pope: June 28, 1943

I am writing you a very cautious answer to yours of June 20, for as the book[1] is going now, I think you have a firm grip on it and will be a much better judge than I as to how to handle

---

[1] *Colcorton*, Scribners, 1944.

it. I think, in the beginning, it was like a brook that got to spreading out and running in various different thin channels, and that now you have channelled it deeply and well, and will have the instinct of how it should flow. A book, of course, has to arise out of the author, and what an editor must fear most is that he will influence the author too much. And so you must make your decisions. The only thing is that I thought, since there is no true love-story in this book and can be none, that the devotion of Danny, which is almost selfless, would be accentuated if he came to realize the whole situation and so assumed the responsibility for the act of murder, for the sake of protecting her — of protecting her conscience and protecting her from any danger there was from the law.

I have liked these last chapters you sent me very well indeed. I think there need be no more change or cutting in them until the proof, when we shall get a new look at the book in that form. One always does get a fresh view in type, somehow.

As for the swamp, I think it is very good, and I am glad you have that element in — if you do err, it is in the direction of having too much, but let it lie for the proof. All your nature writing — if we have to use such a horrible phrase — is admirable. I do think that Johnson could have brought the egret feathers — that that is not too coincidental or melodramatic. Whether the murder should be done before the departure of Beth and Jack is a question. I am rather inclined to think it should be after, but you will now have a better instinct for that problem. But if it were after, it could be led into by Danny's surprise and pleasure to find that Abby had not left as he supposed she had.

I think the reader would be conscious of what is back of the whole thing. But I see no reason why Abby should not read Beth the will. It would be the best way to tell her the situation, the most convincing of the necessity of her getting away with Jab. And even of the advisability of leaving Abby behind. I think she should tell her after Jab has guessed the worst. But do follow your judgment.

I think "Colcorton" is a good title, and a suggestive name. "Slow Flows the Guallo" too closely parallels a Russian novel called, I think, "Slow Flows the Don."

Marjorie[1] seems to be all right, but now her husband[2] has entered the ambulance service and is destined for Africa. I think that upset her, and quite reasonably so. But Southerners just have to be in wars some way. So she expects soon to come to New York, and she is ready to talk about another book, which delights me. Willkie[3] did go to Cross Creek and there was a grand time. Marcia Davenport and her husband Russell were there. Marcia told me all about it, and how they did literally get to a point where they practically slept all afternoon from so fine a feast.

Ever sincerely yours,

TO ANN CHIDESTER

DEAR ANN: JULY 15, 1943

I think you write wonderfully about the rivers, and I am glad you love rivers. I always did, even the little ones, like one they call the Sluice, about eight miles long, that ran from a lake called Little Turkey, through the school ponds at St. Paul's, at Concord, N. H., and finally into the Merrimac. And then we had grand days as boys, on the Connecticut. Those were the logging days there, and we learned to spin a log almost as well as a professional. I think, with all your feeling about the St. Croix, you should write a book of some kind about it, or about it and the Mississippi. Perhaps a novel, and perhaps not. Whatever it was, we should publish it. Perhaps it is a moment when you might better not do a novel. I should feel no doubts at all

[1] Marjorie Kinnan Rawlings.   [2] Norton Baskin.   [3] Wendell Willkie.

about what you could achieve in a non-fiction book on such a subject — the rivers and the river people too.

There was another river that I saw and shall never forget the look of. I daresay in a small way it resembles the Mississippi, which I have never seen except in crossing it. That was the White River in Missouri. I spent a week there in the winter — and it was very cold too — with Ernest Hemingway. There was just a powdering of snow on the steep banks of the river, and on the ground above, where we waited for ducks to drop to the water. It was just like the rivers in the *Harper's Weekly* Civil War pictures, and most wonderful to me. And the woods behind the banks were not second growth, such as I had always seen, but were great trees widely spaced. One could imagine a man riding at a gallop through them. One day, as we were getting back to the houseboat — and we saw a good many of the river people living in houseboats that were just like those Mark Twain told about — we heard a most terrific racket around a curve, and then there came a regular old-time Mississippi steamboat with two funnels, side by side, pouring out wood smoke. To Hemingway this was a commonplace, but to a Vermont Yankee it was like going back eighty or ninety years and coming into Mark Twain's world. I wish I could have taken a trip up and down that White River on that boat.

We got those mistakes with regard to jazz and swing[1] corrected a long time back, but once they get into print, it is hard to get them out of it. They are out now, though.

Always yours,

DEAR ——:   AUG. 30, 1943

A great deal of any novel is written from remembered observation, from actual experience. We rather think that that

[1] In her book, *No Longer Fugitive*, Scribners, 1943.

whole scene,[1] in which the little messenger appeared, was taken from memory, for we know that Nancy Hale worked on just such a magazine as the one in her story. We know that she, like every really intelligent American, respects and probably admires the Jewish race. But characterizing the messenger as a Jew does make him more distinct to the reader, just as would be true if he were characterized as Irish. But probably the messenger she remembered just simply happened to be a Jew and, if so, it would have been absurd to have called him Italian, or anything else. The Jewish race today is certainly facing a terrible crisis, and this naturally makes the members of it sensitive, and we think sometimes unduly so. Not long ago, Americans were universally ridiculed by Europeans, especially in pre-Civil War days. They were sensitive too, and with much less cause than the Jew. But we do not think that writers should be asked to falsify their books on that account, or that harm would come if they do not.

Nancy Hale is at present recovering from an illness, and we cannot communicate with her, but when we do see her we shall speak of this matter to her with the full expectation that she will say that she has nothing but sincere regard for your people, and only used the reference you suggest for reasons of artistic effect.

Ever sincerely yours,

TO ERNEST HEMINGWAY

DEAR ERNEST: SEPT. 2, 1943

Evan Shipman[2] never turned up in the week that he intended to, or at any rate he did not call me up so that we might dine together, as he had planned. He may have found things so

---

[1] In *The Prodigal Women*, by Nancy Hale, Scribners, 1942.   [2] Author of *Free for All*, Scribners, 1935.

pleasant in Windsor[1] that he stayed there for all of his leave. Maybe you will know, and if you do, tell me, because I have a letter for him from Harold Stearns'[2] wife written after Harold's death. She wrote me a very moving letter, too. She said Harold — who did suffer terribly — was most unhappy because he had not made the most of himself. But I believe that is the case with every one of us, even of those who seem to other people to have done well.

I can imagine that Evan could not bear to leave Windsor, because I was up there last weekend and it was wonderful. But I had no time to find out where Evan was, because this was a family celebration of the centenary of our grandparents' marriage, and somehow a lot of the business of running the thing off fell upon me and kept me busy. There were only thirty-five of us there, because all the boys in the next generation to mine are in the Army or Navy, and even several in my generation. Twenty-two in all. And then the difficulties of travel which Louise[3] and I experienced on the way home deterred others. It was quite a good party, though. One of my cousins read off a kind of record of our generation, and one of the items in it was that two of us had spent a night in jail. So when I saw her a few minutes later, I asked if she meant me. She said, "You are the third one that has asked if he were meant, and the two that I knew about aren't even here." Only one had the distinction of having spent a night in his own home town jail in Windsor. He did it on somewhat the same grounds that Thoreau did. He thought the law was wrong and refused to bow to it — although he had to do it the next day in court. I had to transport an enormous gold loving-cup from New York to Windsor, where I left it. And then they made one of my daughters bring it back to me, and here it is in the office, and

---

[1] Windsor, Vermont.   [2] Editor of *America Now: An Inquiry into Civilization in the United States,* Scribners, 1938.   [3] Mrs. Maxwell Perkins.

if you will come up in October, I'll take it around to the Ritz or the Chatham, and get Waldo[1] and Charlie Sweeny,[2] etc., and we'll make proper use of it.

This afternoon —— is coming in with a lot of pictures and a sort of reminiscent manuscript, which I have already declined once. And so have other publishers. I think the portraits are good, and that he is, but one could not sell a book of that kind now, and the paper situation makes it particularly difficult to take it on. But I did tell him I would look at the new pictures he has, and reconsider, but that there was very little hope. Still, I am glad he is coming, for I think he is very good company and that we'll go out and have a cocktail.

Always yours,

TO MARJORIE KINNAN RAWLINGS

April 19, 1944

Dear Marjorie:

I am delighted to hear about Norton,[3] and I hope he will stick to his decision and come back in September. I didn't realize that the time was so far off, though. I had figured that his year was all but up now.

As to the Profile,[4] I thought I got off pretty well, and was very glad that Cowley did wander off, more or less, into a discussion of publishing instead of me. It is making plenty trouble though — all kinds of manuscripts come in to me, on the theory that I was created to put them into publishable shape. And because of the remark that one can tell as much by seeing an author as by reading the manuscript, all sorts of authors insist on being seen as well as read. But it did one very fine thing.

---

[1] Waldo Peirce, the painter. [2] Col. Charles Sweeny, author of *Moment of Truth*, Scribners, 1943. [3] Norton Baskin, husband of Marjorie Kinnan Rawlings. [4] A "Profile," in *The New Yorker* of April 1 and April 8, 1944, by Malcolm Cowley, of which Perkins was the subject.

Very old, and ill, Mrs. John Leal, the widow of the school-teacher I mentioned, in Plainfield, N. J., was simply delighted, I am told. The Plainfield paper told of the Profile and of the fact that John Leal, who was so much admired in the town, was referred to. I had always felt I let John Leal down, and I was glad of this.

My grandson, who is five, was looking at the illustrations in the original edition of "The Yearling"[1] and asked me about the story, so I partly read and partly told him a good deal of it, and when it came to how poor Jody had to shoot Flag, he was extremely distressed. He understood, though, that they could not live if Flag was at large. He sat for a long time pondering the problem of confining Flag successfully, looking almost like an old man while in thought. And then he suddenly brightened, and said, "They could keep him from jumping the fence, with chicken wire stretched over a pen." But I told him Penny couldn't get chicken wire, even if there was any in those days, so then he sank back into thought, and finally he shouted, "They could get rope and stretch a net over." He thought that solved the problem, and it made it seem as if it had happened, to him, and he was happy again. I shouldn't have told him the story until he was old enough to read it all.

I am enclosing a copy of an ad of "Colcorton"[2] which goes into *The Saturday Review*. We would advertise it more, much more, except that we are rationed in advertising too. You can't tell what you can get into a paper, but very little, comparatively.

I was simply delighted by what you said of your novel.

Always yours,

---

[1] By Marjorie Kinnan Rawlings, Scribners, 1938. [2] A novel by Edith Pope, published by Scribners in 1944.

The individual to whom the next letter was written had brought in a manuscript which Perkins thought had merit, in spite of certain rather serious defects. He felt, also, that the author did not have an adequate knowledge of the English language, or a true understanding of American life and American ideas. She, on the other hand, felt that Perkins, and Scribners, were depriving her of her right to give the world a message.

The correspondence with this individual was continued in the letters of May 23, May 25, and May 31, 1944, when Perkins wrote, "I realize that our correspondence is futile and had better be ended." However, in response to another letter, Perkins wrote the letter of November 3, 1944, to be found later in this collection; and, still later, the letters of May 31 and August 16, 1946.

DEAR ——: MAY 19, 1944

Since you tell me you have no copy of your letter, I am returning it herewith. Perhaps you will wish to publish it sometime. It shows that you are one of those who Know and so exempt yourself from the Biblical injunction: "Judge not that ye be not judged."

You ask who I am, and I may as well answer you and have an end to it. I am, or at least should be if I fulfilled myself, John Smith, U. S. A. He is the man who doesn't know much, nor think that he knows much. He starts out with certain ambitions but he gradually accumulates obligations as he goes along, and they continually increase. They begin with his inherited family, and grow with the family that results from his marriage, and further increase with his associates, and those whom he represents. He soon finds that about all he can do, and that not too well, is to fulfill those obligations. He knows that he is a failure, and is bound to be, because he is not in the confidence of God, like some, and does not know God's plan. He does know what he has undertaken to do, and he hopes to Heaven that he will manage, to some considerable extent, to do it. That's what he is serious about, for he can't, in view of his observation of the rest of the world, be very sure about himself, or think that his fate is a matter of moment. He can accept the kiss of death too, as long as he doesn't let himself in for it by his own negligence, which would mean the betrayal of others. Tom Wolfe would have understood perfectly what I am talking about, and Tom Wolfe would be the very first one who would tell you that I never had let him down. His last letter, in pencil, written when he was about to die, shows that. So does the fact that I am still working in his interest as his executor.

About the *New Yorker* Profile[1] I can't exactly understand what you mean, but I can tell you that Profiles in the *New Yorker* are things to dread. I dreaded this one for a couple of years, and even consulted a lawyer as to what means might be taken to prevent its publication. But when it did come out, I said, "I wouldn't mind being like that fellow," and secretly I thought he was a great sight better person than myself.

One of my deepest convictions is that the terrible harms that are done in this world are not done by deliberately evil people, who are not numerous, and are soon found out. They are done by the Good — by those who are so sure they are good that they are sure that God is with them. Nothing can stop them, for they are certain they are right. I think Hitler is one of them. Certainly Martin Luther was one when he tore Europe to tatters. I think your friend Henry Wallace is one, and that he would be perfectly ready to take charge of the whole universe, with the certainty that he could manage it, because he

---

[1] A "Profile" of Perkins, by Malcolm Cowley, in *The New Yorker* of April 1 and April 8, 1944.

knows that God is with him. This world is crowded with Good people who think as George III, who said, "My motives are beneficent and therefore those who oppose me are scoundrels." That's a pretty kind of reasoning, and many of the New Dealers indulge in it.

I would say, "Hate the evil, but beware of the Good. Put your trust in those who think they are not much, and simply do your best and try to meet your responsibilities."

You speak of two books we published. We published "A Guide for the Bedevilled";[1] first, because we think such a House as this should give a chance to those who have something worth saying to say it, and it enabled us, we thought, to help the American principle of equality by which true Americans detest prejudice against minorities. And then we published it because it was a magnificent piece of fiery writing — which is also a consideration for publishers. You say it is anti-Semitic. It is written by a Jew, against injustice and intolerance. And while we have been violently criticized by anti-Semites for it, we have been highly praised by Jews who are regarded as admirable. How do you know you are right?

You refer to "Out of the Night"[2] as having been ghost-written by Isaac Don Levine. Did the book not say that it was written in collaboration with Levine? If it did not, you have a right to criticize it, but if it did, it plainly shows that it was not written by Jan Valtin but by Isaac Don Levine. There is nothing unfair about that and perhaps that book never could have been written except in that way. If it says it was done in collaboration, there was no deception.

Etta Shiber[3] could not write, as she truly says, yet she had a story of intense interest and importance. It could never have been told without a collaborator. Do you now say that it should

---

[1] By Ben Hecht, published by Scribners in 1944. [2] Published in 1941 by Alliance Press. [3] Wrote, in collaboration with Anne and Paul Dupré, *Paris Underground*, Scribners, 1943.

never have been told? It was plainly shown on the title-page that she did not write it, for it said it was by her "in collaboration with Anne and Paul Dupré." What's the matter with that? If you don't like books written in that way, look at the title-page first and then don't read them. Of course, it would have been a better book if Etta Shiber could have written it, but, as it is, it is better than no book at all — at least, from the point of view of those opposed to totalitarian government.

In conclusion, I quote Oliver Cromwell, who once said to Parliament, "Gentlemen, I beseech you by God's blood, consider that thou may'st possibly be wrong." John Smith, U. S. A., is always aware of the fact that he may be, and probably is, wrong. That is tolerance. He simply does his simple best in the world and hopes to God that he will never let anybody down or betray any principle in which he believes.

Ever sincerely yours,

MAY 23, 1944

DEAR ——:

Don't keep saying that we published "Out of the Night,"[1] for we didn't. I don't think we would have, either, for there was something very sinister about the book, I thought. And thank you for calling me a business man. Nobody else ever did that, and I am afraid you couldn't find anyone around here who would.

It is those people who know that they are right because some outside or higher power conveys the conviction to them who do the great damage in the world.

Ever truly yours,

[1] By Jan Valtin in collaboration with Isaac Don Levine, published in 1941 by Alliance Press.

Dear ———: MAY 25, 1944

You do write with such power, such expressiveness, that it is too bad you should not be published. One difficulty is that you are not yet a mistress of English in your writing, though I am sure you are in your understanding; and another is that you have not yet mastered — it seems to me — the technique of the novel. Did you ever consider writing your own story, in straight narrative form, in the third person, as a novel? You could, of course, depart from the facts, whenever you pleased, but that would give you a natural form to follow, and the doing of it might give you a valuable discipline for future writing. This, of course, is none of my business, but one cannot help feeling that the powers you have ought to be used to effect.

I suppose there is no use in continuing our controversy, but you enlarged upon the Martin Luther question. The difference between you and me is that I stand with Erasmus, and you with Luther. It seems to me that the issue joined by them typifies the tragedy of man. Martin Luther acted as he did for the reasons you give. He was outraged by the state of the Church, even though it was improving and had become ashamed of its own abuses. Erasmus begged him to refrain from violence — from bringing things to an issue and breaking everything to pieces. Erasmus loved the good as much, or more, than Luther did, but he believed that the good could not be accomplished by violence — by charging like a mad bull. He believed it could be accomplished only slowly, by patience, and by reason. He tried to hold Luther back — you should read all their correspondence — but so headstrong a man as Luther could not refrain from action. Any man admires Luther, and sympathizes with him, because emotions are stronger in all of us than reason. And so Luther, a man of fine intellect too, but of terrific passions, destroyed Christendom, destroyed Europe, and — although I suppose someone else would have done it in any case, some other man of justifiable but ungovernable rage — brought on the present shambles, which has been recurrent since the destruction of the unity of Europe, of Christendom.

That is just my point. The tragedy of man is that reason and tempered wisdom are always, throughout man's history, overcome by passion and ungoverned emotion. That is man's ruin. Take the Civil War for an instance. Relatively speaking, there was in the South only a handful of slave-owners, and a good many of them realized that slavery was a frightful mistake, a terrible wrong and an economic error. If fifteen years had passed without violence — probably less — this would have been self-evident, and so would the fact that the South could never prevail against the great economic power of the North. There would have been no war. But the men of passion got going. I admire Wendell Phillips and the others, but they wrought harm. They preached Abolition, and that started the men of passion in the South, and that silenced the men of reason, and so that terrible and unnecessary tragedy was brought on by passionate men — by men who knew God was with them. Nobody knows with whom God is. Our knowledge is only finite. Temperate men of reason never think they know what God wants. The men who founded this country *were* men of reason, by some strange chance, Jefferson, Madison, and the others, even Hamilton, and so they were able to compromise, not being sure what was right, and to approximate what *was* right. So we had the Constitution.

I give those two instances to show what I mean — that the fanatics, the ones who are sure when nobody can be sure, are the ones who bring ruin upon us. Emerson's poem, "Brahma," which is almost a literal translation, by the way, says plenty about what men know. Truth one might say is a dome of many-colored glass. One can only see part of a dome at a time. No one can grasp it all optically, and much less mentally. There is some truth in almost every belief, but we can see only a little at a time.

I have read a good deal of your novel about the editor. You obviously regard me with contempt for approving the publication of such books as "The Women on the Porch,"[1] although it seems to me that, if one wants to look at it from a moral point of view, it is of value to show what frustration and futility our present civilization produces. But if I were what you had supposed, if I remained the helpless employee of an organization in which I disbelieved, and which I thought was what you think it is, I should be utterly despicable in my own eyes too. That would be the lowest thing possible.

Then, in the end, you have your editor go out for himself as a publisher, on the basis of certain resolutions. One of these is, to my mind, a complete betrayal of his profession — that he will only publish books which will coincide with his own views. If he is that kind of man, let him speak for himself and be a writer. But the function of a publisher in society is to furnish a means by which anyone of a certain level of intelligence and abilities can express his views. A publisher should not be, as such, a partisan, however strongly partisan he may be as an individual. If he allows his partisanship to govern him in his choice of books, he is a traitor to the public. He is supposed to furnish a forum for the free play of the intellect, in so far as he possibly can. That is the whole American theory — that opinions can be given a means of full expression, and that the public, hearing all of them and considering them, will eventually approximate a right conclusion. Every profession has its own particular code of ethics, its own morality, that its members must adhere to or they betray it. And a primary element in the morality of the publisher is that he shall not

---

[1] A novel by Caroline Gordon, Scribners, 1944.

let his own personal views obstruct the way for the expression of counter-views. I should say that no individual in this House, for instance, is a believer in communism. But when we got so fine a book as "Soviet Communism: A New Civilization," by Beatrice and Sidney Webb, who have been life-long students of social questions, we felt that it was our obligation to publish it. Then the ways of the Russian system would be ably set forth, and the arguments for it, and the American citizen could, from that source and others, form his own opinion. The American idea is that public opinion rules, and the American publisher's idea is that it is his duty to get individual opinions bearing upon issues before the public in order that it may be given the materials from which public opinion may competently crystallize.

Ever sincerely yours,

May 31, 1944

Dear ——:

Your novel has been read by several of us, and we are very sorry that we have had to conclude that we cannot make an offer of publication. It is quite readable and has vitality, but, in general, it is our impression that you have not yet sufficiently mastered the technique which is necessary to present its thesis impressively and logically. Apart from this general consideration, your conception of publishing houses and their function in society is quite contrary to the reality — at least, you have not established its validity. It is clear that publishing houses, even as churches and hospitals, etc., can function only on a stable financial basis. The ideal of publishing would be a forum where all sections of humanity could have their say, whether their object was to instruct, entertain, horrify, etc. Nevertheless, there are certain rules of quality and relevance, which can only be determined by some sort of selection and this the publisher, representing humanity at large, attempts — with many mistakes — to make. Or, to put it differently, artists, saints, and the other more sentient representatives of the human race are, as it were, on the frontiers of time — pioneers and guides to the future. And the publisher, in the capacity mentioned, must make some sort of estimate of the importance and validity of their reports, and there is nothing he can base this on but the abilities to judge that God has given him.

I realize that our correspondence is futile and had better be ended, but I should like to say, if you'll let me, that I knew from your face that you were an utterly sincere and good person.

We are returning the manuscript to you under separate cover.

Ever sincerely yours,

TO ALICE D. BOND

JULY 17, 1944

DEAR MISS BOND:

I am afraid, now, I may be answering your letter at too late a date. I got laid up for two weeks, at a time when I was trying to think of what I could tell you that would help.

It is true that Scott Fitzgerald's "This Side of Paradise"[1] was declined by two publishers, but it was also declined by us, in the first version, and it was I who, Scott being in the Army then, sent it to the two other publishers, and I was afraid to death they would take it. I felt that it showed an amazing talent and that if Scott came safely back from the war, he might revise it — as he did.

So far as I know, S. S. Van Dine was only declined by one

[1] Scribners, 1920.

publisher, when he put the matter of a series of detective stories forward in the form of synopses. When he brought these synopses to us, we immediately accepted all three of them, for I knew that Willard Wright[1] would never do anything otherwise than well, and that a detective story is necessarily relatively artificial and, if done by a skillful and scrupulous writer like Willard, should justify itself, even though he might not have a gift for fiction in general.

As for Thomas Wolfe, he was declined by four or five publishers, but at least two of them had editors who saw that he was a very remarkable writer, and it was only because of what they regarded as the insuperable difficulties of cutting and organizing, etc., and its great length, that it was declined.

You asked about Marjorie Rawlings, but she never wrote a novel until the first one that we published, "South Moon Under."[2] I believe that she has publicly said that she had been trying to write for years for magazines and had said to herself that if a Florida story she sent to *Scribner's*[3] was not accepted, she would give it up. But we took the story,[4] and other stories thereafter, and encouraged her to write a novel.

As a matter of fact, I think the percentage of the very good books — the really notable books — that are declined is higher than the percentage of the highly competent mediocrities. The reason is that the books of the greatest talent are almost always full of trouble, and difficult, and they do not conform to the usual standards. They are often strange. They are different, as were "This Side of Paradise" and "Look Homeward, Angel."

I cannot tell you about any living authors, because authors generally do not like to have declinations told about, naturally enough. I do hope I am not writing you too late.

You ask about Marcia Davenport — we immediately ac-

---

[1] Willard Huntington Wright, author, under the pen-name S. S. Van Dine, of the Philo Vance mysteries, published by Scribners. [2] Scribners, 1933. [3] *Scribner's Magazine.* [4] "Cracker Chidlings," published in the February, 1931, issue.

cepted her first book, "Mozart," even though not a very great deal of it was written. One could tell from what we saw of the manuscript that she had skill, and from what we saw of her that she was unconquerable and would do what she undertook.

I hope this letter may help you, but I am afraid it won't.

Ever sincerely yours,

TO JOSEPH STANLEY PENNELL

JULY 26, 1944

DEAR STAN:

I suppose you have already seen the enclosed picture. I send it because Brady might have taken it on one of the battlefields of Maryland or Virginia. You only have to imagine horses, in place of the mechanical vehicles. The trouble with reviewers, and with editors, is so simple that nobody gets it. They ought to just take a book and give themselves to it, and read it like a regular citizen and see whether they like it or not. They ought not to apply their standards and frames of reference, and all that, to it, until afterwards. But you cannot make them do it. It is something that only simple-minded people do perhaps. I know that, because of editors that have a magnificent equipment and appreciation too, and yet when it comes to some book that needs to be revised, they can only think of its revision, not in terms of the writer's intent and capacities, but in the terms of some classic that they measure everything of that kind against. If it is a book about a prostitute, it has to be thought of in terms of "Moll Flanders" or "Maggie" — which I never read. Therefore, anything true in the original — which, of course, is very rare — baffles them because they haven't anything with which to compare it directly. They ought to judge books the way they judge people. When they meet a person and talk to him, they do not say that he does not resemble some other person, or does resemble him, or make any such comparison. They just size him up on his own terms. That's the only way to judge. It is one of those things that are so simple, and that when you say it, it does not seem to mean anything. But it is because of that, that many a reviewer and an editor is nothing like what he has the abilities to be.

Yours

SEPT. 19, 1944

DEAR ———:

I think your novel will be here today. I called up Mrs. Otis,[1] and so she said — and you will know how eagerly it will be read by me, and by Jack.[2]

I was not surprised at your letter,[3] because I learned many years ago that all an executor gets for what he does is abuse — at least, at the moment when he does it. I can only tell you that I am required to do the best I can for the estate, and that I would certainly be to blame, even legally liable, if, in representing Tom's heirs, I neglected their financial advantage. To Scribners, or to me, there is no advantage whatever. I never yet saw a movie of a book that I was not disappointed in, and yet I never knew a book to be hurt even by a bad movie, but often helped by what is called a good one. That, too, I had to consider. Anyhow, no one has to go to a movie and a book is not transmuted into a picture. It still exists, no less than before.

But I did not make this sale without the uttermost care and all the protection I could get, which was little. I went first to see one of the movies which this particular producer, Ripley,[4]

---

[1] Elizabeth Otis of McIntosh & Otis, literary agents.   [2] John Hall Wheelock, an editor at Scribners.   [3] The writer had expressed disapproval of the sale of *Look Homeward, Angel* to a motion-picture producer. Perkins, as executor of the estate of Thomas Wolfe, had made the sale.   [4] Arthur Ripley of Monter-Ripley Productions.

put on, in a preview. It was called "Voice in the Wind." I also insisted upon having the approval of the scenario writer, in whom I have confidence. When I showed Jack your letter, he, who knew nothing much about the matter, said, "Well, if only you could get the producer of 'Voice in the Wind' you need fear nothing." I do worry though, and expect abuse. But Tom always wanted a movie production, if it could be a good one, and would have made such an arrangement as I have made. At any rate, it is for me to act upon my own judgment, after reflection and consultation, and all the few precautions available, regardless of however many people may be made mad as hell, and who they may be.

Always yours,

TO WILLIAM B. WISDOM

SEPTEMBER 22, 1944

DEAR MR. WISDOM:

The trouble with these lists of novels and novelists lies largely in definition anyhow. I think if a man was simply talking to you over a drink, he might give you a very different list from what he would when he sits down to prepare one for the SRL,[1] for then he begins to think of academic standards, and he might say that Tom[2] did not fit well with the definition. God knows Tom fitted well with no definition, but was a very great writer.

With what you say, I am in pretty close agreement. I have always read Dos[3] with fascination, but the fascination of his writings was that of amazingly revealing *documents*. His books will be valuable to the social historian. They will not long survive as novels, hardly even as fiction. And Lewis[4] is a remarkable journalist, a satiric journalist. His importance is not

[1] *Saturday Review of Literature.* [2] Thomas Wolfe. [3] Dos Passos. [4] Sinclair Lewis.

in his writing as creation, but in his amazing observation. Anyhow, I always thought that he never got beyond the late Victorians as a writer of fiction.

Cabell[1] I never tried hard to read, but had little success with him in the little I did. And if I really read him, I might feel very differently. Cather[2] I should put very high, and Ellen Glasgow for her urbanity and on technical grounds. Nathan[3] I always felt a kind of irrational impatience with.

Hem's[4] best writings, his truly magical ones, are his stories, and especially the quiet stories. But I did think that, as a novel, "A Farewell"[5] was more completely successful than "The Bell,"[6] though not the equal of "The Bell" as literature. I thought Hem did astonishing things in "A Farewell," and followed them all the way through the book. He showed how everything is conditioned, and indeed contaminated, by war — and how a purely physical attempt at seduction grew, in spite of everything, into love.

As to Steinbeck,[7] I was never fully convinced, though later writings may convince me. And Faulkner[8] has seemed to me, so far, to have been a magnificent virtuoso. But I am told his later short stories would disprove this, and that what would make one think he was what I said, came rather from the deliberate purpose of shocking people into listening to him.

Always yours,

Oct. 3, 1944

Dear ———:

It is very hard for me to express a certain uneasiness I feel about ———, because it is really instinctive, though backed by

[1] James Branch Cabell. [2] Willa Cather. [3] Robert Nathan. [4] Ernest Hemingway. [5] *A Farewell to Arms*, Scribners, 1929. [6] *For Whom the Bell Tolls*, Scribners, 1940. [7] John Steinbeck. [8] William Faulkner.

experience. It is, first, that books written in anticipation of events and developments often lose a great deal of relevance they are intended to have because things develop quite, or somewhat, differently.

Another consideration is that a writer does best what comes entirely from himself, and not so well in carrying out the ideas of others. This I know, considerably, from having myself suggested books to writers who had nothing at the moment and wanted to write. Such books were always below their best, though sometimes successful.

A third reason is that the best fiction does not arise out of an idea at all, but the idea, or argument, arises out of the human elements and characters as they naturally develop. And this seems to apply particularly to ——, because her nature is to begin a book without knowing the conclusion, or even the steps of development, so that the development and conclusions come from the situation and the people.

Your idea I think is a good one except for the reasons given above, and they *may* not apply. I cannot tell about it. Apart from an uneasy feeling that comes from these considerations, I should be all for the plan. Anyhow, if —— wants to do it, as I think she does very much, we could be sure that the outcome would be what we should regard with great favor — even though it fell below her best work. We are for whatever she may do. Anyhow, she has at present to complete "——," and I thought we might be able to see more clearly what the probabilities for "——" would be by the time that was done.

Ever sincerely yours,

The following letter is addressed to the same individual to whom Perkins had written on May 19, 23, 25, and 31. She had asserted that Grosset & Dunlap had been "bought" by Scrib-

*ners, and the other publishers, in order to establish a sort of
monopoly and prevent the publication of good books at lower
prices. In this letter, Perkins endeavors to clear up that misconception.*

Nov. 3, 1944

DEAR ———:

The trouble is, in this Grosset and Dunlap matter, you are
not acquainted with the facts. You are right in saying that
Grosset & Dunlap only reprinted other people's books, and any
publisher was glad to have them reprint any of their books,
after a certain period — with us, two years — unless they had
sold that right to some other reprint house. There was, therefore, no restriction except in that one respect — and, for a long
time, there was no other reprint house — as to what they should
publish. They were always in friendly coöperation with us, and
with most of the other publishers, and everyone would have
been glad to have had them continue on their own as reprint
publishers. But the deaths of large owners of stock of the company left the ownership in the hands of widows and such people
as could not manage the business. These people naturally
wanted to dispose of it, but they were very anxious that it
should go into good hands. We, and certain other publishers,
were also very anxious to keep it out of bad hands. That is why
the sale and purchase were made, and they were not made
with premeditation on the part of the purchasers, but very
quickly indeed, almost one might say overnight, and for the
good of the book business in general. It is evident from these
facts that all your argument about a cartel is wholly beside the
point.

You refer later to Thomas Jefferson, and I should like to
say that I have always regarded him as the greatest of all

political philosophers, and of statesmen. But it seems to me that I am one of the very few Jeffersonians now extant. Jefferson believed in as little government as possible, and in as wide a diffusion of power as possible. He thought that concentration of power in the federal government was likely to end in the loss of the people's liberties — that power corrupts those who hold it, and increasingly as they hold more. All this is what I believe, but I find that people in general now have no fear of the concentration of power, and are for it, and that great numbers of them believe that the more government, the better. The whole world seems to have been hypnotized into the acceptance of the principles of totalitarianism, which is the utter antithesis of Jeffersonianism.

I don't know, of course, how they felt about Dickens in Russia, but in this country he has been perhaps the most beloved of all English writers, and the only reason his books are in rather small type is that they are very large books indeed, especially when they have the wonderful Cruikshank illustrations, and those by other artists. Until a few years ago, we were the publishers, in this country, of three editions of Dickens, illustrated and well printed. We gave them up, after many years, because at one time the demand fell too low to justify us in continuing them. But I think there is now a revival of interest in Dickens, and I should hope we might resume them when the paper shortage ends.

My own personal view is that America's future will be safer under Jefferson than Hamilton, but I am afraid that since even the Democratic Party, which used to come nearer to Jeffersonianism, is now apparently even more for the extension of the powers of the Federal government, and their concentration, than any other, there isn't much hope in that regard. But I should like to say too, that I think those who regard Hamilton as Fascistically inclined have never taken the trouble to read him. Let them read "The Federalist Papers," one of the wisest and greatest books in the world. He, more than any other single man — and largely through these papers — brought about the adoption of the United States Constitution. Can the man who fought so valiantly for the principles in the Constitution, at the time when its adoption was under debate, be regarded as Fascist?

Sincerely yours,

Nov. 13, 1944

DEAR ——:

Although we do not in general believe in discussing the reasons for decision upon a publication — for we think it should speak for itself, and that time will bring the right answer concerning one that is questioned — we are glad to write you regarding "The History of Rome Hanks,"[1] in view of the openminded spirit in which you have written.

To begin with, it has seemed to us that a publisher's first allegiance is to talent, which is very rare and valuable. It is with that that a publisher is primarily concerned. And so when we read "The History of Rome Hanks," realizing that its publication would involve many difficulties and dangers, some of them arising from the element in it to which you refer, it was said here, "We must find a way to publish it." It was our unvaried experience that books containing what you refer to as "dirty," particularly in the use of words, are thereby seriously injured in their sales — and, if only on that account, we should prefer that such words were not used. But if they belong, if they are the words that would actually be used in the circumstances of the book, then artistically they should be used, and an author feels as if he were playing false in evading them.

[1] Novel by Joseph Stanley Pennell, Scribners, 1944.

In this particular book, a great deal of what you speak of as dirty results from what was, in fact, one of the most terrible curses of the Civil War, dysentery. No one could picture the way that war was and leave that element out of it. And Mr. Pennell was bent upon picturing the war as it was.

But, that apart, this book pictures immorality and vice as horrible, as in fact they are. It would in no way draw anyone toward them, but would certainly repel them. The chapter, for instance, of a St. Louis street, and the houses, is equivalent to a Doré horror picture, and would act as a deterrent to vice. There are many books published to which no objection is made which would have the opposite effect, so that the question comes down to one of taste. But in literature, at any rate, that is an extremely difficult question. What could one say in regard to it in considering Dean Swift's "Gulliver's Travels," or Rabelais' writings, or a couple of hundred others of the great classics? Many people would prefer not to read them, would find them offensive, and we can perfectly well understand that point of view. But one can readily judge a book in this respect before buying it, and can avoid it. But, in truth, nobody could be actually hurt by it.

We took the book because it seemed to us to reveal a new and remarkable talent, the most obvious example of which is perhaps the recreation of Pickett's Charge. But we are never certain of our judgment, and we waited with great interest for the reviews. As it was a first novel, the probabilities were against its getting much attention or receiving very emphatic approval. But it got both. The *New York Times* in fact gave it the front page of the Book Review section, and the *New York Herald Tribune* gave it a very large part of the second page. These are the two most important book-reviewing papers in the country, and both of them thought as we did about this book and the talent of the author. And, indeed, all but a minute number of the other reviews in the country took the same view. It seemed to us, therefore, that our judgment had been confirmed.

Ever sincerely yours,

TO GEOFFREY PARSONS

DEC. 4, 1944

DEAR GEOFFREY:

With regard to the inquiry for the Century Association about James Boyd, I have written to Struthers Burt, who knew him as well as anybody in the world, to ask him to send an excellent article he wrote for a paper in Southern Pines when Jim died. It is odd it should be so hard to think of anecdotes about Jim, in view of the fact that he had a very sharply defined character. He was of Scotch descent, and took pride in it, as was shown by the fact that he almost always wore plaid socks, and often a plaid tie — whether designating any particular clan or not, I do not know. He had the dry humor of the Scotch, and the shrewdness about people. His critical faculty was highly developed, and he would talk well and revealingly about almost anything, including politics — and with a philosophical detachment. He often said that he should have been a critic of literature rather than a novelist. And although this was not true, his judgment upon contemporary writers was full of understanding and his range of sympathy was such that he had the highest admiration both for Ernest Hemingway and Thomas Wolfe, whom many consider to be poles apart. His outright arguments with Tom — whose faults he was, of course, aware of — were, I think, helpful.

As the editor of a weekly newspaper in Southern Pines, he wrote a column about an imaginary native character which exhibited his own point of view on social and political develop-

ments in this country. I hope you have this, for it is very revealing and might be quoted from. The columns were published in
a pamphlet, and I could get them if you need them, I think.

Jim was also convivial. Once, a good many years ago, in the
Prohibition era, before the speakeasies were well known, he
arrived in town with all the ingredients of a mint julep except
the mint. It was a broiling afternoon, and he was determined
to get that — although I should have been satisfied enough with
the other ingredients in some other form. We spent an hour
on Sixth Avenue, inquiring in every likely place, and finally
got what we wanted and went to the Plaza and enjoyed the
results. Scotch persistence.

There was told one very amusing story which would have
been characteristic of Jim, if true. Struthers Burt is a fighting
idealist, a crusader. One of the things he crusades against is
billboard advertising on the roads. Several years ago he was
called a number of times on the telephone, apparently by different people, who accused him of hypocrisy in that there was
a sign just outside Southern Pines which said, "Welcome to
Southern Pines, home of the famous novelist, Struthers Burt."
If you know Struthers, you will know that this reduced him to
a fiery particle. He motored full speed to where the sign was
said to be, and there it was. He drove fast to his lawyer. But
the lawyer thought that, first of all, he ought to see the sign
himself, and they went back to the spot. There was no sign.
I was told that this was Jim's doing, and it would have been
characteristic of him except that he was not addicted to practical jokes. But I never quite liked to ask Struthers, and I
always forgot to ask Jim.

There is no use in saying that Jim was a wonderful husband,
father, and friend. He was completely loyal. He had terrible
handicaps. He was always suffering with the sinus affliction that
killed him, and he never gave in to it to any degree. He would

never speak of it unless asked about it, and then always hope-
fully, although it was wasting him away. But even before that,
as a boy, he was laid low with infantile paralysis, and never did
completely recover. He was Master of Hounds in Southern
Pines, but he could ride only by balance, or almost that, because
he had no grip in his knees. He rode in spite of *that,* and he
wrote in spite of the other. It was a heroic life, really, though
almost no one knows it.

I'll send the Southern Pines paper as soon as Struthers sends
it to me.

Always yours,

TO CHRISTINE WESTON

DECEMBER 13, 1944

DEAR CHRISTINE:

I read the story[1] almost a week ago, and upon finishing it
had expected to write you immediately of the pleasure I got
from it, with the idea of going right ahead in the regular way,
with a view to publication. But I was deterred by the feeling
with which I left it, that it might be so revised as to become a
true little masterpiece, but that as it stood it was prevented
from being that by being a combination of elements which are
not easily compatible. The natural tale of events that could
be actual, with the highly fantastic. And so it could be revised
in one of two ways, and in either case to great advantage, I
believe. I wish I could talk to you, for I don't know whether
you would be willing to consider the suggestions, but Henry
Volkening[2] says that he has heard no more about your coming
here, and we are still early in the winter. You only said you

[1] *Bhimsa, the Dancing Bear, a Fairy Tale for Young Readers,* Scribners, 1945.
[2] Of Russell & Volkening, literary agents.

would be down sometime during the winter. I'll, therefore, at least make a preliminary attempt to write, for you always have been willing to consider suggestions. If you are not, you can simply stop at this point. But in spite of the pleasure I got in the reading, I cannot get over my feeling that in view of your particular equipment, and of your great talent, you are missing a chance.

I think that if you did revise, and made the book wholly a fantasy, because the presence of the other elements makes it too difficult to accept fantasy, you would have to make the story all but totally unreal from the start — for the fairy tale does have its own wild logic, I should think. When Alice gazes upon the looking-glass, and then passes through it, you are prepared for anything. The falling asleep and having a dream is perhaps an outworn device, though was it not used in those Wizard of Oz books, which all children do adore? A more usual method is that of the old fairy tale, which prepares one also for anything in the world by beginning with "Once upon a time" — for way back in the dim past almost anything might have happened. But when you have a very natural opening, when you have the little English boy with his parents away and his only companion asleep, old Lal, and then the sudden sound of the drum and the cymbals, one expects a natural story of actual events, or close to actual — and, after all, the wonders of India, to the American child, are enough to give such a narrative all the variety and color and charm that anyone could want — and then, by the time the two boys and the bear are summoned by the prince, everything begins to become fantastic, and sometimes even, I should say, un-Indian, particularly the submarine in the river. Not that anything at all is not permissible in a fantasy, but one has begun to feel that what they are going to find out about is the way things would seem to a child in India, so that the fantasies lose some of their value.

But then, after the escape from the robber tribe, you come to that moving song, "Do you know where the snow leopard dwells?" and, at the beginning of that chapter, Thirteen, you revert to the natural, or natural enough story, and with splendid effect.

It was when I came to that point that the expectations you had aroused by the first chapter seemed to be realized and made me regret that the entire story had not been written in that way, and that what might actually have happened, or almost so, had not been held to throughout.

Suppose the story were revised to that effect. Then, I should say, it ought to begin not very differently from the way Chapter Two begins, so that almost immediately we would know of this little boy, lonely and bored, nothing to do, with a dreary day before him. And then he hears the drum and then the cymbals, and then he sees Bhimsa. And finally David goes off, just as he does, with Gopala and Bhimsa. And, by the way, Bhimsa is grand, and almost always truly in the character of the bear, and all I would say about him is that the more you make of him the better. And so they set out, and then the course of events, in a large sense, could be just as it is except that I do not think Bhimsa ought to imitate a fat woman on roller skates, because Gopala, who trained him, would never have known of roller skates.

Now would it be too unreasonable for the two boys and the bears to be summoned by an actual prince, a boy? Or for the actual prince to want to keep them for himself? Couldn't strange, though actually possible and wholly Indian, things happen before the actual prince, so that the reader would be really getting a series of pictures of India, which is a wonderful land to children? And then couldn't they escape from there in some really possible way, and go on and come upon the estate of his uncle, a man who found the company of animals preferable to that of men? And couldn't wonderful, though really natural, things happen while they were there? But thereafter they fell in with the robber tribe, and that wouldn't perhaps need so much change. And finally, as I said, you come into those wonderful last chapters, which are all but natural. It would simply mean that the motive of the writer would then be not to give a fantasy but to use the possibilities of India to tell the story of how these boys went together and made their way with old Bhimsa, and finally got, as you have them do, back to Gopala's home in the mountains. I don't mean that there should not be strangeness — which is quite compatible with the scene and wonders in it. It seems to me that India, to the American child-reader, gives you infinite opportunities. Certainly one can encounter anything in the company of an Indian prince. But you might then have a wholly natural story which no one but you, with your material and talent, could possibly have written.

I won't go further, though I could in details, because all this may be unwelcome. I simply want to lay the matter before you, because I cannot get away from a deep sense that you might turn the dancing bear — which, by the way, I think ought to be called "Bhimsa," with the rest in a separate line — into a truly wonderful and unforgettable natural tale.

Always yours,

Dear ——:　　　　　　　　　　　　　　　　Dec. 26, 1944

You are now consulting me on a very ticklish question. You remember Punch's advice to those contemplating matrimony. The last man who consulted me on this question — but didn't wait for an answer — sent me the girl's picture to help me come to a conclusion. When he finally presented the bride, she was much better than the picture, and I thought he had done very well indeed. I really think it is one question that a man must decide for himself. But certainly, from a practical stand-point, it does not make it any easier to follow the generally unprofitable career of a novelist. I guess we had better wait until you come in after New Years, for that is only a week away.

Many thanks for writing.

Ever sincerely yours,

DEAR ——— :   JAN. 24, 1945

We remember your former letter with regard to "Rome Hanks,"[1] which we fully answered, and we very much doubt whether the lady you refer to, who questions the sanity of the author, is as well qualified to judge of its merits as the large number of critics who have expressed their admiration for it. We have not read Caldwell's "Tragic Ground,"[2] but you may have noticed that when the case got to the Magistrate's Court in Boston, it was thrown out with ridicule, and that the police-man who made the arrest received something approaching a reprimand for it. We think that "Rome Hanks," which has sold in the original edition barely short of 100,000 copies and is being published in the Armed Services edition, and by a Book Club[3] in a large popular edition, received an astonishing success in sales for a book which could only be appreciated by a public of unusual intelligence. We may point out that no public is "compelled to read" a book, and that anyone who took pleasure in what you object to in this book would give it very slight attention because it would make no sense to him.

Ever truly yours,

[1] A novel by Joseph Stanley Pennell, Scribners, 1944.   [2] Novel by Erskine Cald-well, prosecuted by Sumner Anti-Vice Society.   [3] The Dollar Book Club.

TO R. W. COWDEN

DEAR MR. COWDEN:

FEB. 9, 1945

I fully appreciate the compliment of being asked to be one of the judges of the Hopwood[1] fiction contest, but I must, with deep regret, decline. It is my conviction that an editor should be even more obscure than a child, who should be seen. The editor should be neither seen nor heard, or so I think. And so I have made it a rule to do nothing but the regular editorial work, and not to speak, or lecture, or act as a judge, or to take on anything on the outside, even when greatly tempted, as now.

Ever sincerely yours,

TO ERNEST HEMINGWAY

DEAR ERNEST:

APRIL 19, 1945

I knew it would be mighty hard for you to get adjusted after all that. I know you knew it too, in your head, but I thought you probably would be worried by feeling completely fit and yet not able to get going. I am dead sure it will be all right, but I know it will be tough too. But I think you ought to take it easily. Get out into that old Gulf Stream, where things always seem to be all right, not necessarily for you yourself, but in the big way. Probably they are really all right, that way too. When you say, "It is all done with people," you touch on what is the great tragedy of life, I think. That nothing is ever in a condition of purity. I think that is the great surprise to a boy who goes into anything — that it is never the way he thought

[1] Avery Hopwood Award, given each year by the University of Michigan for distinguished work in the field of creative writing by regularly enrolled students of the university.

it would be. It is all bitched up with other things that do not belong in it. That has always been true in this business. It is true, as you say, in everything about war. A campaign is not conducted on pure military principles, but is all messed up with political, financial, and otherwise foreign elements. Everything is that way. Though, in art, everything can be excluded. But not easily. This is too much to write about in a letter, but it really is the most shocking discovery a boy makes when he gets into anything. Remember Prince Andrei looking up at the stars, after the artillery officer got the rough deal, and thinking everything was so different from what he had thought it was going to be?

I had a note from Charlie Sweeny[1] today, from Utah. The address is Box 2391, R.F.D. #4, Murray 7, Utah. In answering it, I did bring in again the hope that he would do the book we had talked about.[2] It would be out of all he has learned through a mighty crowded life, and that is what good books come out of. He seemed in good spirits though, in this short note. He liked that Venturi book on painting.[3] So did I. There are some people that nobody ought ever to quarrel with, and he is one of them. It is easy to see how enraging he might be, but I would take anything he gave, and stand it, because I would know that he was all right. I guess that just means what everyone knows, that whatever some people may do, even if it is very bad, is right for you. And if it was very bad, it is because there is something wrong with them for the moment, or maybe wrong always. But if so, it must be accepted, because you know they themselves really are all right.

I am talking too much, and I have got to stop.

Always yours,

---

[1] Colonel Charles Sweeny, soldier and writer, author of *Moment of Truth*, Scribners, 1943. [2] A volume of reminiscences. [3] Lionello Venturi, *Painting and Painters*, Scribners, 1945.

The next letter was written in response to one from a young man, at that time in service over-seas during the War, who had asked Perkins' advice with regard to a writing career and had sent him the manuscript of a story.

TO JOHN H. MULLIKEN, JR.

DEAR MR. MULLIKEN: MAY 17, 1945

I shall be greatly interested to read the story when it comes. I should think you had seen plenty by now, but I do not think you need be impatient to put it into writing. I think, in truth, that the best writing of all is done long after the events it is concerned with, when they have been digested and reflected upon unconsciously, and the writer has completely realized them in himself. It is good journalistic writing that is done quickly while everything is still new, but not the best writing. Long ago I went to visit Ernest Hemingway, after he had been a couple of years in Key West. We went fishing every day in those many-colored waters, and then also in the deep-blue Gulf Stream. It was all completely new to me, and wonderfully interesting — there was so much to know that nobody would ever have suspected, about even fishing. I said to Hemingway, "Why don't you write about all this?" and he said, "I will in time, but I couldn't do it yet," and, seeing I did not get his meaning, he pointed to a pelican that was clumsily flapping along, and said, "See that pelican? I don't know yet what his part is in the scheme of things." He did know factually in his head, but he meant that it all had to become so deeply familiar that you knew it emotionally, as if by instinct, and that that only came after a long time, and through long unconscious reflection. I don't mean that you should not write about all this now, but that the best of it can only come after all the experience has been yours for a long time, and you have absorbed it and can see it in perspective. So don't worry about the time element.

As to perhaps a couple of years of college, I should think that that might be of great advantage, in a general sense, but don't try to learn about writing there. Learn something else. Learn about writing from reading. That is the right way to do it. But then it can only be done by those who have eyes and ears, by seeing and listening. Very few of the great writers had that formal education, and many of them never mastered spelling or grammar. They got their vocabulary by reading and hearing. But the way they teach literature and writing in colleges is harmful. It results in one getting into the habit of seeing everything through a kind of film of past literature, and not seeing it directly with one's own senses. It makes it so that whenever a man wants to write, for instance, of an amiable, drunken old Irish rascal, he cannot do it as he really sees him, but has to do it considerably as Thackeray saw him and pictured him in Captain Costigan.[1] I would say that a couple of years in the newspaper business was much better for one who wanted to be a writer than a couple of years in college. But there are, of course, other advantages that come from the college.

Anyhow, since you seem likely to be over there for quite a long time further, I am sending you another of those little books,[2] on the chance that you have not read Hemingway.

Ever sincerely yours,

There follows another letter to a young man on active war-time duty who wanted to be a writer, as was his father, the novelist James Boyd.

[1] In *The Newcomes.*   [2] A Hemingway reprint, in the Armed Services Edition

TO JAMES BOYD, JR.

Dear Jim:[1]   June 22, 1945

I have sent "Eighteen Poems"[2] to Lawrence Bemis.[3] I do think you ought to read all that you possibly can — though I should hope that it would not all be in contemporary books. But they certainly should be read too. I suppose you have at command all these Armed Services Editions, and they have made very good selections. But certainly much reading is what a young writer should do. As for finished writing, I should suppose it would be impossible in your circumstances, but I don't think that much matters now. You see plenty, and you hear plenty, and that is much more important even than reading. You remember how when Swift was a young man he would go to the inns on the highways and sit in the bars and listen to the teamsters and coachmen talk. He never used the language that he heard — and I suppose he really listened just from interest anyhow — but the rhythm, the tempo of living speech is in the talk of the regular run of people. And so, though you can't write as you wish now, you are probably going unconsciously through the best education you could have. Seeing, hearing, and reading.

I was mightily interested by what you said of Okinawa. That must have been something. I suppose you know what your mother wrote me, that your brother[4] got the Silver Star in France. Probably that is old news to you, and maybe you won't even think it means much, being in the midst of it all. I hope I'll see you soon, but I suppose the Pacific Coast will be the only dry land you will be on for some time yet.

[1] James Boyd, Jr., a son of James Boyd, was, at this time, in the U. S. Coast Guard, on active duty in the Pacific.   [2] Collection of posthumous poems by James Boyd, published by Scribners in 1944.   [3] A friend of James Boyd, Jr.   [4] Daniel Lamont Boyd, a corporal with the Combat Engineers of the 35th Infantry Division.

What I wanted to say was that, as to being a writer, I don't think you need worry that you can't really work on writing itself. What really makes writing is done in the head, where impressions are stored up, and it is done with the eye and the ear. The agony comes later, when it has to be done with the hand, and that part of it can gain greatly from seeing how others do it, by reading.

Good luck,

TO NANCY HALE

DEC. 19, 1945

DEAR NANCY:

I know exactly how you feel about the distortion of truth for praiseworthy motives. What is there to tie to but truth? Nothing. If we do not adhere to that, we are done for — not that I don't sympathize with those who say the truth can't be known. Anyhow, it is with truth that publishing is concerned, and I think that 1946, our centennial,[1] will be a stormy year.

I hope Mark[2] will get adjusted in St. Paul's. It must be just that he hasn't got the hang of things, or perhaps that he is rebellious against them. If by some chance somebody would just happen to give him the right shove at the right moment, it might all straighten out for him. I know, before midyears in my Freshman year, I was dead certain that I would be fired, and was going to enlist in the Army. And then an upper-class-man to whom I said this took me to my room and in twenty minutes showed me how to work, and I passed every single examination. You have probably just got to let him alone, and hope it will turn out right. Since you liked "Teresa,"[3] I am

---

[1] The centennial of the founding of the House of Scribner in 1846. [2] Son of Nancy Hale, then at St. Paul's School. [3] *Teresa or Her Demon Lover*, a book about Byron and Teresa Guiccioli, by Austin K. Gray, Scribners, 1945.

sending you a book that is very much better and considerably about the same thing, "For Thee the Best."[1] Don't bother to thank me for these. I only hope I shall see you soon.

Always yours,

TO JAMES BOYD, JR.

JAN. 4, 1946

DEAR JIM:[2]

I delayed answering your letter because I wanted to quote from Scott Fitzgerald, and it took me a long time to find the paragraph:

"So many writers, Conrad for instance, have been aided by being brought up in a métier utterly unrelated to literature. It gives an abundance of material and, more important, an attitude from which to view the world. So much writing nowadays suffers both from lack of an attitude and from sheer lack of any material, save what is accumulated in a purely social life."

About twenty years ago, I was talking to Galsworthy in London about Scott Fitzgerald. I wanted to enlist his interest, and perhaps his help in England. But he was not sympathetic and, curiously enough, he said almost exactly what Scott said, many years later, in the quotation. He said these writers who become writers at the start are invariably disappointments. It is much better for a man to have been something else than a writer, so that he has viewed the world from a fixed position.

I thought that perhaps you might be able to infer from this quotation and anecdote some meaning for yourself in your per-

[1] A novel about Byron's last years, by Mark Aldanov, Scribners, 1945.   [2] James Boyd, Jr., son of James Boyd, served in the U. S. Coast Guard, on active duty, first in the Atlantic, then in the Pacific.

plexity. You have in fact had several years at sea, and in war, and perhaps that has done for you what Galsworthy and Fitzgerald thought so important. You are the only one who can tell, if you can. But, as for the question of the newspaper and style, I don't think there is much in it. Just off-hand, here are four who began as reporters: Ernest Hemingway, Edmund Wilson, Stanley Pennell, Stephen Crane. I could name a good many more, who did not have a style but came out of the newspaper profession to be noted writers. Dreiser did, for one. I do think writing for a paper, when you must produce, say, half a column in half an hour, with a copy-boy standing by to tear the half sheets out of your machine, does tend to sloppy writing perhaps. But great writers have done it. Charles Dickens did it. I think if one has the nature to develop a style, he will certainly do it. And that working for a newspaper will not prevent it.

Anyhow, I fully understand your restlessness, and I do think you ought to do something. Next time you come to New York, we'll have a drink and a talk, I hope. But nobody could have gone through what you have and not have difficulty in getting adjusted. That is just inevitable.

Yours,

TO ANN CHIDESTER

JAN. 31, 1946

DEAR ANN:

I waited to answer your letter until that young son of Stu Preston[1] came in. I had a date with him, and finally I went out with him for tea, as we call it. I enjoyed talking to him, and my fear would be that he is too like his father, who was almost faultless and was universally liked both in school and college.

---

[1] Stuart Preston, a friend and classmate of Perkins.

This boy seemed quite a bit like Stu. I read what I judge came from letters he had written home in the war, and they did show that he had a natural expressiveness in him, and an awareness. That is about all you could say. They certainly did not show that he might not turn out to be a good writer, but there was nothing to make you feel a confidence that he would. I was beguiled into giving him advice as to what kind of courses he should take in Harvard, and what he should avoid. In truth, I think it would probably be better if he did not go back there at all. Anyhow, I'll see him again, I think, and I should want to help him for the sake of his father even if he were not your friend.

Your letter gave me pleasure because of the spirit of it, and what you said about your feeling about the new book.[1] I'm glad you see Sinclair Lewis. I was talking to his English publisher about business matters, and then he spoke of Lewis, and I said, "Everything about him is good. Even the bad in him is good-bad," and Frere[2] said, "That is exactly right, and he is the only man I know of of whom that could be said."

I also come from a town that had a penitentiary in it, and sometime we ought to talk about penitentiaries. I never could feel it was a horrible place, even when once or twice I went in to see convicts. Still, the sun of Vermont shone on it, and there was a beautiful view of Mt. Ascutney from the cells at the back. Because of knowing it from childhood, and the prisoners they used to let work in gardens, and all, I could not think of it as the horror that I suppose it really is.

Always yours,

---

[1] *Mama Maria's*, Scribners, 1947. [2] Frere-Reeves of William Heinemann, Ltd., London.

MARCH 27, 1946

DEAR MR. JONES:

I was greatly pleased by the last sentence in your letter, telling of how "a host of hazy memories come back clear and sharp" from looking at your manuscripts. I remember reading somewhere what I thought was a very true statement, to the effect that anybody could find out if he was a writer. If he were a writer, when he tried to write, out of some particular day, he found in the effort that he could recall exactly how the light fell and how the temperature felt, and all the quality of it. Most people cannot do it. If they can do it, they may never be successful in a pecuniary sense, but that ability is at the bottom of writing, I am sure. Not that they would use that day exactly, but that it would be part of the frame of reference, for instance, if they were writing fiction. They would use that day in the fiction, and they could get the exact feel of the day.

Now this is something that I have told many writers, and I do not believe any of them have done it. Most of them keep note-books, and they certainly should. But they should keep them this way, I think: They should get a loose-leaf note-book and put into it preferably stiff cards, and they should make notes all the time about everything that interests or catches attention. Then, each thing should have a separate page, and at the top of the page should be put some key word. The key word might, for instance, be some topic like, say, "Fear." Then, just let the cards accumulate for quite a period, and then group them together under the key words. I think if a writer did that for ten years, all those memories would come back to him, as you say, and he would have an immense fund to draw upon. One can write about nothing unless it is, in some sense, out of one's life — that is, out of oneself. I remember telling Sherwood

Anderson, who had all his unsystematic note-books, about this, and he thought it was wonderful. But I don't believe he ever did it, nor anyone else that I suggested it to, including myself.

Let me know occasionally how things go.

Ever sincerely yours,

The letter that follows is, once more, addressed to the individual to whom Perkins had written on May 19, 23, 25, 31 and November 3, 1944.

MAY 31, 1946

DEAR ——— :

What I said to you about your writing was true. It has passion and power, but it is not publishable. Your mastery of the English language is not sufficient to enable you at present to write a book to which we could hope to do justice. Besides, I do not think that you understand the fundamental American principles of freedom. Under our theory, the rule is by the considered public opinion of the people, and this depends upon a free press. A free press furnishes the channels for information. The information appears then in magazines, newspapers, and books. Some of what appears may be even deliberately misleading. But when it all has appeared, there is the material from which an adult public may form its opinion, and that opinion, in our theory, rules. When we published "I Chose Freedom,"[1] we foresaw that we would meet violent criticism and opposition. But it is a publisher's function to furnish the means for informing the public on matters of controversy. We should, therefore, have betrayed our profession at the cardinal point of its ethics, if we had refrained because of fear of complications, or of reprisals.

[1] By Victor Kravchenko, Scribners, 1946.

I do not know what your background is, but you have not yet acquired a sufficient command of our language nor, I think, of our principles.

Ever sincerely yours,

The trial referred to in the following letter took place in St. Augustine, Florida, in connection with the suit for libel brought against Marjorie Kinnan Rawlings. This suit centered about the name of one of the characters in Mrs. Rawlings' book, "Cross Creek," published by Scribners in 1942.

TO MARJORIE KINNAN RAWLINGS

JUNE 10, 1946

DEAR MARJORIE:

I have just read with great amusement and interest the accounts of the trial in the St. Augustine paper, which I guess Mr. May[1] sent up to Whitney Darrow.[2] We ought now to be able to get some literary publicity, at any rate. We are sending the clippings over to the *Publishers' Weekly,* and we can use them elsewhere too. Don't you think that —— was put up to sue, that she never would have done it on her own account?

I read to Mr. Kravchenko[3] some of what you said about his book, and I told him that I thought the way you had felt about Russia, and about attacks on Russia, was the way ninety per cent of our own most intelligent, tolerant people still did feel. They cannot believe that things are as they are. But I know of it from other sources than Kravchenko. Leigh White[4] was over there, as a correspondent, a couple of years ago. He was

---

[1] Philip S. May, attorney, of Crawford & May, Jacksonville, Florida. [2] A vice-president of Charles Scribner's Sons. [3] Victor Kravchenko, author of *I Chose Freedom*, Scribners, 1946. [4] Author of *The Long Balkan Night*, Scribners, 1944.

very far to the Left then, and he thought he was going to the Promised Land. He wrote, a month or so back, from Europe, to ask if we would have the courage to publish a book he described, to be called "Two Worlds." He said that, along side it, Bill White's[1] book would seem like communist propaganda. And the reason for it is simply that a totalitarian country must become tyrannous, must be a police state. Even if it starts with the best intentions and under the best men, it will end up that way. It is hard to see what we are coming to here, but the people who laid down the principles of our government realized the terrible danger of concentrated power, and set up a system for the diffusion of power. The idea was expressed by Lord Acton when he said, "Power always corrupts, and absolute power corrupts absolutely." I think we are in an awful situation. But, anyhow, you have this case off your mind, and better forget all such things as communism and totalitarianism, etc., and just write your own book. I remember well how many anxious nights I got through happily by just thinking about "The Yearling,"[2] and I hope for one more such experience.

I know how terribly hard is such a fight as you have gone through — how horrible all that has to do with law and courts is. If my father had not died when I was seventeen, I should probably have been a lawyer — although, even then, I did plan to be a newspaperman. But the family pressure was pretty strong the other way. I have always been grateful that I escaped the family fate. In the instance of Tom, he simply could not take it. It was for that reason that we settled the lawsuit,[3] although we never did tell him so. He was so tormented that he could do nothing but drink and brood. It was

---

[1] William C. White, author of *These Russians*, Scribners, 1931.   [2] By Marjorie Kinnan Rawlings, published by Scribners in 1938.   [3] Suit for libel brought against Thomas Wolfe and settled out of court. The plaintiff alleged that one of the characters in a short story by Wolfe, in his volume *From Death to Morning*, Scribners, 1935, was identifiable as herself and that the characterization was damaging.

absolutely necessary to get the thing out of the way, and this was only done with his apparently satisfied agreement. But afterward he did think that we had let him down. So, after seeing him go through some preliminaries, I can well imagine the strain you have been under.

Yours,

TO NICHOLAS MURRAY BUTLER

JUNE 26, 1946

DEAR PRESIDENT BUTLER:[1]

Charlie Scribner[2] and I were both deeply touched by your letter, and I shall nevertheless cling to the hope that there may be another book, by some chance. I know that you have still much that you could say, to the advantage of the world. And we should, as we always have, take pride in making your words available as publishers.

When I heard of your misfortune,[3] I had meant to write to tell you how important you had been in my life, at the beginning. In 1907, when I had just become a reporter on the *New York Times,* Mr. Ochs[4] gave a luncheon in the Times Building to the staff. You were the only speaker. I listened avidly to every word. Several days later, it was announced that a prize of fifty dollars would be given to the reporter who could give the best account of the affair, and of what you said. I thought it would be useless for me to compete, but that it would not be sportsmanlike not to. But I waited until the last minute and, having finished the story, I clattered off on the typewriter what I remembered of what you said, and just made the deadline. I thought no more about it, until one day I came into the

---

[1] President of Columbia University. [2] Charles Scribner, president of Charles Scribner's Sons. [3] His blindness. [4] Adolph S. Ochs, publisher of the New York *Times.*

office and two or three people came up and congratulated me; for what, I did not know. I had actually won the prize, and although I was given a good many black looks by star reporters, I nevertheless gained great prestige and whatever there was of ill feeling, that a cub should have beaten the rest, soon melted away. One might say that that incident gave me my real start, and I have always been grateful to you.

We are to publish "The World Today"[1] on July 15, but I think that copies are already in the hands of the Carnegie Endowment. When I saw the jacket on the completed book, I instantly wished that you could. It is a beautiful picture, and exactly right.

Ever sincerely yours,

The following is again addressed to the person to whom Perkins had written the letters dated May 19, 23, 25, 31 and November 3, 1944 and May 31, 1946. This correspondent was a great admirer of the work of Thomas Wolfe, but asserted that Wolfe had turned against Perkins on the ground that the latter was a believer in the capitalist system. And so he was, but Tom had never "turned against" Max, for this or for any other reason. This misconception was based upon the now famous letter, in Wolfe's "You Can't Go Home Again," which Webber, the hero of the novel, addresses to Foxhall Morton Edwards, a character very clearly modelled after Maxwell Evarts Perkins. In rebuttal, Perkins enclosed, with his letter, a copy of the letter that Wolfe had written him, almost on the day of his death, the last that Wolfe ever wrote. This letter (see page 141 of this book) expresses Tom's deep affection and admiration for his old friend and editor.

---

[1] By Nicholas Murray Butler, Scribners, 1946.

AUGUST 16, 1946

DEAR ———:

Didn't I once show you the very last thing that Thomas Wolfe ever wrote — a letter to me, written almost on the day that his illness in Seattle took its fatal turn? I thought I did, the first day you came in, but in case I did not, I enclose a copy of it. The original I gave to the magnificent collection, perhaps the most complete of any author's literary estate, that is to be given[1] soon to Harvard, to be in the library that Tom loved. This letter may show you that things were not as you imagine them to have been after Tom went to another publisher,[2] by whom three[3] of his books were published after his death, with my coöperation.

The letter you refer to, at the end of "You Can't Go Home Again," is often thought by people to have been an actual letter sent to me. It was not. It is fiction, though its basis does rest upon Tom's relations with me. But our political divergence was actually of no great importance. It was something on the same principle as that of Erasmus and Luther (I realize the absurdity of suggesting any comparison between me and Erasmus). Those two both wanted the same thing, but Erasmus, a temperate man who thought that violence always defeated its own purpose, felt that the end should be worked toward gradually. Luther was impetuous and violent, and could not wait. I think Tom did have a foreboding of death, but he was no social outcast. To the contrary, he was greatly in demand, and enjoyed it. His plans were to go straight on with his writing and to live as he had always done. I think there is no danger but that that magnificent letter will be available in his books and in other books forever, and I think too that it was expressive of a great development.

[1] Gift of William B. Wisdom.   [2] Harper & Brothers.   [3] *The Web and the Rock, You Can't Go Home Again, The Hills Beyond.*

By the way, Franz Schoenberner is no hack reviewer. He is a very notable person, who left Germany on account of the Nazis, against whose coming he had fought bravely and brilliantly as editor of *Simplicissimus*. I was greatly interested and pleased by the article,[1] because of the character of the author and the fact that he had only lived here two years. He can see Tom in perspective, and more objectively than we Americans.

Ever sincerely yours,

TO G. P. BRETT, JR.

DEAR MR. BRETT:[2]   SEPT. 27, 1946

I am afraid I cannot coöperate with you as fully as I should wish in this matter because I did not read "Forever Amber."[3] I did look it over, to see what it was like, and my impression was that it was an honest piece of work and that, in respect to the great events of the Restoration and the character of the King and his brother, it was historically good — particularly the plague and the fire. I thought, too, that the ending was quite admirable. From what I saw of those doings that might result in what might be legally called obscenity, I should not suppose that there was anything in the book that could rightly be so described. The events were rather referred to as happening, than described. There was no attempt, that I could see, at salaciousness.

That is all I can say about the book because, as you know, a man becomes an editor because he loves books and then finds that he cannot possibly get time to read the books of any other publisher than the one he works for. That is too bad.

As to censorship of literature, while I must agree that there

[1] About Thomas Wolfe.   [2] President of the Macmillan Company.   [3] A novel by Kathleen Winsor, Macmillan, 1944.

are sometimes books which are deliberately contrived to appeal to vicious instincts, I believe that freedom of speech is the very basis of this nation, and that what damage, if any, may come from such books should be risked because of the much greater damage that would come if the principles of censorship were introduced and progressed. Nobody knows who is qualified to exercise censorship. I have read the opinions of various people of high repute, in the *Journal American* "Crusade" against salacious or obscene books, and most of them seem to me to have no understanding of literature at all. They constantly assert that writers introduced an element of salaciousness, as they called it, into books to make them sell. A true writer never wants to introduce that element. He does it because his book is a revelation of life — and life should be revealed as it is — and he generally hates it just as much as any genteel reader or censor, and generally much more, for he is bound to be a sensitive person if he is a true writer.

Ever sincerely yours,

TO TAYLOR CALDWELL

DEAR JANET:[1]   Nov. 18, 1946

I am sending you today through page 221.[2] I have not in-dicated many cuts, but all you can do will be valuable. One thing that bothers me is that Frank grows up too slowly — and when you come to his poems, I do not think anyone fourteen, or even fifteen, could be believed to have written them. He is very well done, and so is Paul but, "Sentimental Tommy" and "Oliver Twist" to the contrary, people do prefer to read about characters at least in their late teens, and the sooner you can get him there without sacrificing the admirable portrayal and

[1] Taylor Caldwell, in private life Mrs. Marcus Reback. [2] Of her novel, *There Was a Time*, Scribners, 1947.

incident, the better. And since the story is much more focussed upon this one character, other material is less important than it would have been in your other books, and can be cut.

In my reading, I have been trying to think of some way of giving the story more plot. Being the story of the growth of one who has in him genius, and of how this is deterred and developed in spite of everything, it does not need anything like as much plot as "This Side of Innocence,"[1] for instance. It isn't that kind of story. But if it had a little more, it would be good. If there were hints and suggestions to the reader that what occurred at a certain point was going to lead to something else, it would create a greater degree of suspense. Don't you think that girl that finally set Frank free, you might say, might even be seen by Frank at points in these pages? To do this would require some changes later, but not many. She could come as a child to Bison, to visit the uncle who made her his heir, and could just be occasionally seen, and not known at all. But the emphasis could be put upon her that could lead the reader to expect her to reappear. When Frank and Paul were rambling around, and Paul was responding to the beauty of trees and woods and all, he might easily on occasion see this girl and respond to her charm and grace, or whatever qualities you would give her. By the way, that little scene where the boys see the two little girls sitting on the fence is most admirable.

Always yours,

TO TAYLOR CALDWELL

DEAR JANET: DEC. 31, 1946

I am sending you a life of Thackeray,[2] and you will find that in the literary world of that day there was plenty of envy,

[1] By Taylor Caldwell, Scribners, 1946. [2] *The Showman of Vanity Fair*, by Lionel Stevenson, Scribners, 1946.

malice and hatred. There was even more in the Elizabethan day, and it resulted in a lot of amazingly good writing. That is always true, in the literary world as well as in others, and one must simply accept it, I suppose. It is absurd to say that writers are not good because their books sell in great numbers. How about Tolstoi — and he said that a writer's importance was to be gauged by the amount of pleasure and satisfaction that he gave.

Jack[1] is getting on well with the proof[2] and is finding great pleasure in reading it, and he has shown me the slight cuts that he has made, and his corrections. I am looking forward eagerly to seeing what you can send me of the book you are doing.

I am sorry that you are back among the blizzards, but really we are doing very well this winter — that is, I suppose Buffalo is relatively doing as well as New York. We have had no snow, and I have only worn an overcoat for about four or five days. A winter generally goes through its course the way it starts, so we may be lucky this time.

Another book you ought to read when you get around to it is "Of Making Many Books,"[3] because that shows the way writers are, too.

My best to Marcus.   Always yours,

TO ANN CHIDESTER

JAN. 6, 1947

DEAR ANN:

I do not think anyone can read "War and Peace" too much. I read it six times, and pieces of it to Johnny and Jerry.[4] It is

[1] John Hall Wheelock, an editor at Scribner's. [2] Of *There Was a Time,* by Taylor Caldwell, Scribners, 1947. [3] By Roger Burlingame, a book about Scribner authors and books, issued by Scribners on the occasion of their completing a hundred years of publishing, 1846–1946. [4] John and Jeremiah Gorsline, his grandsons.

said to be vastly better in the original, in point of style and language, but I really think maybe it is better for us that we do have to read it in a translation, for I think it might be too much of an influence, that one might tend to be overwhelmed by it, the other way, and to imitate it. I read "Smoke,"[1] and I know what you mean. When Scott[2] was writing "Tender Is the Night"[3] — he didn't think he ought to talk about the books he was doing, and so put it this way — he said that the whole motif was taken from Ludendorf's[4] memoirs. They were moving up the guns for the great Spring offensive in 1918, and Ludendorf said, "The song of the frogs on the river drowned the rumble of our artillery." When he told me this, it puzzled me, but when I read the book I realized that there was all this beautiful veneer, and rottenness and horror underneath. I am only saying this because of what you said about "The Great Gatsby."[5]

Anyway, you can feel sure that everybody here is for "Mama Maria's."[6]

Always yours,

DEAR ———:   FEB. 17, 1947

We are grateful for your letter about "I Chose Freedom."[7] We think the professor to whom you submitted it took exactly the right position. He believes in the free play of the intellect, and in discussion, as the only basis for a republic, and we think he is right. We took exactly the same position: we think that a partisan publisher is betraying his profession. He cannot publish at a loss, and so he must regard the economic factor, but he should be a channel for freedom of expression. You say that

---

[1] By Turgenev.   [2] F. Scott Fitzgerald.   [3] Scribners, 1934.   [4] Eric von Ludendorf, a German general, field-marshal in the First World War.   [5] By F. Scott Fitzgerald, Scribners, 1925.   [6] By Ann Chidester, Scribners, 1947.   [7] By Victor Kravchenko, Scribners, 1946.

you were surprised that we should stoop to publish this book. We did not, and we do not stoop. We know the author of this book. We carefully examined his authenticity and his history, because we thought that what he wrote might have a great influence, and that it was our duty to be as confident as one possibly could be of his honesty and knowledge. We found very good sources in this country, even in our own State Department, to support him. Whatever doubts we had, at the time of publication — and they were very slight — have been completely obliterated by our continued acquaintance with him. There is no question of his honesty and sincerity.

Now, as to the other matter. As I say, we as publishers are not partisan, but your side of the picture is not the only side. You think that there is a great and powerful nation with whom we may be at war, and that the way to avoid war is to be gentle, and compromising, and appeasing. Perhaps you are right. But I may remind you that just exactly such a situation existed in the 1930's, and there are those who think that if we had not been so gentle and appeasing, we might have avoided the horrible affliction of the last war. You give one point of view, but there is that other one, and the cases are not dissimilar. Hitler said he would Nazify the world, in "Mein Kampf." Lenin and Stalin have said they would communize the world, and there are those who think they are working at it. What we publishers think is that our function is to bring everything out into the open, on the theory that we have an adult population that knows values, or can learn them, and let them decide.

Ever sincerely yours,

The letter to the novelist and writer, Marcia Davenport, which follows, exemplifies the kind of detailed and constructive criticism which only an editor of unusual perception could offer.

The Scribner files reveal many instances in which Perkins made similar detailed suggestions, to a great variety of writers, but the following, like one or two other letters of the same sort in this collection, has been selected as representative.

TO MARCIA DAVENPORT

APRIL 28, 1947

DEAR MARCIA:

I think you have written a notable book[1] in a first draught but that it needs, as any book, to be revised. The revision should be almost only a matter of emphasis, for the scheme is right. Having borne the heat of the battle, you must not fail it now. It is a book about a person, Jessie, but it is also about New York, and that must never be forgotten. Jessie is a New Yorker who came out of the East Side and the West Side. In one week many things occur, quite naturally, which change her life and herself. In telling of these you should always keep the reader aware of New York, as you mostly do: when Jessie recalls the past, she should still be aware of the present, in motors, cabs, or walking, or in bed, or in a bath — as people always are. New York is a foremost character in the novel. Jessie is in a crisis of her own life, in New York, but in all her reflections, here and there, she is in the place she came out of, New York, and is aware of it. So you give New York, top to bottom, and that alone is a great thing to do. Make Jessie more aware, as she goes about in cars, cabs and afoot, of the way New York is, of how Fifth Avenue looks in the haze of afternoon, or whatever, even when she is lost in the past. This means that you should emphasize what you have already done. A person, like Jessie, walks or drives along a street in deep reflection, but is still aware of how it

[1] *East Side, West Side*, Scribners, 1947.

looks, and of its *quality*. So get that in more, by a touch here
and there, to make this book realize one of its great motives,
to give New York as only an East Side, West Side New Yorker
knows it. You have done this, really, but emphasize it — and
the fact that these Park Avenuers, etc., don't belong to it, don't
really like it, but that the children of immigrants who never
got out of it, even Jessie and Mark and others, do belong and
love it and couldn't for long be anywhere else. So make the
book say that, by blending Jessie's present with the past as she
recalls it. The reader must be aware of time and place, as it is
and as she remembers it. That is what you intended, and means
only an occasional reference to give a sense — by sight or smell
or whatever — of a spot of New York. In truth, I only know
this from what you have said and written, so you have done it.
But strengthen it. For instance, you tell of her in a taxicab as
being *oblivious* to the ugliness of the street. I think she should
be *aware*. People are oblivious only momentarily. And in this
book that gives New York through Jessie, you must not have
her oblivious unless she has to be — which would be briefly.
I ought not to be telling you, because you told me: maybe the
biggest thing this book can do is to give a realization of this
unique place, New York.

But the book is also about Jessie, who is an indigenous New
Yorker, as her mother, the child of immigrants, was. Her character and talent brought her into wealth, and into the society
of the upper East Side, but never even blurred her sense of
reality, her sense of values. Jessie, her daughter, would have
inherited and learned that sense of things, and so, as you have
it, she would, as she did, have worked. (I think you should
have had her work on the *World,* and not on a literary-sound-
ing review.) She gave up working when she married — this
should be made plain — which was even more natural for her
when the depression made those who had money, or some, feel

ashamed to keep a job from someone who needed it. But in
the week of the book, and early in it, I think you should show
that it was on Jessie's conscience that she was not pulling her
weight, as it would be. And at the end of the book you should
show, perhaps even in only a paragraph, that she was through
with that, that this week of crisis had changed her, and re-
stored her sense of values — those of her mother and, I hope
we could say, of all true New Yorkers. Anyhow, New Yorkers
are not fooled by any pomps and vanities or by the sinful lusts
of the flesh. They know them for what they are, and may like
them, but they reverence nothing. Jessie is real and not un-
human, but she is too much always in the right and Brandon
too much in the wrong. About that I don't know what you can
do, except by having Jessie realize that in some ways she had
been exasperating, and by the use of two more outside scenes.
You have the one where the two women who knew her recall
Rosa Landan. One could say this violated the scheme of your
book — that all should be presented through Jessie's senses.
That scene is essential, I think. But it would be less obtrusive
if you added *two* others, and one of them could be where people
commented on Jessie, and more or less unfavorably. But the
great thing is to have Jessie come out of this book as a woman
different from when she went in. That you must do. She's been
through too much to be the same. It was a week of culmina-
tion. It must end, must indicate a changed life for Jessie. Must
be conclusive.

So much for generalizations — forgive me for telling you what
I know you know and most of which you told me — and now
to come to particulars. Perhaps for that I should have kept the
manuscript by me. But I did make notations on the margin,
up to the last hundred or hundred and fifty pages. There was
nothing to be said against them, I thought, except that some
of the speeches were too long to be natural, though great

novelists have made them so and perhaps rightly. Writing, like drawing, is an art, and whatever conveys the *meaning* is justified. But I think, as we are today, that when Mark talks so long among his people, without interruption and a fresh start, or even Jerome Block (who is grand), the effect is reduced, because it seems unnatural. Just consider this a little. If I'm right, a few trifling interpolations, here and there, will make amends.

You say you will have to rewrite the first chapter in the light of the last, and that is right in principle, but I have no fault to find with it. But work it in there that she has worked and thinks she should. And I think there should be more about Matthew Kernan.

I put a note on page 30, which said: "Generalizations are no use — give one specific thing and let the action say it." Can't recall the instance, but it's true. By the way, don't they still have an orchestra on the Staten Island boats — they do on others — and would you be phony to have one play for Jessie and Mark, some old-time song? They could ask for it. Even if not true, I think it would be fair. They have music on the ferry to Blauvelt.

I should have kept the manuscript, but look at notes on pages. When you have people talking, you have a scene. You must interrupt with explanatory paragraphs, but shorten them as much as you can. Dialogue is *action*. You can't take the reader's attention from it much without impairing its effect. Think of watching a duel, with someone explaining the *why* of it. I think this was about Millicent, that there you do too much explaining. The action and dialogue, which is action, should do it. They can't do it altogether, but you don't trust them enough. You must interpolate and explain, but you tend to overdo it.

The truth is you're right, you can't see a book before the

end. It must be revised in the light of the end. Now there are two weak scenes in this book, where you were "planting" things that have to be there. They are weak only at the start, where you tell, expositionally, of the various people present. Ideally, you should let them come in and *reveal* themselves in talk and action. You can't, but I think you should trust more to the talk and action. One scene is the committee meeting and the other is the Stillman dinner. (Let me put this in as I think of it: You must make people talk, as they do, in elision. Not, "You will," but "You'll" etc., all through.)

On page 55, or thereabouts, I have made a note that your exposition stops the action for too long, that too much is explained that comes out anyhow.

Lorraine and the dog are very good, and might even be somewhat enlarged upon. She is a real type, all over New York's East Side.

A little thereafter, Jessie is preparing dinner, shelling peas. And she remembers about Brandon and how he had acted. In this, while she is remembering, you should still have Jessie aware of New York.

Wherever you bring in the sounds of the East River, and the scene, you always do wonders, and I don't think you could overdo it.

Chapter 6, page 111. The Stillmans' dinner party. I have commented on this. It just needs to be pulled together and organized. More should be said by the action and the talk. It gets to be all right when Mark turns up, but I think you might make more of Stillman's telephonitis, and if you could explain the characters by what they did and said, in the early part of the chapter, it would be better. Then they go home. Just emphasize New York. Couldn't you make more of their drive up, I think, Fifth Avenue in the dark, in brief description, which you do excellently well. But about Mark and herself, I think you explain what the reader gets by inference. What they say and do tells all. You tend to explain too much. You must explain, but your tendency is to distrust your own narrative and dialogue.

I may be getting out of order, not having the manuscript, but when they have that dinner before the play, you explain too much. Once they get to talking, everything is right.

Now we come to Thursday. My notes say, "Cut down Anna and Sarah somewhat." The cat, Putzl, is good and he, or she, should be brought in several times, later in the story, and not just here.

Now we come to the committee meeting. Make the people come out through talk and act, just as far as you possibly can. Avoid all possible exposition. You introduce characters, such as Althea Crowe, who reveal themselves in what they say and do. But then you stop the narrative to explain what should come out in the movement of the story.

When Mark comes to dine with Jessie, you have the chance to bring out all about her work — the work she did on the *World* — and why she isn't doing it now. She could just simply say it. She could tell why she stopped.

Wednesday. This is where she remembers the agonizing time when, because Brandon wanted it, she was pregnant. Helen Lee comes and, after Helen Lee goes, she remembers. But even here, along with her remembrance, you should keep her aware of the present. It is Jessie *now,* remembering her mother's death.

I think the brief chapter which breaks into the scheme of the book, where Serena and her friend, waiting for Serena's car, talk of Jessie, is admirable. But since you have to have this chapter, I think it would be well, as I have said, to have two other chapters, and in one of them you could have people talk about Jessie in a way to show that she was fallible herself.

Iris's call is good, very effective in showing the aspect of

New York life that she represents. If anything, it might be enlarged upon.

Then, when Jessie is in her bath she remembers. This is a good example of what I mean. She would be absorbed in her memories, but still she would be aware of her bath, and of the sound of the river, and of New York. She should realize at the same time, through interpolations of the present, both the past and the present.

Again, after they realize the deadly character of Rosa's illness and go there to dinner, which is good, Brandon wants her to have a child. She agrees to it. This is told in memory and somehow, during those memories, the reader should be aware of what was going on in the present. I forget exactly where she was, but at one time her memories come while she is walking. There, too, I think you ought to break in upon her abstractions with things she notices, so that the reader will be conscious of the present, as she would be, even while the concentration is upon the past. Always the present and New York should be kept in.

I did think that perhaps you overdo Brandon's brutality during the period when she was in all those agonies of pregnancy. I have a note, "Around page 319: too obstetrical and should be cut, and compressed."

Then, we come to her going to market, and that is very good. And then, later, to the theater. There is the dinner party at the night club, before it, and there you begin again with too much generalization. Try to make the people stand out through the dialogue and action. I think they almost would do it alone, but you do not put enough confidence into your dialogue and action.

Then you come to the play. Everything is right with this, excepting that it would be better if you could give some running account of the action of the play. I know what play it was, I suppose, and I realize that you do not want to put that failure before the reader, for the sake of the author. But couldn't you just give snatches of some imaginary play, so as to make the whole thing more actual? Couldn't you invent a play, of which you would only have to give trifles, that was somewhat parallel to the real one?

The Elizabeth Betts incident of the party is extremely good. The rest, I think, might stand compression.

You really know all about this book yourself. It is true that Althea's loyalty — though one knows right away what kind of person she was and that she would be loyal — should be based upon something more than the reader is given. I do think you should account for this, for her strong feeling for Jessie, through Jessie's memory.

I do have some fear that the murder runs too far toward melodrama, but not so much in what quite plausibly happens. But, in revision, I would think of that danger. When Serena Lowdon tells them off, she does it wonderfully. Even so, I would try to compress what she says, because I think she too speaks at greater length than people actually do speak at unless they have been prepared in advance, which she was not. She was speaking out of her emotions and her character, without forethought. I have argued to that effect about Mark's talk to his people, which is very good, as they are, and about Bloch. Mark begins to speak on page 530, I think. I would try to have more questions thrown in while he is speaking.

I have referred to it before. It is on page 593, where you have Jessie oblivious. The story is told through Jessie's senses almost wholly, and she must not be oblivious. You might be, for a block or so, but when you were stopped by a traffic light it would bring you back to awareness of the present.

I have referred to the Staten Island ferry. I hope you can find it rightful to have music on it, and that maybe they could ask for some old New York song. I think you could do it, even if they do not any longer have three-piece orchestras there.

If this book can give the quality of New York and show the wonderful people, mostly the descendants of immigrants, as the real New Yorkers, and also at the same time show the corruption among people of wealth and supposedly of culture, who just live here without belonging, it will be a very great achievement in that alone. It could be simply the story of Jessie, a woman whose life comes to a week of crisis in which she must come to conclusions with all the most important things in her life. That would be enough in itself. But if you can only get all this meaning into it — and it is in it, in fact — about New York, and also the situation the world is in, which comes out when she goes with Mark to visit his Czech relatives, you will have done wonders. To accomplish this, you need only to intensify throughout what actually is there — and I think you would naturally do this in the revision, anyhow. It is largely a matter of compression, and not so much of that, really. It is, as you said, that you can't know a book until you come to the end of it, and then all the rest must be modified to fit that.

Always yours,

TO ALAN PATON

MAY 6, 1947

DEAR MR. PATON:

I am sending you our contract for the publication of "Cry, the Beloved Country."[1] You will see that we are limiting ourselves to the United States and Canada because of your wish to arrange publication in South Africa. I do think, though, that that should be done in connection with a London publisher, and

[1] By Alan Paton, Scribners, 1948.

since Jonathan Cape[1] turned up here, I told him I would let him see the manuscript. He is a good publisher, and if he is interested he will write to you, or will report to me.

I think the book is a very fine one, and you come to realize in the end that the real protagonist is the beautiful and tragic land of South Africa, but if you come to the human hero, it is the Zulu pastor,[2] and he is grand. One might say that the last third of the book is something of an anti-climax, but I don't think one should look at it in a conventional way. It gives an extraordinary realization of the country and of the race problem, not as a problem but as a situation. It is a sad book, but that is as it should be. So was the Iliad and so is the Bible. But as Ecclesiastes says, "The earth endureth forever."

I suppose this letter will be in Johannesburg when you get there, for I am sending it air mail. We'll await your corrections impatiently, in order to get into type.

Ever sincerely yours,

TO JAMES JONES

MAY 9, 1947

DEAR MR. JONES:

I hope you may get to New York, and that we may have a talk. "The Laughter"[3] manuscript has come, and I'll hold it until I see you anyhow.

Did you ever read a good book about the Elizabethans? It was those people, I think, and perhaps also François Villon, that I was thinking of when I said that about there not being enough great rascals among the writers. Marlowe, Greene, Nash, and a dozen others, were always in all kinds of trouble,

---

[1] Publisher of *Cry, the Beloved Country* in England.   [2] Stephen Kumalo.   [3] A novel by James Jones, not yet published.

and quite a bit of their writing was done in envy, malice, and hate. It was because they were so crowded with emotions that they were in trouble, and that some of them were actually rascals. Yet some of them were magnificent men, in truth, including Greene, who left his wife in the country and went to London and went to the devil as fast as he could, and then wrote one of the most moving letters that ever was written to a woman, just before he died. And he was such a great writer because he was capable of all the rest. But one could talk of such things indefinitely, and talking would be better than writing.

Now, although this matter does not concern you for the moment, since you are not writing about people you know, though one must write from his own frame of reference as somebody called it — that is, he must really write in some sense out of his experience — I do not think that for one to write about people he knows is the betrayal it is often represented as being. A daughter of Tolstoi's once told me that most of the people in "War and Peace" were identifiable to anyone in the Tolstoi family, and many of them were derived from them. Nobody could call him an S.O.B. I remember the horror with which I realized, when working with Thomas Wolfe on his manuscript of "The Angel,"[1] that all these people were almost completely real, that the book was literally autobiographical. I had thought that it was only so in the way that "David Copperfield" was, or Thackeray's "Pendennis." Tom saw how I felt, from my expression, I suppose, and he said, "But you don't understand. I think that they are great people." He meant his mother and father, and so on. Anyhow, the book was a great book, and there wasn't anything to be done about it, but it did give great pain for a time. In the end, everybody in it was glad he was in it. And, anyhow, Tom was doing the only thing he could do,

[1] *Look Homeward, Angel*, Scribners, 1929.

and the thing he had to do. And it was a horrible crime that
he should have departed from his inevitable scheme by trying
to change his mother into an aunt, and himself, who had been
Eugene, into George Webber.[1] He should never have violated
his own plan. Well, Tom could certainly not have been called
a rascal, he was more like an archangel, but he did have that
turbulent nature that those others had which sometimes makes
a man both an archangel and a rascal. We all think that Frank
Harris was a notable writer, and he really did come mighty
close to being an S.O.B., if not quite.

But if you come to New York, we could talk about these
things, and I hope you will.

                              Ever sincerely yours,

                    TO JAMES JONES

                                        MAY 28, 1947

DEAR MR. JONES:

I have read your letter several times, but I do not know the
book[2] well enough to be able to visualize it as a whole, and so
I cannot fully understand the significance of the ways in which
you are dealing with the parts. But wherever I can understand
them, I agree with what you say. For instance, the motivation
in the case of Prew — his having blinded the man, etc. — seems
to me a distinct improvement and, in fact, almost everything
you say seems to me to go in the right direction. For instance,
the shooting of Prew seems to me very good and dramatic. And

---

[1] These changes were made by Wolfe after he left Scribners, and appear in the
three books published by Harper & Bros.: *The Web and the Rock*, 1939; *You Can't
Go Home Again*, 1940; *The Hills Beyond*, 1941. The changes were made in an
effort to escape the charge that his writing was solely autobiographical.   [2] Perkins
here refers to the manuscript, as yet unfinished at that time, of James Jones's novel
of World War II, to be published by Scribners in the near future under the title
From Here to Eternity.

I think your plot — about which you ought not to concern your-self so much — is right, if you can adhere to your principle, that the events must rise out of the actual characters and their environments.

I share your distrust for the artificiality of plots but, after all, the greatest of all novels had several of them, "War and Peace." And do you remember the extraordinary coincidence of the, supposedly killed at Austerlitz, Andrei returning to his father's estate on the very night when the little Princess was to die in childbirth? I think it would be much better to read that book over and over, to the neglect of books on the art of fiction.

But when you come to such books, I could name you, and could probably get you, much better ones than you have been reading, except for Ellen Glasgow — and didn't she say in there[1] somewhere that a writer should read all of them and then *forget* them? For instance, there is one we published by Henry James,[2] made up from prefaces, and there was one called "The Art of the Novel," I think, by Lubbock,[3] and some book[4] which gathered together Chekov's comment on fiction, in letters which were wonderful. And E. M. Forster wrote very well on fiction in a book[5] I know I have but cannot recall the name of, in which he finally said that the novel never could be wholly satis-factory because, in the end, a writer could not avoid the ar-tificiality of accounting for all its significant characters. In life, a lot of them just disappear, but once you have fixed the reader's interest upon a character, you can't let that happen, and if you account for him near the end by having a telegram announce his death, which would be natural enough in life, it seems phony. But I won't send you any of these books until you

[1] In *A Certain Measure: An Interpretation of Prose Fiction*, Doubleday, 1943.
[2] *The Art of the Novel, Critical Prefaces to the New York Edition of His Works*, by Henry James, with an Introduction by R. P. Blackmur, Scribners, 1934. [3] *The Craft of Fiction* by Percy Lubbock, Scribners, 1921. [4] *Letters on the Short Story, the Drama, and Other Literary Topics*, selected and edited by Louis S. Friedland, Minton, Balch, 1924. [5] *Aspects of the Novel*, Harcourt, Brace, 1927.

finish your novel, for I do not think you ought to read about writing while you are writing.

Yesterday, without naming you, I was trying to explain to a prominent and able writer what you were trying to get across in your book, and the great difficulties of it. It would have been much easier to make a man writer understand, but I think she did, for she is very intuitive. Then I told her you had been reading "——," and she was shocked by that and agreed with me that while writing you should not be reading about writing. But then she spoke of a book[1] which was not about writing, but which by inference enormously illuminates the problem. I have sent you that. I had read it years ago and thought it most revealing. It is concerned with painting, and is derived from the lectures of Robert Henri.

I can understand the value of "The Last Tycoon,"[2] and that it was enhanced for you in not having been completed. But, of course, each writer must have his own method. Hemingway didn't know, except in the most general sense, the story he was going to unfold in "For Whom the Bell Tolls,"[3] and, by the way, it took him five years, I think, to write that. He is not nearly through the one he has been working on now for two and a half years. You are all right on time, except for the fact that time is the enemy of us all, and especially of the writer. But don't become obsessed with that feeling, as Tom Wolfe did.

I do get a little afraid that in thinking of the theory, and so much of the plot — though I suppose you cannot avoid it — you may become sort of muscle-bound. That is, you must be flexible. A deft man may toss his hat across the office and hang it on a hook if he just naturally does it, but he will always miss if he does it consciously. That is a ridiculous and extreme analogy, but there is something in it.   Ever sincerely yours,

[1] *The Art Spirit*, compiled by Margery Ryerson, Lippincott, 1923.   [2] By Scott Fitzgerald, Scribners, 1941.   [3] Scribners, 1940.

MAY 29, 1947

DEAR ——— :

The point is that any sort of censorship is extremely dangerous. Nobody is wise enough to be a censor. When the Catholic
Church and the *Journal American* were campaigning against
obscenity in books, many opinions were published by men of
eminence in support of the campaign. I read all of them. Not
one of these men knew what good writers are about. Almost
every one said that they introduced what you call "sexy material" into their books in order to make them sell. Good writers
never do that. Good writers are much more sensitive than other
people, both to the beautiful and the ugly, both to virtue and
to vice. They all hate vice, but it is part of what they see, and
what they must tell to reveal reality, and to make others aware
of it. You named certain writers to whom the most prudish
could not object. I would maintain that such writers too would
be impaired if we were not allowed free play of expression.
Scott, Tennyson, and Irving would not have been what they
were, were it not for such writers as Chaucer, Shakespeare,
and all those Elizabethans, who all had in them many passages
that people who hold your view regard as obscene.

And, after all, what is the "argument" of "The Heller"?[1]
It is that there is a state of society here which causes some
young people to act in the way this girl did — and to that
extent this book is a severe criticism of American society — but
that there is also, even in such young people, or at least in the
one in this book, a basic wholesomeness and loyalty which leads
the reader to conclude that her marriage will be good, and that
she will lead a loyal and wholesome life, though not — because
of the defects of our society — upon a high level. It often puz-
zles me when people think that matters connected with sex

[1] A novel by William E. Henning, Scribners, 1947.

should be suppressed. Sex itself cannot be suppressed, and the efforts to do it, it seems to me, generally result in greater damage than it can do itself. After all, it was not an invention of man, but of God. We are not to blame for it. We are to blame, perhaps, for the abuse of it, but that usually comes from ignorance, which results from suppression and censorship. The way to kill germs and maggots is to bring them into the open, where they are recognized for what they are. It is when they are allowed to propagate under stones and in darkness that they can grow strong and more harmful.

You speak contemptuously of the author of this book. We are informed that since 1929, when he was eighteen and was graduated from high school, he has been an artist, a mural painter and, in order to carry on economically, a commercial artist at times. He had always certain literary aspirations, and at one time published a magazine which, of course, could not have been a commercial success. He married in 1940, and then gave many hours out of every twenty-four to learning to write. He thinks that his first stories were not very good, and they were not published. Then he finally produced "The Heller." He says: "I like the freshness of people of eighteen; they're real personalities by that time, they exist in a world of first-hand experiences. When they meet each other on the street, do they stop, piously talk about the weather and politics? No. They let out a heartfelt scream, and then it is how was your date, whadja wear, whendja get in, whadja do? They're concerned about things that actually happened, and happened to *them*. Working all day and writing all night takes most of my time, but when my wife can pry me loose I enjoy such ordinary things as movies, swimming, dancing." It seems to me that, in view of these facts, your estimate of him is inaccurate.

Ever sincerely yours,

JUNE 4, 1947

DEAR KATHARINE:

I had been thinking about you and Struthers.[1] I had meant to write. "Close Pursuit"[2] has sold about 15,000 copies. I think that it showed that you have a great talent for what we call the "historical novel." That would lead me to favor your doing the story of two American families, which would be in some degree a historical novel. I would vote for that, rather than for the psychological one. But you must write what you want to write, and I am not trying to beguile you.

I am deeply sorry that Struthers is not well enough for anything. I know he had a bad time, but I had hoped that everything was right by now. I would like to hear more about the way he is. There is nothing that I'd like better than having a talk with you and Struthers. Maybe we can do it at the end of the summer.

Do you remember when you wrote "The Branding Iron"[3] that I said you had used about seven plots in one book? It is a curious thing anyone could have such wealth of invention, but I think that even now you tend to too much plot. Even in "Close Pursuit," I think you did, and I tried to think of ways of simplification. But the whole thing was so closely interwoven that it seemed to me no change should be suggested. But in this new book, which I hope will be the tale of the two families, do consider whether I am not right in thinking that you carry a remarkable virtue somewhat too far in plotting.

I saw young James Boyd yesterday, and we talked about Nat's[4] book, though he had not really read it. As for prices, I

---

[1] Struthers Burt, the writer, husband of Katharine Newlin Burt.　[2] A novel by Katharine Newlin Burt, Scribners, 1947.　[3] Scribners, 1919.　[4] Nathaniel Burt, whose book of poems, *Rooms in a House and Other Poems,* was issued by Scribners in 1947.

am afraid you will be more appalled as time goes on. Costs of manufacture have risen one hundred percent in the last six years, mostly on account of increased wages.

My best to Struthers.

Always yours,

JUNE 4, 1947

DEAR ——:

This is in answer to your letter of May 29[1] with regard to certain passages in the tale of Aladdin in "The Arabian Nights." We deeply sympathize, as individuals, with the development of better understanding among all groups, but we do not think that in this country there should be any groups, as was the intention of its Founders, and we deplore, as individuals, the development of group consciousness. While we are, therefore, wholly in favor of the intentions of your League,[2] it does not seem to us as publishers that it would be proper for us to edit a classic of some centuries' standing. Only the author would have the right to do that, it seems to us, and if we did it, we should in some degree betray an obligation to our profession.

Nowadays, publishers are under pressure from all sorts of groups. What if they should trim their books to suit every point of view and every element of religious and racial pride? What, then, would remain of that one relatively free realm left, the republic of letters?

Ever sincerely yours,

---

[1] A letter requesting the removal, in future editions, of certain passages involving Jewish characters.   [2] The Anti-Defamation League.

INDEX

INDEX

"Absolution," by F. Scott Fitzgerald, 36, 47

Across the Busy Years, by Nicholas Murray Butler, 145, 169

Acton, Lord, 276

Adams, James Truslow, 185, 190, 195

"Adjuster," by F. Scott Fitzgerald, 47

Adventures of General Marbot, 153

Aldanov, Mark, 270 n.

Aleck Maury, Sportsman, by Caroline Gordon, 86

All Good Americans, by Jerome Bahr, 118

American, The, by James Truslow Adams, 185, 190

American As He Is, The, by Nicholas M. Butler, 145

American Earth, by Erskine Caldwell, 66 n.

American Fiction, by Joseph Warren Beach, 188

American Mercury, the, 36

Americanization of Edward Bok, The, by Edward Bok, 35

America's Coming-of-Age, by Van Wyck Brooks, 9, 10 n.

Anatomy of Bibliomania, 83

Anderson, Sherwood, 165, 167, 224, 274

Angels on Toast, by Dawn Powell, 165 n., 175 n.

Annals of the Poets, by Chard Powers Smith, 80

Anti-Defamation League, the, 303

Arabian Nights, The, 303

Arizona, 28

Arlen, Michael, 139 n.

Armed Services Editions, 263, 267, 268

Armies March, The, by John Cudahy, 210

Art of the Novel, The, by Henry James, 298 n.

Art Spirit, The, compiled by Margery Ryerson, 299 n.

Artillery of Time, by Chard Powers Smith, 146, 194

Asheville, N. C., 130 n.

Aspects of the Novel, by E. M. Forster, 298 n.

Aswell, Edward, 228

Athens, 14

Atlantic Monthly, the, 170, 229 n.

Austen, Jane, 191, 195

Awakening, by John Galsworthy, 27, 28

"Baby Party," by F. Scott Fitzgerald, 47

Bahr, Jerome, 118 n.

Baker, Ray Stannard, 169, 171

Barrie, Sir James M., 38, 207, 208

Barrie, the Story of J. M. B., by Denis Mackail, 185 n.

Baskin, Norton, 232, 236

Basso, Hamilton, 105, 130, 134, 159

Bastard, The, by Erskine Caldwell, 67

Beach, Joseph Warren, 188

Beautiful and Damned, The, by F. Scott Fitzgerald, 22 n., 30, 32

"Beauty Persists," by Struthers Burt, 45

Bemis, Lawrence, 268

Bergman, Ingrid, 207

Bernstein, Aline, 187, 224

Bessie, Alvah, 154

Best Short Stories of 1925, The, edited by Edward O'Brien, 47

Between the Dark and the Daylight, by Nancy Hale, 210 n.

Bhimsa, the Dancing Bear, by Christine Weston, 257–262

Bierce, Ambrose, 201 n., 205, 206

Binns, Archie, 147

Birch, Reginald, 57

Bishop, John Peale, 188

Blackmur, R. P., 298 n.

Blood, Sweat and Tears, by Winston Churchill, 162 n.

Bok, Edward, 33
Bond, Alice D., 246
Book of My Youth, The, by Ray Stannard Baker, 171
Book of the Month Club, the, 128
Boswell, James, 145, 147
Boyd, Betty Grace, 216
Boyd, Daniel Lamont, 268 and n.
Boyd, James, 41, 49, 50, 55, 65, 89, 257–259, 267, 268
Boyd, Mrs. James, 41, 42
Boyd, James, Jr., 268, 270, 302
Boyd, Madeleine, 60, 61, 71
Boyd, Thomas, 56, 203, 216 n.
Brace, Donald, 151
Brady, Mathew B., 248
"Brahma," by Emerson, 243
Branding Iron, The, by Katharine Newlin Burt, 302
Brandt, Carl, 193
Brett, G. P., Jr., 280
Brickell, Herschel, 95, 113
Bridges, Robert, 22
Briffault, Robert, 110 n., 136, 227
Broken Journey, A, by Morley Callaghan, 75
Brontë, Charlotte, 191
Brooks, Alden, 204, 214
Brooks, Corinne, 214
Brooks, Van Wyck, 9, 10, 30, 48, 224
Brown, Mrs. Slater, 206
Brownell, William Crary, 9, 10, 26, 42
Browning, Robert, 208
Bryan, William Jennings, 168, 169
Burial of the Guns, The, by Thomas Nelson Page, 202
Burke, W. J., 149
Burlingame, Roger, 56
Burns, Robert, 80
Burt, Katharine Newlin, 51 n., 55, 302
Burt, Nathaniel, 302
Burt, Struthers, 43, 44, 51, 55, 164 n., 227, 257–259, 302
Butler, Nicholas Murray, 145, 169, 277
Butler, Samuel, 22
Byron, Lord, 80, 269 n., 270 n.

Caballa, by Thornton Wilder, 80
Cabell, James Branch, 251
Caldwell, Erskine, 66, 263

Caldwell, Taylor, 137 n., 142, 227, 281, 282
Callaghan, Morley, 74
Canby, Henry Seidel, 57
Cape, Jonathan, 78, 157, 295
Caravan, by John Galsworthy, 63
Carlyle, Thomas, 34, 207, 208
Carter, John, 189, 190
Cather, Willa, 251
Catholic Church, The, 300
Certain Measure, A, by Ellen Glasgow, 298 n.
Chamberlain, John, 102
Chapin, Joseph Hawley, 43, 56, 57
Chatham Walk, 91
Chelsea Hotel, the, 134
Cherio's Restaurant, 147
Chidester, Ann, 199, 232, 271, 283
Children's Homer, The, Padraic Colum's, 225
Churchill, Winston S., 161, 162, 181, 189, 190, 201, 211
Civil War, the, 126, 182, 243
Clarendon, Lord, 47, 161
Cloister and the Hearth, The, 195
Close Pursuit, by Katharine Newlin Burt, 302
Clough, Arthur, 189
Cohn, Captain Louis H., 64
Colcorton, by Edith Pope, 230–232, 237
Colum, Mary M., 47, 128
Colum, Padraic, 224, 225
Concord, N. H., 232
Connecticut River, the, 232
Copeland, Charles Townsend, 145, 149, 160, 189, 191
Cosmopolitan, the, 52
"Countryside, The," by Struthers Burt, 45
Courthouse Square, by Hamilton Basso, 105, 134
Cowboys North and South, by Will James, 42
Cowden, R. W., 264
Cowley, Malcolm, 236
"Cracker Chidlings," by Marjorie Rawlings, 247
Craft of Fiction, The, by Percy Lubbock, 298 n.
Crane, Stephen, 201, 271

Unknown War, The, by Winston Churchill, 161

Valley of Decision, The, by Marcia Davenport, 196
Van Dine, S. S., 53 n., 214, 227, 246, 247
Van Gelder, Robert, 209
Venturi, Lionello, 265
Villon, François, 295
"Voice in the Wind," 250
Volkening, Henry, 259
von Schlieffen, 211

Wallace, Henry, 239
War and Peace, by Tolstoi, 2, 36, 64, 129, 144, 201, 265, 283, 296, 298
Wartels, Nat, 203
Web and the Rock, The, by Thomas Wolfe, 183, 227 n., 228 n., 279 n., 297 n.
Webb, Beatrice and Sidney, 245
Weber, William C., 157
Wecter, Dixon, 168, 182, 184
Weed, Clive, 57
Weeks, Edward, 170
Wells, H. G., 181
Wendell, Barrett, 190, 191
Wertenbaker, Mrs. Charles, 126; *see also* Nancy Hale
West with the Night, by B. Markham, 204
Weston, Christine, 227, 259
Wheelock, John Hall, 44, 45, 71, 102, 123, 148, 249, 250, 283
When I Grew Up to Middle Age, by Struthers Burt, 44, 45
When the Whippoorwill, by Marjorie Kinnan Rawlings, 150, 193
White, Leigh, 275
White, William C., 276
White River, The, 151, 232
Why I Am An American, 164, 167 n.
Wilcox, Charles, 205
Wilder, Thornton, 80
Will Shakspere and the Dyer's Hand, by Alden Brooks, 204, 214
Willkie, Wendell, 232

Wilson, Edmund, 188, 224 and n., 229, 271
Windsor, Vermont, 163, 220, 235
Wine of the Country, by Hamilton Basso, 159
Winter in Taos, by Mabel Dodge Luhan, 117
Wisdom, William B., 183, 187, 223, 250, 279
Wister, Owen, 154
Wizard of Oz, The, 260
Wolfe, Fred, 104, 133, 139, 140
Wolfe, Thomas, 2, 60, 61, 68–72, 77, 88, 90, 91, 93, 98–101, 104, 106, 110, 115, 116, 118, 119, 121, 130, 132–135, 139, 140, 142, 148, 179, 183, 184, 187, 188, 200, 208, 224–229, 239, 247, 249, 250, 257, 276, 278, 279, 296, 297, 299
Women on the Porch, The, by Caroline Gordon, 244
Worcester *Spy,* the, 34
World and Thomas Kelly, The, by Arthur Train, 16
World Today, The, by Nicholas Murray Butler, 278
World Was My Garden, The, by David Fairchild, 192
Wound and the Bow, The, by Edmund Wilson, 188
Wright, Willard Huntington, 53, 214 n., 215, 247; *see also* S. S. Van Dine
Writers in Crisis, by Maxwell Geismar, 188, 222
Writing and Writers, by Robert Van Gelder, 209 n.
Wyckoff, Irma, 188 n., 225

Yearling, The, by Marjorie Kinnan Rawlings, 83, 86, 113, 135, 139, 193, 237, 276
You Can't Go Home Again, by Thomas Wolfe, 183 n., 227 n., 228 n., 278, 279 n., 297 n.
Young, Stark, 45, 58, 61, 94, 95, 103, 192
Young Pandora, by Ann Chidester, 199

John Hall Wheelock (1886–1978), the editor of this volume, was for many years a colleague and close associate of Max Perkins at Scribners, and succeeded him as Senior Editor. He was also a distinguished poet, whom Allen Tate called "one of the best poets in English." His most recent volume, published posthumously, is *This Blessed Earth*.

Marcia Davenport, one of Max Perkins's most gifted writers, first came to Scribner's as the author of the highly acclaimed biography of Mozart, which was followed by five successful novels and, most recently, by her autobiography, *Too Strong for Fantasy*.

Crichton, Kyle, 137
Cromwell, Oliver, 241
Cross Creek, 232
Cross Creek, by Marjorie Kinnan Rawlings, 164, 175–180, 275
Cruikshank, George, 254
Cry, the Beloved Country, by Alan Paton, 294
Cudahy, John, 210

Darrow, Whitney, 69, 71, 72, 275
Davenport, Marcia, 79, 196, 227, 232, 247, 285, 286
Davenport, Russell, 79, 232
David Copperfield, by Charles Dickens, 144
Death in the Afternoon, by Ernest Hemingway, 77, 78, 90
Decline of the West, by Spengler, 47
Defoe, Daniel, 2, 131, 161
Dickens, Charles, 254, 271
Dodd, Mead & Co., 162
Dodge, Mabel, *see* Luhan
Dollar Book Club, The, 263
Don Quixote, 114
Dorrance, Ward, 148
Dos Passos, John, 58, 73, 181, 250
Doubleday & Co., 68
Dreiser, Theodore, 48, 271
Drums, by James Boyd, 41
Duffield, Pitts, 10
Dunn, Charles F., 44, 45
Dupré, Anne and Paul, 240 n., 241
"Dust," by Struthers Burt, 45
Dwell in the Wilderness, by Alvah Bessie, 154 n.
Dynasty of Death, The, by Taylor Caldwell, 137, 143

East Side, West Side, by Marcia Davenport, 286
Eastman, Max, 209
Eighteen Poems, by James Boyd, 268
Elizabethans, The, 295, 300
Emerson, Ralph Waldo, 243
Empire on the Seven Seas, by James Truslow Adams, 195
England, 211, 212
Erasmus, 125, 182, 242, 279
Etchison, Annie Laurie, 192
Europa, by Robert Briffault, 110

Europa in Limbo, by Robert Briffault, 137
Evans, C. S., 64
Evarts, Mary, 218, 219, 220
Evarts, William (cousin), 221
Evarts, William Maxwell (grandfather), 218 n., 220

Fairchild, David, 192
Falconry, by Russell and Sargent, 155 n.
Farewell to Arms, A, by Ernest Hemingway, 193, 251
Farrar, John, 164
Faulkner, William, 251
Fear of Books, The, by Holbrook Jackson, 83
Federalist Papers, The, by Alexander Hamilton, 255
Fifth Column, The, by Ernest Hemingway, 159
Fifth Column and the First Forty-Nine, The, by Ernest Hemingway, 97
Fitzgerald, F. Scott, 5, 19–21, 26, 29–31, 36, 38, 46, 58, 59, 69–71, 77–79, 87, 88, 95, 96, 130, 158, 191, 222, 223, 227, 246, 247, 270, 271, 284, 299 n.
Fitzgerald, Zelda (Mrs. F. Scott), 36, 79
Fix Bayonets, by John W. Thomason, Jr., 47, 181 n.
Fleming, Peter, 91 n.
For Thee the Best, by Mark Aldanov, 270
For Whom the Bell Tolls, by Ernest Hemingway, 152, 156, 159, 162, 164, 174, 193, 207 n., 251, 299
Ford, Ford Maddox, 127, 128
Forever Amber, by Kathleen Winsor, 280 n.
Forster, E. M., 298
Forsyte Saga, The, by John Galsworth, 63
France, Anatole, 31
Frank, Waldo, 224
Franklin, Sidney, 95
Free for All, by Evan Shipman, 91
Freeman, Douglas Southall, 103, 205 n.

Frere-Reeves, A. S., 106, 272
Friede, Donald, 199
Friedland, Louis S., 298 n.
From Death to Morning, by Thomas Wolfe, 104, 106, 118 n., 276 n.
From Here to Eternity, by James Jones, 297 n.
From These Roots, by Mary M. Columbus, 128 n.

Galsworthy, John, 27–29, 38, 46, 63, 69, 185, 208, 270, 271
Galsworthy, Mrs. John, 29, 46, 65
Garden, Mary, 19, 25
Garden of Adonis, The, by Caroline Gordon, 103, 130
Geismar, Maxwell, 188, 222
George III, 215, 240
Gettysburg, Pa., 78, 146
Gilkyson, Walter, 45
Glasgow, Ellen, 151, 251, 298
Golden Apples, by Marjorie Kinnan Rawlings, 87, 88 n., 92
"Golden Wedding, The," by Ring Lardner, 32, 33
Gone to Texas, by John W. Thomason, Jr., 114
Gordon, Caroline, *see* Tate
Gorsline, John and Jeremiah, 283
Grant, General Ulysses S., 2
Gray, Austin K., 269 n.
Great Gatsby, The, by F. Scott Fitzgerald, 38–41, 46, 59, 159, 284
Green Hat, The, by Michael Arlen, 139
Green Hills of Africa, by Ernest Hemingway, 96, 97
Greene, Evarts, 34
Greene, Robert, 295, 296
Greene Murder Case, The, by S. S. Van Dine, 53
Grosset & Dunlap, 252, 253
Guide for the Bedevilled, A, by Ben Hecht, 240
Gulliver's Travels, by Jonathan Swift, 256

Hale, Edward Everett, 208
Hale, Lucretia, 208

Hale, Nancy, 126 n., 191, 208, 209, 227, 234, 269
Hale, Nathan, 208
Hamilton, Alexander, 243, 254
Hamlet, MacLeish's, 77
Hansen, Harry, 57
Harper and Bros., 134 n., 183, 227, 228, 279 n.
Harpers Weekly, 233
Harris, Frank, 297
Harrison, Benjamin, 220, 221
Harvard University, 2, 9, 279
Heaven Trees, by Stark Young, 45
Hecht, Ben, 240 n.
Heinemann, William, Ltd., 64 n., 69, 106 n.
Heller, The, by William E. Henning, 300, 301
Hemingway, Ernest, 48, 58, 73, 77, 78, 90, 94, 95, 117, 118 n., 129, 148, 151–153, 155, 156, 159, 162, 164, 174, 193, 200, 203, 204, 208, 209, 227, 228, 233, 234, 251, 257, 264, 266, 267, 271, 299
Hemingway, John (Bumby), 94, 155
Henning, William E., 300 n., 301
Henri, Robert, 299
Hero in America, The, by Dixon Wecter, 168, 183, 184
Hills Beyond, The, by Thomas Wolfe, 279 n., 297 n.
History of Rome Hanks, The, by Joseph Stanley Pennell, 255, 263
History of the Rebellion in England, Clarendon's 47, 161
Hitler, Adolf, 210, 212, 239, 285
Hogg, James, 36
Hollister, Paul, 161
Homer, 155, 225
Hoover, Herbert, 196
Hoppin, Frederic T., 10
Hopwood Award, Avery, 264
Houghton Mifflin & Co., 77
"How to Live on Thirty-six Thousand," by F. Scott Fitzgerald, 36
How to Write Short Stories, by Ring Lardner, 37
Huckleberry Finn, by Mark Twain, 43
Huebsch, Benjamin, 9, 168
Hughes, Major, 56

Huneker, James, 18, 25, **26**
Hunt, Frazier, 153

I Chose Freedom, by Victor Kravchenko, 274, 284
"I Have a Rendez-vous with Death," by Alan Seeger, 80 n.
In Chancery, by John Galsworthy, 28
In Memoriam, by Alfred Tennyson, 80
"Incident at Owl Creek," by Ambrose Bierce, 201
Indian Summer of a Forsyte, the, by John Galsworthy, 28
Institute Cultural Argentine Norteamericano, 145
Irving, Washington, 300

Jackson, Andrew, 186
Jackson, Holbrook, 83
Jackson, Thomas J. (Stonewall), 103
James, Henry, 298
James, Will, 42, 131, 227
Jeb Stuart, by John W. Thomason, Jr., 52 n.
Jefferson, Thomas, 186, 243, 253, 254
Jinglebob, by Phillip Rollins, 132
Johnson, Clifford, 91 n.
Johnson, Samuel, 145
Jones, James, 273, 295, 297
Journal American, the, 281, 300
Journal to Stella, Swift's, 105
Joyce, James, 120
Judge Comes of Age, A, by John C. Knox, 175 n.

K19, by Thomas Wolfe, 123
Keats, John, 80
Kenyon College, 187
Key West, Florida, 77, 79, 95, 266
"Killer, The," by John W. Thomason, Jr., 52
Kipling, Rudyard, 207
Kit Brandon, by Sherwood Anderson, 166, 167
Knollenberg, Mr., Yale Librarian, 208
Knox, John C., 175 n.
Knudsen, William S., 213
Kravchenko, Victor, 274 n., 275, 285

Ladies' Day, by Chard Powers Smith, 194
Lardner, Ring W., 32, 37, 96
Last Tycoon, The, by F. Scott Fitzgerald, 191, 192, 299
"Laughter, The," by James Jones, 295
Lawrence, Bishop William, 189
Leal, Mr. and Mrs. John, 237
Lee's Lieutenants, by Douglas S. Freeman, 205
Lemmon, Elizabeth, 159, 222
Lenin, 125, 285
Letters on the Short Story, the Drama, and Other Literary Topics, edited by Friedland, 298 n.
Levine, Isaac Don, 240
Lewis, Sinclair, 64, 72, 102, 250, 272
Life of Emerson, The, by Van Wyck Brooks, 48
Lincoln, Abraham, 212, 223
Lit (The Nassau Lit), Princeton University, 202
Little Lord Fauntleroy, by Frances Burnett, 57 n.
Little Turkey Lake, 232
Liveright, 48
Long, Huey, 105
Long, Ray, 52
Long Hunt, by James Boyd, 65
Look Homeward, Angel, by Thomas Wolfe, 60, 61, 64, 68–72, 100, 112, 183, 227, 229, 247, 249, 296
Lost Adventurer, The, by Walter Gilkyson, 45
"Love in the Night," by F. Scott Fitzgerald, 47
"Lovely Lady, The," by Struthers Burt, 45
Ludendorf, Eric von, 284
Luhan, Mabel Dodge, 104, 117, 118
Luther, Martin, 125, 182, 239, 242, 279

Mackail, Denis, 185 n.
MacLeish, Archibald, 77, 79
Madison, 243
Mama Maria's, by Ann Chidester, 272, 284
Man of Property, A, by John Galsworthy, 28

Mannerhouse, by Thomas Wolfe, 187
Marching On, by James Boyd, 49–51
Markham, B., 204 n.
Marlborough, Duke of, Churchill's Life of, 161
Marlowe, Christopher, 80, 295
Marquand, John, 58
Masters, Edgar Lee, 134
Maugham, Somerset, 181
May, Philip S., 275
Mein Kampf, by Adolf Hitler, 285
Melancholy Tale of "Me," The, by E. H. Sothern, 14
Mellen, Ida M., 165 n.
Memoirs, by Sherwood Anderson, 166, 167
Memoirs of a Cavalier, Defoe's, 131, 161
Men at War, 200, 204
Men In Battle, by Alvah Bessie, 154 n.
Mencken, H. L., 37
Merrimac River, 232
Methuen & Co., 134
Michigan, University of, 264
Miller, Henry, 229
Mississippi River, the, 233
Modern Library, the, 90
Monter-Ripley Productions, 249 n.
"Mountain Prayer," by Struthers Burt, 45
Mozart, by Marcia Davenport, 79, 248
Muench, Irma Wyckoff, 188 n., 225
Mulliken, John H., Jr., 266
Murray Hill Merchants and Manufacturers Club, The, 57
My Day in Court, by Arthur Train, 127, 129, 138
My Life, by Leon Trotsky, 67
My Road to Destiny, by Taylor Caldwell, 143

Napoleon Bonaparte, 2, 147, 212
Nash, Thomas, 295
Nathan, Robert, 251
Nation, The, 68
National Arts Club, the, 26
Native American, by Ray Stannard Baker, 169, 171
Nelson, Donald M., 213
New Canaan, Conn., 48
New Republic, the, 64, 68

New Yorker, the, Profile in, 236, 239
Newcomes, The, by Thackeray, 267 n.
"No Door," by Thomas Wolfe, 118 n.
No Longer Fugitive, by Ann Chidester, 233 n.
Note Books, Samuel Butler's, 22
Nowell, Elizabeth, 124, 126, 130, 132, 133, 140

O Lost, by Thomas Wolfe, 60, 61
O'Brien, Edward, 47
Ochs, Adolph S., 277
Of Making Many Books, by Roger Burlingame, 283
Of Time and the River, by Thomas Wolfe, 88, 90, 93, 98–101, 104, 106, 120, 122, 183, 200, 227, 228
Old Lady, The, by J. M. Barrie, 207
Old Testament, The, 30
"One of My Oldest Friends," by F. Scott Fitzgerald, 47
Ordeal of Mark Twain, The, by Van Wyck Brooks, 30 n.
Other Side, The, by Struthers Burt, 55
Otis, Elizabeth, 249
"Our Own Movie Queen," by F. Scott Fitzgerald, 47
Our Times: the United States, 1900–1925, by Mark Sullivan, 48
Out of the Night, by Jan Valtin, 240, 241

"Pack Trip," by Struthers Burt, 45
Page, Thomas Nelson, 202
Painted Veils, by James Huneker, 25
Painting and Painters, by Lionello Venturi, 265
Paris France, by Gertrude Stein, 163
Paris Underground, by Etta Shiber, 240 n.
Parsons, Geoffrey, 257
Paton, Alan, 294
Peirce, Waldo, 58, 118, 146, 153, 155, 157, 206, 236
Pendennis, by Thackeray, 144
Penhally, by Caroline Gordon, 74
Pennell, Joseph Stanley, 248, 255 n., 256, 263 n., 271
Perkins, Edward Clifford, 220

Perkins, Edward N., 218–222
Perkins, Elizabeth Hoar (Evarts), 220–222
Perkins, Louise (Mrs. Maxwell E.), 39, 94, 102, 157, 235
Perkins, Nancy G., 146
Phelps, William Lyon, 190, 207, 218, 220
Phillips, Wendell, 243
Pirate Junk, by Clifford Johnson, 91
Plato, 110
Players Club, The, 56, 57
Plays, by John Galsworthy, 63
Poems, by Alan Seeger, 80 n.
Pogany, William Andrew ("Willy"), 225
"Poor Fool, The," by Erskine Caldwell, 66
Pope, Edith, 230
Powell, Dawn, 164, 175
Practical Cat Book, The, by Ida M. Mellen, 165
Preston, Stuart, 271, 272
Princeton *Lit,* 202
Printer's Ink, 37
Problems of Lasting Peace, The, by Herbert Hoover, 196
Prodigal Women, The, by Nancy Hale, 127, 191, 208, 209, 234
Profile, *New Yorker,* 236, 239
"Pursuit," by Struthers Burt, 45
"Pusher-in-the-Face," by F. Scott Fitzgerald, 47

Rabelais, François, 256
Randall, David, 225
Rawlings, Marjorie Kinnan, 83, 85, 87, 92, 113, 135, 137, 150, 163, 164 n., 175, 193, 227, 232, 236, 247, 275
Reback, Marcus, 283
Reback, Mrs. Marcus, *see* Taylor Caldwell
"Renewal," by Struthers Burt, 44
Reynolds, Paul, 31, 47
Ripley, Arthur, 249
"River, The," by Struthers Burt, 45
River House, by Stark Young, 61
R. E. Lee, by Douglas S. Freeman, 103 n.
Roberts, Margaret (Mrs. J. M.), 229

Roll River, by James Boyd, 89
Rollins, Philip A., 132
Roof, The, by John Galsworthy, 63
Rooms in a House and Other Poems, by Nathaniel Burt, 302 n.
Roosevelt, Franklin D., 125, 186, 213
Roosevelt, Theodore, 168
Rousseau, Jean-Jacques, 12, 183
Roving Commission, A, by Winston Churchill, 161, 181
Russell, William F., 155 n.
Ryerson, Margery, 299 n.

St. Croix River, 232
St. Paul's School, 232
Saint's Progress, by John Galsworthy, 28
Sanctuary, The, Edward Bok's, 35
Sargent, William D., 155 n.
Saturday Review of Literature, the, 63, 102, 110, 237, 250
Saunders, Marion, 199
Sauters, the, 65
Schoenberner, Franz, 280
Scott, Sir Walter, 195, 300
Scribner, Charles (1854–1930), 38, 39, 65
Scribner, Charles (President of Charles Scribner's Sons), 57, 97, 112, 161, 162, 212, 277
Scribner, Charles, Jr., 202
Scribner's Magazine, 26, 28, 44, 45, 47, 137, 188, 247
Scribner's Sons, Charles, 115, 116, 132, 133, 252, 269
Seeger, Alan, 80
"Sensible Thing," by F. Scott Fitzgerald, 47
Shadows of the Sun, by Alejandro Perez, 95 n.
Shakespeare, William, 300
Shelley, Percy Bysshe, 36, 80
Sherman, General, 219
Sherwood, Robert, 180
Shiber, Etta, 240, 241
Shipman, Evan, 91, 206, 234, 235
Shock of Recognition, The, by Edmund Wilson, 224
Showman of Vanity Fair, The, by Lionel Stevenson, 282
Silcox, Louise, 167

Six Short Plays, by John Galsworthy, 29

Sluice River, the, 232

Smith, Chard Powers, 80, 146 n., 194

Smoke, by Turgenev, 284

So Red the Rose, by Stark Young, 94, 95, 192

Son of the Gods, A, by Ambrose Bierce, 205

Sothern, E. H., 14

South Moon Under, by Marjorie Kinnan Rawlings, 84, 85, 87, 92, 247

Southern Pines, N. C., 55, 257–259

Soviet Communism: A New Civilization, by Beatrice and Sidney Webb, 245

Spain, 118

Spengler, his *Decline of the West,* 47

Spoon River Anthology, by Edgar Lee Masters, 134 n.

"Spring Freshets," by Turgenev, 97

Spy, the Worcester, 34

Stalin, Josef, 285

Stearns, Harold, 235

Steeplejack, by James Huneker, 18, 19, 25, 26

Stein, Gertrude, 104, 118, 163

Steinbeck, John, 251

Stevenson, Lionel, 282 n.

Story of a Novel, The, by Thomas Wolfe, 110

Strange Fugitive, by Morley Callaghan, 75

Strater, Mike, 98, 206

Sullivan, Mark, 48

Sun Also Rises, The, by Ernest Hemingway, 48, 157

Sweeny, Col. Charles, 153, 155, 157, 202, 236, 265

Swift, Jonathan, 2, 105, 256, 268

Taine, Hippolyte, 8

Tate, Allen, 73, 147

Tate, Caroline Gordon (Mrs. Allen), 74, 86, 103, 130, 148, 244

Tender Is the Night, by F. Scott Fitzgerald, 58, 88, 95, 284

Tennyson, Alfred, 80, 300

Teresa or Her Demon Lover, by Austin Gray, 269

Terry, John, 188, 215, 224

Thackeray, William Makepeace, 267, 282

There Are No Giants, by Taylor Caldwell, 143

There Shall Be No Night, by Robert Sherwood, 180 n.

There Was a Time, by Taylor Caldwell, 281, 283

These Russians, by William C. White, 276

This Side of Innocence, by Taylor Caldwell, 282

This Side of Paradise, by F. Scott Fitzgerald, 19–21, 246, 247

"Thistle, The," by Tolstoi, 156, 202

Thomas Wolfe's Letters to His Mother, 215 n.

Thomason, John W., Jr., 47, 52, 55, 85, 114, 153, 180, 202, 215, 217, 227

Thompson, Raymond, 215

Thoreau, 235

Three Soldiers, by Dos Passos, 181

Through the Wheat, by Thomas Boyd, 203, 216 n., 217

Times, the London, 104, 106

Times, the New York, 2, 63, 102, 110, 256, 277

To Let, by John Galsworthy, 28, 29

Tobacco Road, by Erskine Caldwell, 66 n.

Tolstoi, Leo, 2, 30, 129, 155, 156, 201, 202, 283, 296

Torrents of Spring, The, by Ernest Hemingway, 48

Tragic Ground, by Erskine Caldwell, 263

Train, Arthur, 16, 23, 127, 138, 164 n., 204, 227

Trelawny, Edward John, 36, 80

Tribune, the New York *Herald,* 102, 110, 256

Trotsky, Leon, 67

Tugwell, Rex, 215

Turgenev, Ivan, 97

Tutt and Mr. Tutt, by Arthur Train, 23, 24

Twain, Mark, 233

Twice Thirty, by Edward Bok, 33

"Two Consciences, The," by Mary M. Colum, 128

Two Persons, by Edward Bok, 35